T0380611

Cold War University

❖❖ STUDIES IN AMERICAN THOUGHT ❖❖
AND CULTURE

Series Editor

Paul S. Boyer

❖

Advisory Board

Charles M. Capper

Mary Kupiec Cayton

Lizabeth Cohen

Nan Enstad

James B. Gilbert

Karen Halttunen

Michael Kammen

James T. Kloppenberg

Colleen McDannell

Joan S. Rubin

P. Sterling Stuckey

Robert B. Westbrook

Cold War University

*Madison and the New Left
in the Sixties*

Matthew Levin

THE UNIVERSITY OF WISCONSIN PRESS

The University of Wisconsin Press
1930 Monroe Street, 3rd Floor
Madison, Wisconsin 53711-2059
uwpress.wisc.edu

3 Henrietta Street
London WC2E 8LU, England
eurospanbookstore.com

Copyright © 2013
The Board of Regents of the University of Wisconsin System
All rights reserved. No part of this publication may be reproduced, stored in a retrieval system, or transmitted, in any format or by any means, digital, electronic, mechanical, photocopying, recording, or otherwise, or conveyed via the Internet or a website without written permission of the University of Wisconsin Press, except in the case of brief quotations embedded in critical articles and reviews.

Printed in the United States of America

Library of Congress Cataloging-in-Publication Data

Levin, Matthew, 1973–
Cold War university : Madison and the New Left in the sixties / Matthew Levin.
        p.   cm. — (Studies in American thought and culture)
Includes bibliographical references and index.
ISBN 978-0-299-29284-3 (pbk.: alk. paper)
ISBN 978-0-299-29283-6 (e-book)
1. University of Wisconsin—Political activity—History.
2. University of Wisconsin—Madison—Political activity—History.
3. New Left—Wisconsin—Madison—History.
4. Students—Political activity—Wisconsin—Madison—History—20th century.
5. Madison (Wis.)—Intellectual life—20th century.
6. Madison (Wis.)—History—20th century.
I. Title.   II. Series: Studies in American thought and culture.
F589.M15L48 2013
977.5'83—dc23
2012035302

Contents

Acknowledgments

There are many people who assisted with and supported this project over several years. I would like to thank Tony Michels and Jeremi Suri especially for their longstanding encouragement and for helping me focus my ideas and writing. Many people shared generously in recounting memories of Madison in the 1950s and 1960s, and this project would not have been the same without their time and thoughtfulness. The staff members at the Wisconsin Historical Society and the University of Wisconsin Archives were immensely helpful as I conducted research, and Gwen Walker, editor at the University of Wisconsin Press, and the late Paul Boyer offered help and encouragement at crucial points. The anonymous readers for the UW Press spent considerable time reading the manuscript carefully; their extensive comments did much to improve the final product. Finally, I would like to thank my parents for the lifelong encouragement they have offered and especially Alder, Taye, Isaac, and Nicole for sustaining me through the years that it took to complete this project.

Cold War University

Introduction

It was a warm spring afternoon on May 16, 1966, the day of the first large-scale confrontation between students and administrators at the University of Wisconsin in Madison. Known afterward simply as the "draft sit-in," the confrontation came on the heels of a failed meeting between university president Fred Harvey Harrington and leaders of a recently formed student group, the Committee on the University and the Draft; with Harrington declaring that he would not give in to their demands, approximately four hundred students conducted a quick vote and then filed into the university's recently built Administration Building. The university, for its part, did not try to oust the demonstrators from the building. City and campus police remained nearby, but their directions were to take no action as long as the students did not damage property or interfere with university functions. Occupying the first floor of the building, near the campus's eastern edge, the students would stay for more than seventy-two hours. They busied themselves with speeches, debates, singing, and even studying; those in the building on the first night of the protest watched a screening of Charlie Chaplin's *Modern Times*, a Depression-era classic of social protest that parodied the mechanization and dehumanization of modern society.[1]

Among the many factors that led to the sit-in, a tactic adopted most recently from the civil rights movement, the immediate context was the escalation of the Vietnam War and the increasing threat of the military draft. Building on a long tradition of student activism in Madison, the campus antiwar movement had developed rapidly over the previous year, in response especially to the U.S. bombing of North Vietnam that began in early 1965, while draft protest had emerged even more recently. College students had enjoyed a blanket deferment from the draft system under earlier rules, but President Lyndon Johnson's decision to double draft calls in July 1965 meant a shift in policy. In early 1966, the Selective Service System adopted a program similar to that from the Korean War, using students' rank-in-class information and the results of the recently reintroduced Selective Service College Qualification Test to determine which students would retain their deferments and which would be eligible for the draft. As protests emerged on several university campuses around the country, the first test in Madison was scheduled for May 14; a small group of students picketed the test site, while a group of two hundred students met and approved a letter to President Harrington, demanding that the university cease any and all cooperation with the Selective Service System. Specifically, students wanted the administration to stop offering campus space for the draft exams and to end its policy of providing students with rank-in-class information that would be used to determine draft eligibility.[2]

The student group that led the protest, the Committee on the University and the Draft, was an ad hoc, or impromptu, group formed in the weeks leading up to the protest. Though lacking a formal leadership structure (a more permanent group, the Wisconsin Draft Resistance Union, would emerge that fall), organizers included graduate students like Evan Stark (sociology) and Robert Cohen (philosophy) as well as a contingent of undergraduates, many of them history majors, like future investigative journalist and *60 Minutes* producer Lowell Bergman. One prominent argument against the draft was that it was discriminatory; with a deferment system that protected many students from the draft, it threatened to turn the University of Wisconsin into a "sanctuary for middle-class youth," a bastion of privilege that left blacks and poor whites more vulnerable to the draft. Protesters also argued that grades were a poor criteria on which to base life and death decisions, a point echoed by a number of teaching assistants and professors as well.[3]

The sit-in revealed student anger at the draft system, but its most pointed target was the university itself, especially its role in facilitating the draft and, by extension, the war in Vietnam. While university officials believed that their actions, including hosting the draft tests and releasing students' rank-in-class information, did not imply an endorsement of the draft system or the war, dissenting students saw the issue from a much different perspective. A leaflet issued by student protesters accused the university of betraying its ideals by cooperating with the military, while another criticism asserted that the university had essentially become a part of the Selective Service System. With headlines from Vietnam forming the backdrop for the protest—"World Peace Hinges on Viet, LBJ Claims," "Ky Troops, Tanks Move in on Rebels," and "Threat of Open Civil War: Fighting Flares in Da Nang" are just a sampling of headlines in one of the city's daily newspapers during the sit-in—members of the student group drew the connection between what they considered the university's tacit support for the draft and support for American foreign policy in Vietnam.[4]

For at least a week, the sit-in held the attention of much of the campus and the city. Though sometimes tempered with ambivalence about the students' tactics, public support came from a variety of corners, including the usually conservative Inter-Fraternity Council, the Wisconsin Student Association (the university's student government), a group of fifteen campus clergy members, and Wisconsin senator Gaylord Nelson, who declared that he was in agreement with the principled concerns raised by the student activists. On the other side were groups like the UW Young Republicans, which passed a resolution condemning the sit-in on a close vote of 21–20, and a campus chapter of the conservative Young Americans for Freedom, which proclaimed the sit-in just one more example of "extremist left-wing activity" in Madison. Conservatives in the state legislature, less than a mile down the road from the students ensconced in the Administration Building, unleashed by far the most venom. Republican state senator Gordon Roseleip, a long-time critic of campus activists, claimed that the demonstration was communist controlled, while Republican assemblyman Harold Froehlich drew on long-standing stereotypes of campus protesters when he suggested that a bill to increase out-of-state tuition, then under consideration in the legislature, would decrease the number of "New Yorkers sitting in buildings who should be in class."[5]

With no end in sight—the group vowed to continue the demonstration until its demands were met—it was not clear if the uneasy peace between the student activists and university authorities would hold. Both sides were acutely aware of the protests that were slowly spreading through the nation's campuses, protests first sparked by the University of California, Berkeley's Free Speech Movement in 1964, and some believed that Madison might be the next campus to witness a violent clash. Attempting to defuse the situation, Chancellor Robben Fleming, who led the Madison campus of the University of Wisconsin and who would later express some sympathy for the goals of the protesters, if not their tactics, organized a meeting in front of the university's historic Bascom Hall on Wednesday, two days after the sit-in began. Before a crowd of several thousand, including all but a token force of the protesters who had stayed in the Administration Building, Fleming, President Harrington, and a few student leaders spoke, with Fleming agreeing to one of the protesters' demands by scheduling a special faculty meeting for the next Monday. Some faculty members also tried their own personal intervention, meeting with students in the Administration Building and urging them not to push the protest too far. Historian William Appleman Williams, known as a strong opponent of the war, told students that they "functioned as the conscience of the university," but he encouraged them to work on persuading faculty members in order to change university policy. Another sympathetic and well-liked history professor, German-born George Mosse, warned the students of the negative effect that continuing the sit-in would have on faculty opinion.[6]

The students did ultimately call off the sit-in, but if they were hopeful that the faculty could be persuaded, they would be sorely disappointed. After listening to a number of presentations, including one from a group of students speaking *against* the protest, the special faculty meeting rejected two separate resolutions that contained sharp indictments of the university's relationship with the draft and the military, one of them offered by William Appleman Williams on behalf of the student protesters and the other by another professor sympathetic to the protest, historian Harvey Goldberg. Instead, the faculty approved a rather generic statement of concern over the issues raised by the sit-in. While continuing the policies of providing rank-in-class information to students and making available university facilities for draft examinations, the meeting authorized the creation of a student-faculty committee to investigate the university's relationship to the Selective Service System. Moreover, though a last-minute amendment offered by George Mosse deleted a declaration that the faculty was "unalterably opposed to coercive methods" like those used by the student protesters, it was clear that many at the university were disturbed by the means employed at the sit-in, an issue that would emerge with greater force during future confrontations.[7]

The draft sit-in never regained momentum after the faculty meeting, with final exams just days away and most students leaving for summer break, but the spotlight that it placed on the university's cooperation with the draft would resonate throughout the era. Following up on the anger at the university—a reporter for the campus newspaper, the *Daily Cardinal*, described a gathering of one thousand students after the special faculty meeting as "thick with charges of 'faculty betrayal' . . . [as] speaker after speaker rose to denounce 'faculty collusion with the military'"—the Committee on the University and the Draft met again in the fall, broadening its focus to include a more general criticism of the university and its functions. Students also met that fall to form the Wisconsin Draft Resistance Union, a group that played an active role throughout the rest of the sixties in counseling students and opposing the draft. For their part, the editors of the *Cardinal*, hardly a bastion of student radicalism in 1966, suggested that the sit-in had raised a number of issues that needed further attention, including the university's relationship with the federal government. The *Cardinal* editors could have little idea exactly how much attention this relationship would attract in the years to come, both in Madison and throughout the nation.[8]

❖

The draft sit-in is not the most remembered of sixties protests at the University of Wisconsin, perhaps because it ended peacefully, but it sits in many ways at the center of the era's history. In Madison, it represented the strength of the New Left, the movement of mostly young people who put forward a radical challenge to America's legacy of imperialism, capitalism, and racism. Wisconsin was one of the first campuses in the country to develop a strident student movement, and it was well known throughout the nation for its activism and sometimes its intellectual force. The draft sit-in drew on a long tradition of student protest that pushes backward the beginning of the era that we know as "the sixties," and the university also brought together a mix of political and intellectual traditions that highlights Madison's distinctive history. Beginning with the state of Wisconsin's political culture, born in the early twentieth-century Progressive Era, and including a core of unorthodox faculty members as well as a mix of home-grown Midwest radicals and East Coast Jewish students, the draft sit-in drew on roots much deeper than the recent escalation of the Vietnam War.

Yet even as the University of Wisconsin has its own distinctive history of the sixties, it also points to a broader history of the era, especially the changes that had taken place in American higher education since the end of World War II and the tensions that were beginning to emerge on the nation's campuses. Like many of the country's leading universities, Wisconsin had developed increasingly close ties with the federal government in the postwar years, ties that reflected the important place of higher education in the nation's life and especially the crucial role that universities played in the Cold War struggle with the Soviet Union. Wisconsin was one of many "Cold War universities" that developed during these years, buttressed by a massive influx of federal dollars that helped expand and reshape the campus even as it contributed to the development of a powerful protest movement. This was the contradiction in American higher education that emerged during these years, with universities becoming increasingly central to the Cold War struggle even as they became centers of protest against Cold War policies. The draft sit-in's focus on the university's cooperation with the Selective Service System began the process of exposing this contradiction, a task that would be mirrored on campuses across the nation as symbols of universities' relationship with the federal government, and especially the government's prosecution of the Vietnam War, came under increasing attack. The war was certainly the essential issue for protesters after its escalation in 1965, but the draft sit-in, and later campus confrontations in Madison, show how an increasingly confrontational strain of protest was focused and fueled by the changes in Cold War–era higher education.[9]

❖

Wisconsin had developed a reputation for political organization and activism in the first half of the twentieth century, and this tradition carried over into the 1950s as well, belying the popular stereotype of that era's youth as a "silent generation." While other leading public universities, like the University of Michigan and the University of California, are well remembered for the deep scars left by McCarthyism, the period of strident anticommunism in the late 1940s and 1950s named after Wisconsin's own junior senator, Madison students often pushed the boundaries of McCarthy-era consensus. Though much more limited than their 1960s counterparts, several student organizations sustained a liberal and sometimes even radical politics, opposing campus-based ROTC, supporting civil rights, criticizing the excesses of domestic anticommunism, and developing a critique of American foreign policy long before the war in Vietnam exposed rifts in Cold War dogma. In a mark of the particular atmosphere in Madison, the UW was the only university in the nation to have an officially recognized chapter of the Labor Youth League, the youth group of the Communist Party, in the early and middle 1950s. Well before Berkeley's 1964–65 Free Speech Movement heralded the arrival of a powerful New Left, before young people gathered in Michigan in 1962 to produce the famous "Port Huron Statement," and even before Students for a Democratic Society, the largest New Left organization, was born in 1960, students in Madison were exploring new directions in radical politics. *Studies on the Left*, a journal established by Madison students in 1959, was perhaps the most concrete example, and its potent critique of American liberalism and foreign policy would resonate widely throughout the New Left in later years.[10]

Crucially important to these developments was Madison's dynamic intellectual and activist culture, one that blended East and Midwest, radical, liberal, and sometimes even conservative. Along with an unorthodox faculty, led by radical historian William Appleman Williams, the mix of students in Madison included an important contingent of out-of-state students, many of them Jews from New York or New Jersey, as well as home-grown Wisconsin and Midwest radicals. Indeed, while Jewish students were attracted to the university because of its national reputation for academic excellence, its historically open admissions policy, and its tradition of political activism, they were often overrepresented in left-leaning student organizations, a pattern that was replicated at many other universities as well. In Madison, that prominence brought regular condemnation of "New Yorkers" and various attempts to limit out-of-state enrollment. Still, Jewish students drew on an ethnic background that included family and community traditions of radical political activism and played a crucial role in campus politics, contributing to the development of new political directions even as they provided a link to the Old Left, the constellation of leftist organizations that existed in the first half of the twentieth century.[11]

Along with the prominence of Jewish students in the New Left, Wisconsin also had its own unorthodox roots. The state had been at the forefront of the Progressive movement in the early twentieth century, a movement that sought to curb political corruption and limit the power of special interests, and Wisconsin was known throughout the nation as a "laboratory for democracy" for its reformist policies. The state even had its own Progressive icon in Robert LaFollette, a graduate of the UW and Wisconsin governor, senator, and presidential candidate. Even as the reformist zeal faded after World War I, Progressives maintained an important presence in state politics, with brothers Philip LaFollette and Robert LaFollette Jr. continuing to serve in statewide office into the 1930s and 1940s, respectively, sometimes running as members of the Wisconsin Progressive Party and sometimes as reformist Republicans. Moreover, while most Progressives remained committed to capitalism even as they sought to reform it, Milwaukee-area residents, just seventy-five miles east of Madison, elected in 1910 the nation's first socialist congressman, Victor Berger, as well as the first socialist mayor of a major American city, Emil Seidel. Milwaukee's socialists were known for their concern with honest government and city services rather than any kind of radical program—"sewer socialists," they were sometimes called—and played an important role in the city's politics for several decades. While Victor Berger endured a rocky tenure in the House of Representatives, winning election in 1918 while under indictment for violating the Espionage Act and twice being refused his seat by members of the House, socialists occupied Milwaukee's mayor's office from 1916 to 1940 and again from 1948 to 1960.[12]

This heritage helped establish the University of Wisconsin's vibrant political culture in the postwar years. Even though public universities were especially susceptible to the era's hard-blowing political winds, Wisconsin administrators generally avoided the worst excesses of domestic anticommunism in the early years of the Cold War. Postwar university president Edwin Broun (E. B.) Fred joined other leaders of higher education in his opposition to communists on the faculty, but Wisconsin was home to a number of irreverent professors, including Williams, whose scholarly criticism of American foreign policy earned him attention from the House Committee on Un-American Activities, law professor William Rice, a long-time campus defender of civil liberties, historian George Mosse, an expert on European political history, and soils science professor Francis Hole, a Quaker and dedicated pacifist. Fred also fended off efforts to impose a faculty loyalty oath in Madison, and he and other Madison administrators generally tolerated radical student activity while keeping the campus open to even the most controversial speakers. Such was the university's commitment to a relatively open and strident exchange of ideas that Chancellor Fleming would praise students occupying the university's Administration Building in 1966 for their "disciplined behavior" and would add that students had proved that "the right to protest, which is essential in a democratic society, can be handled in a responsible manner at Wisconsin."[13]

❖

Even as the University of Wisconsin has its own distinctive history of the sixties, it was also a part of the significant transformation in American higher education in the decades after World War II, a transformation that would influence the draft sit-in as well as other events around the nation. Universities already played an important part in American life, and they provided especially critical services during the Second World War, but the Cold War pointed to a new role for the nation's colleges and universities. The Cold War led to changes in the texture of students' lives—shaping their fears, their language, even their humor—but it left a particularly lasting mark on the relationship between higher education and the federal government, with higher education becoming increasingly vital to America's technological, economic, and even military strength, all crucial fronts in the struggle with the Soviet Union. Some scholars have suggested that universities became part of a "military-industrial-academic complex," but whether or not one agrees with this term's negative overtones, their increasingly close relationship to the nation's security undoubtedly transformed many of the country's institutions of higher education, including Wisconsin, into "Cold War universities." This transformation would have profound implications for the future of university education as well as the course of social activism in the 1960s.[14]

The most distinct marker of universities' new role in the Cold War era was the rapid escalation of federal dollars flowing into higher education. Federal monies supported many programs, including area studies, languages, graduate fellowships, and building construction, but the central component of the university-federal government relationship was scientific research. The growth of research funding was especially evident in the several years after the Soviet Union launched Sputnik in 1957, an event that prompted concern that the United States was falling behind the Russians in science and technology; with funding increasing steadily throughout the early Cold War years, the federal government by the early 1960s was spending more than one billion dollars per year for university research. The majority of funds came from the Department of Defense and the Atomic Energy Commission in the immediate postwar years, while these agencies were later joined by the National Science Foundation, established in 1950, and the National Aeronautics and Space Administration, established in 1958. The National Institutes of Health also become a major supporter of university research, with federal dollars from all these agencies supporting everything from small research projects sponsored by individual professors to centers and institutes that employed a large number of researchers, some of them only marginally connected to the universities that officially housed them.[15]

Research dollars and other funds went to many universities by the 1960s, but they were especially concentrated in a smaller number of institutions that had long been regarded as the nation's leading centers of academic research. Several private universities were among this group, including MIT, Harvard, Columbia, Chicago, Yale, and the University of Pennsylvania, while the leading public universities included the University of California, Berkeley, the University of Michigan, and the University of Wisconsin. Indeed, Berkeley, Michigan, and Wisconsin had each developed ties with the federal government even before the Cold War, and they were linked as the only three public universities among the fourteen institutions that chartered the Association of American Universities in 1900, an organization committed to both undergraduate education and advanced graduate study and research. Wisconsin usually ranked slightly below Michigan and Berkeley in terms of federal government funding—one 1966 ranking put Michigan first among all universities, Berkeley eighth, and Wisconsin twelfth—but it too saw a massive increase in federal dollars in the first two decades of the Cold War. Total federal support in Madison, from research and other funds, rose thirteenfold during the 1950s, with the trend continuing into the 1960s as well. Between 1960 and 1966, the year of the draft sit-in, federal research spending at Wisconsin increased almost three times, to a total of $24.7 million; this was quite a contrast with the university's entire research budget fifteen years earlier, which had totaled only $4.2 million, including federal, state, and private monies.[16]

Yet even as Cold War universities developed at Wisconsin and many other institutions, there emerged a contradiction in American higher education, with universities becoming increasingly central to the Cold War struggle even as they became centers of protest against Cold War policies. Other historians, too, have noted how Cold War research and other ties to the federal government became targets for student protesters in the sixties, a point borne out by Madison's draft sit-in as well as later campus controversies in Madison and around the nation. Yet it was not only Cold War–related research and other explicit federal government ties that spurred campus protests; the incredible expansion of higher education, much of it underwritten by those same federal dollars, also helped fuel the era's upheaval. Even as universities struggled with the consequences of federal funds on a number of fronts, including fear of federal control, the increasing emphasis on research, and the fact that some fields benefited more than others from the nation's new priorities, it was the dramatic growth of campus enrollments that was the most outstanding feature of Cold War–era higher education.[17]

While any consideration of the increase in the number of students has to take into account the effects of the baby boom as well as the increasing importance of a college degree to successful employment, the expansion of colleges and universities in the 1950s and 1960s was also a significant imperative of the Cold War. If anyone had doubted the importance of higher education to America's security, the 1958 National Defense Education Act made the connection explicit, and the federal dollars flowing to universities subsidized rapid growth. From 2,102,000 in 1951, the nation's student population reached 4,145,000 in 1961 and a remarkable 8,949,000 in 1971 (the first baby boomers, born in 1946, did not reach college age until 1964). At the UW, the numbers tell a similar story, with enrollment trending upward from a low of just over thirteen thousand students in 1953 and growing every year through 1969, when there were more than thirty-five thousand students on the Madison campus.[18]

The increasing number of students did not guarantee a powerful movement based in the nation's universities and colleges, but as one historian has put it, it helped create the "infrastructure" for the era's upheaval. Trained in research and steeped in critical inquiry, disillusioned with the increasing scale of university education and convinced that higher education had shifted from its moorings, students on crowded campuses found it easier to organize their generational cohort as the sixties developed. Moreover, the reality of the New Left is that it was always a minority movement, even among university students, and even on notably activist campuses like the University of Wisconsin and the University of California, Berkeley. At campuses like the University of Texas at Austin, Southern Illinois University, and Penn State University, which did not have extensive traditions of student protest and usually possessed a more conservative faculty and administration, the New Left often drew an even smaller percentage of students. There would certainly have been a New Left even if university enrollment had stayed constant through the early decades of the Cold War, but burgeoning student populations, made possible to a significant degree by the influx of federal government support, amplified the voice of student radicals. In Madison, where the student population at the time of the 1966 draft sit-in was more than double its low in 1953, the rapid increase made it possible to gather four hundred students to occupy the Administration Building, a thousand students for an hours-long late-night meeting, and several thousand for a Bascom Hill gathering. These numbers would help establish the New Left as a powerful movement in America's social, cultural, and political history.[19]

❖

The following chapters trace the history of the sixties in Madison. Although the great clashes of the middle and late sixties generated the most headlines at the time and command particular attention in most histories written about the era, including an entire collection of books on 1968 in particular, the first three chapters emphasize the importance of the early postwar years in the beginnings of the New Left. Starting with the dramatic changes at the University of Wisconsin and in higher education more generally in the early years of the Cold War, additional topics include the liberal and leftist student organizations that survived and sometimes even thrived during the McCarthy era as well as the emergence of a vital intellectual culture in the 1950s and early 1960s. The final three chapters trace the development of a more activist movement on Madison's campus in the 1960s, including the influence of the civil rights movement, the beginning of the antiwar movement, the climactic protest against the university and representatives of Dow Chemical Company in 1967, and the many directions that the movement took in the late 1960s and early 1970s. The final chapters also trace some of the challenges the New Left faced as well as the emergence of a conservative student movement, a development that would have increasing significance at the end of the sixties and into the following decades.[20]

Ultimately, Madison offers a window into the history of a compelling period in America's past. Though some have argued that the New Left did not leave the same kind of institutional legacy as the development of modern conservatism, which has dominated much of American politics in the last few decades, the campus movements of the sixties were part of a fundamental shift in the nation's cultural and social footing, one that stretches from race and gender relations to the emergence of a powerful environmental movement and the expansion of democracy to politically marginalized groups. Madison was a center of the political and cultural activism that helped establish this shift, a key in the emergence and development of a New Left that would present a powerful challenge to Cold War orthodoxy. Rooted in the contradiction of Cold War universities and heightened and exposed by the war in Vietnam, the New Left would leave an immediate and significant mark on American history even as it continues to reverberate in our own time.

1

Cold War University

Higher Education after World War II

Standing before the University of Wisconsin's graduating class of 1948, General Omar Bradley, hero of World War II and a key player in the 1944 invasion of Normandy, spoke with a determined gravity. That summer, there were many reasons to be pessimistic about the future, and the events that had shaken the world over the past several months and years hung heavy in Bradley's words: "The great powers have joined in a struggle for the hearts and minds of people," Bradley said, "calling on them to choose between a free and captive life. This struggle must eventually resolve itself either in peaceful settlement of fundamental differences or it must erupt eventually in the violence and convulsion of war."[1]

On that warm afternoon, everyone knew the struggle to which Bradley referred. Usually a time for celebration, the joy of graduation was tempered by the knowledge that Wisconsin's graduates, and indeed all Americans, faced a world that was burdened by the developing Cold War. Thoughts about jobs and families intermingled with the reality of a worldwide struggle with an indefinite horizon, of the Cold War and the onset of the atomic age. Peace, as Bradley declared, required vigilance and strength: "Peace is a fragile and fugitive blessing for which millions have given their lives. But it cannot be easily fashioned from the wreckage of this last war. It must be constructed by sacrifice, by courage, by patience, among people who value it highly enough to defend it. It demands moral leadership, adherence to principle, and the willingness of nations to sustain it with such strength as it shall need for enforcement." Calling on the graduates before him to bring faith to a "tired world," Bradley reminded them that they could not ignore the events taking place in the world around them. They were confronted by a choice: either forge an equitable and sustainable peace or risk chaos and disaster. Sitting on the sidelines was no longer an option. "You are implicated in the destiny of a world from which you cannot escape," Bradley concluded. "Either you work for peace and prosper with it. Or you abandon the world to aggression and perish."[2]

Bradley's speech depicted a particularly stark future for Wisconsin's young graduating class, reflecting as it did the mood of the nation during that harrowing summer. In raising the Cold War as a fundamental issue in young people's lives, however, it was much less remarkable. Ever since the end of World War II and for many years after General Bradley spoke, the Cold War was a powerful reality for students. Sometimes in ways that were clearly identifiable, such as the looming of the draft or the regular threats to political discourse, and sometimes in ways that were less noticeable, like the creep of Cold War militarization into students' daily lives and the deepening relationship between the federal government and the university, the Cold War was much more than a struggle in some faraway place. The domestic battle against communism was a social, cultural, and political struggle for the home front, one that influenced the lives of all Americans.

Even as the Cold War affected the lives of students, it also left an indelible mark on universities themselves. The two decades following the end of World War II witnessed the phenomenal growth of scientific research on university campuses, a shift in higher education toward technical training, and a massive increase in enrollments, all within the context of a rapidly developing relationship between the federal government and the academic world. Though emerging for a variety of reasons and affecting the nation's universities unevenly, the general trends, as well as their intimate relationship to the Cold War, are unmistakable. At Wisconsin, the unprecedented flow of Cold War–related funds in the postwar years underwrote significant changes, and the university became embroiled in the nation's struggle in a way that altered the principle of "service" that had been part of the university's proud tradition since the turn of the century. Wisconsin, like many institutions of higher education, became a "Cold War university." Increasingly supported by the federal government, it played an increasingly crucial role in the broad and multifaceted struggle with the Soviet Union.

This transformation would also, however, reveal tensions in Cold War–era higher education. Even as universities became more important to the nation's politics, culture, and even its defense, the incredible expansion of universities, underwritten in large part by the federal government, would have unintended consequences. The federal government invested in universities because of their role in producing scientific knowledge as well as a highly trained workforce, but as enrollments swelled and universities became centers of Cold War dissent, the partnership between the federal government and higher education would provoke increasing scrutiny. While the framework for this partnership was constructed in the late 1940s and 1950s, it would not be until the 1960s that the effects of the Cold War on the university would be fully realized; these effects would help lay the foundation for the powerful protest movement that dominated the era.

❖

The city of Madison, home to the University of Wisconsin, was first settled in the early nineteenth century, as Americans began to move into south central Wisconsin, an area that had long been home to a number of Native American tribes. The first Europeans to enter Wisconsin were French, in the seventeenth century, but their main interest was the fur trade, and they established few settlements, preferring to trade with the Native Americans instead. The territory was ceded to the British after the Seven Years' War and then to the United States after the American Revolution; it was a few decades later that James Doty, a judge in the Michigan Territory, which included Wisconsin at the time, established the city. With land in the Madison area going on sale at the federal land office in Green Bay in 1835, significant settlement began within just a few years, the population increasing to more than six thousand by the time of the Civil War. By the beginning of the twentieth century, the city's original settlers had mixed with mostly German and Norwegian immigrants, along with small communities of Irish, Jews, Italians, African Americans, and others.[3]

Nestled on an isthmus between two lakes, Madison was a picturesque spot, but it was selected first as territorial capital and then as state capital because of its central location between the cities and shipping routes that lay on the state's eastern edge, along Lake Michigan, and the mining industry in the southwest part of the state. It developed some manufacturing over the remainder of the nineteenth century, including the factories of Norwegian immigrant John Anders Johnson on the east side of the city, but it was never dominated by any particular industry, sustained instead by the business of the state capital and, beginning in 1848, the University of Wisconsin. A century later, in 1948, *Life* magazine rated Madison the best city in America, a standout for its natural beauty, prosperous economy, and abundant cultural opportunities.[4]

The establishment of the University of Wisconsin in 1848 coincided with Wisconsin's transition from territory to state the same year, with citizens agreeing that a prominent public university was a requisite for a great state. The first university class met in February 1849 under the direction of mathematics professor John Sterling, while the campus's first building, North Hall, was completed in 1851, resting near the top of a hill on what was then the far western edge of the city. The building had a beautiful view of Madison, the surrounding land, and nearby Lake Mendota; significantly, it was only about a mile away from the state capitol, this proximity perhaps influencing the sometimes stormy relationship between the state government and some segments of the campus. North Hall was complete with living as well as classroom space and still remains in use as a campus building, along with South Hall, University Hall (the first building meant solely for instruction and later renamed Bascom Hall), and other early buildings. The first female students were admitted in 1863, during the Civil War, and the university graduated its first PhD, future university president Charles Van Hise, in 1892, the same year that the *Daily Cardinal*, the student newspaper still in circulation today, started publication.[5]

Wisconsin continued to develop into one of the nation's leading universities during the first half of the twentieth century. It was one of three public universities that helped found the Association of American Universities in 1900, an organization dedicated to graduate-level research as well as undergraduate teaching (the other two were the University of Michigan and the University of California, Berkeley), and it became especially famous for the "Wisconsin Idea" during the early 1900s Progressive Era. Professors at Wisconsin pioneered a close collaboration between the university and the state government for the purpose of improving government and solving public problems, and their model became well known around the country, often captured in the expression that "the boundaries of the university are the boundaries of the state." Meanwhile, 1916 saw the completion of a new campus building, named after the university's first professor, mathematician John Sterling. Sterling Hall originally housed the departments of physics and political economy; more than fifty years later, when it was also home to the Army Mathematics Research Center, it would be the site of one of the nation's worst bombings, a key marker in sixties upheaval.

Madison was also at the center of administrative changes in the state's system of higher education, changes that reflected the growth of higher education and its increasing importance in American society. The University of Wisconsin had initially included just the Madison campus, but it had expanded over the years to include the University of Wisconsin–Milwaukee (added in 1956), UW–Green Bay (1968), UW–Parkside (1968), as well as several freshman and sophomore centers. And while the UW president had previously been in charge of the Madison campus as well as other operations throughout the state, President Fred Harvey Harrington split these responsibilities in 1963, creating the position of provost and, a few years later, chancellor to oversee daily operations in Madison. In 1971, an even larger merger would take place, combining the several institutions within the UW with a number of campuses that had been organized previously as Wisconsin State Universities. The resulting University of Wisconsin System would eventually include twenty-six campuses throughout the state and be governed by a single Board of Regents, with most of its members appointed by the governor and serving nine-year terms.[6]

In Madison, these administrative changes were matched with the tumult of World War II and the years that followed. While the end of the war might have suggested a return to normalcy at Wisconsin and elsewhere in higher education, the reality was a continued rush of changes. The crush of returning GIs in particular stretched the university's resources to their limits. Compared with the prewar peak enrollment of about twelve thousand students in the late 1930s and significantly lower numbers during much of the war, 1946 enrollment jumped past eighteen thousand, about half of them veterans. To accommodate all these students, courses began at 7:45 a.m. on weekday mornings and were scheduled on Saturday mornings as well; even with the use of Quonset huts and other temporary buildings, some classes had to be held off campus. The housing shortage was just as daunting, especially since a good number of returning GIs were married and had children. Many faculty and Madison residents opened their homes, dorms were crammed full, and the university set up a trailer park near the football stadium, Camp Randall, for veterans and their families. Even so, the university was never able to adequately accommodate the crush of students.

The developing Cold War also loomed over the campus at midcentury, though student and campus life at the University of Wisconsin seemed little affected in some ways. Social life on campus centered on dating and beer, much as it had for many years. In addition to the prom, house formals, and even skating and toboggan parties, beer suppers were popular, and Madison had bars that served beer to students eighteen and older, including the German-themed Rathskeller in the campus's Memorial Union. A cursory look at the *Daily Cardinal*, the student paper, indicates that despite a good deal of attention to issues like racial discrimination and academic freedom in the postwar years, more mundane issues were often prominent. The paper covered national and international news (how much seems to have depended on the interest of the paper's staff and the resources available at any given time), but the paper's usual eight or twelve pages reveal a particular emphasis on local campus happenings, society news, upcoming events, and campus sports.

Telling is the criticism of campus apathy that regularly came from the newspaper's editors, as are the generally pedestrian concerns that took up most of the efforts of the university's student government. In the published platforms of students running for Wisconsin Student Association office in fall 1955, for example, campus issues were paramount. Several hopefuls were especially concerned about recent attempts to raise the drinking age, while almost every platform mentioned the need to raise the minimum wage for student workers and included plans to push for more student parking. Two of the twelve students running for the Student Senate mentioned their support for an end to discrimination on campus, an issue that had emerged because of publicity surrounding two university-approved women's houses that continued to ask for racial and religious information on their applications.[7]

Many students might have preferred to ignore the events taking place outside of their relatively isolated midwestern city, but even if most of them did not discuss foreign policy in the dorm hallways or fret daily over the dangers of nuclear destruction, the Cold War impacted their lives in a number of ways. In particular, though it lacked the same intensity that had come with World War II, the militarization of campus life, the continued mobilization and preparation for future wars, was one of the long-lasting consequences of the Cold War. The need to maintain a high level of preparedness meant that compulsory ROTC for male students and civil defense became a normal part of university life, and except for parts of 1947 and 1948, students were susceptible to the draft throughout the postwar years. More broadly, the world instability that marked the Cold War permeated life at the university in less obvious ways as well, infiltrating humor and even reshaping the language of the era, reminding students that they lived in a world constantly threatened with war.

The continuation of compulsory Reserve Officer Training Corps (ROTC) courses after the end of World War II was perhaps the most obvious sign of mobilization for the Cold War. A land grant institution, Wisconsin was required under the 1862 Morrill Act to offer courses in military tactics, but these had been voluntary for most of the university's history. Indeed, Wisconsin had been the first university in the nation to challenge the compulsory system that had started during World War I, when ROTC was established; yet after World War II, when ROTC once again became compulsory for all male students, the state legislature declined to return to a voluntary system. The continued mobilization of the Cold War meant the need for a steady stream of officers, and all male students were required to take ROTC courses in their first and second years, with successive coursework being optional. Many Americans justified compulsory ROTC as crucial to the national defense and as a sign of patriotism, while broader arguments for the program included the benefits of military and civilian interaction. Like Wisconsin, about two-thirds of land grant institutions and one-half of other colleges required ROTC in the 1950s.[8]

Although the mere existence of ROTC on campus would become a key target of student activists in the 1960s, as perhaps the most visible connection between the military and higher education, the debate during the early years of the Cold War remained focused on the compulsory nature of the program. Debate over the issue came up in the pages of the *Cardinal* almost every year in the late 1940s and 1950s, and while some students defended compulsory ROTC because of the continued need for preparedness and many others made their opinion known by continuing in the voluntary program during their junior and senior years, many opposed the requirement as intrusive and militarily unnecessary. A 1949 campus survey indicated that, two to one, students favored making ROTC voluntary (though the survey did not ask about abolishing ROTC altogether, a question that had been rejected by 80 percent of students in a 1927 poll), while ROTC's annual spring review was the focus of two rare student protests, first in 1950 and again in 1957. Summarizing student opinion during much of the postwar period, the *Cardinal* editorialized in 1957 that compulsory ROTC was a waste of taxpayer money and student time; a voluntary program, the paper suggested, would be more effective for those students who wanted to participate.[9]

Though not as intrusive as ROTC, at least for male students, the Cold War–inspired threat of nuclear war also meant the creation of a program for civil defense at the UW. With the emergence of the Soviet Union as an atomic power in 1949, Wisconsin followed the federal government's lead in turning its attention to planning for a nuclear attack, forming a Committee on Civil Defense in 1950 to coordinate the university's efforts. Charged with working with city and county authorities and drawing up plans in case of a nuclear emergency, the Committee on Civil Defense was concerned with an attack on Madison but also gave attention to a possible attack on Chicago or Milwaukee and the role that Madison could play as an evacuation center. The committee catalogued the campus's human and physical resources that might be put to use in case of an emergency and attempted to maintain campus readiness, which included preparing students for the possibility of an attack. The committee posted information throughout campus, and in a 1951 memo to leaders of campus residences ominously declared, "The consequences of an ATOMIC BOMB dropped in Wisconsin may directly affect you."[10]

One of the most pressing issues for male students, of course, was the draft. Discontinued in 1947 under the pressure to demobilize, the reprieve did not last long, as the worsening international situation, combined with a lack of volunteers, led to its return in June 1948. Under that draft law, college students were allowed to postpone induction until the end of the academic year, and Congress also placed increasing emphasis on maintaining the nation's scientific manpower, which meant that many students were able to get deferments and avoid service. In actuality, draft calls were relatively light, except during the Korean War, and even then deferments were available for many students. A UW report found that most students were exempt from the draft either because of their age, physical disqualifications, or deferments as students or ROTC cadets: in 1952, only 8 percent of students were classified as 1-A, eligible for immediate induction. In a twist that would be repeated during Vietnam, at least some students protested their own deferments, arguing that the deferment program was a form of economic discrimination against those who could not afford to attend college. This echoed a concern among some policymakers that the selectivity of the draft threatened the ideals of universal service and shared sacrifice.[11]

One suggestion for sharing the burden of military service, proposed by President Truman after World War II and raised periodically into the 1950s, was universal military training (UMT). Plans varied, but most consisted of a short period of training, perhaps six months, for all young men, which would create a manpower reserve in case of a national emergency. But despite what some called the "democratic" element of UMT, at least some students at the UW were not persuaded. A debate raged in the pages of the *Cardinal* in the spring of 1948, and while the *Cardinal* editors claimed that UMT was necessary in light of the international situation, at least some students disagreed, contending that UMT was inconsistent with America's heritage. Drawing on their experience as soldiers, members of the campus chapter of the American Veterans Committee, a liberal alternative to the more conservative American Legion, voiced their own opposition to UMT. Writing on behalf of the group, one veteran suggested that the real need was to work for peace, not preparation for more wars. Besides, he said, anyone who argued that UMT would be good moral or educational training, two of the arguments sometimes made for the program, had never been anywhere near an army or navy base.[12]

In addition to discussion of the draft and the possibility of UMT, a steady stream of global events also interrupted normal university life, reminding students that the world remained a dangerous place. Students were occasionally confronted with newspaper headlines like the one in the October 15, 1948, *Cardinal*: "War Imminent and Expected, According to State Dept. Statements," and the spring 1948 communist coup in Czechoslovakia, in particular, raised a good deal of anxiety on campus, including concern over potential changes to the draft. More than 150 students attended a panel discussion on "postwar blues" in early March of that year, expressing concern over the failure of the United Nations and the potential for another war, and crowds of students gathered in the Memorial Union to listen to President Harry Truman's March 17 speech before Congress regarding the situation in Czechoslovakia Along with general support for Truman, the *Cardinal* reported what it called campus "jitters." As the paper put it, the Czech crisis raised a number of questions about America's part in the developing Cold War, questions that had no firm answers: "Americans are wondering just how far Soviet influence will extend on the European continent. They are wondering just how far we can and should go to halt its advances. They are wondering—in light of new developments— just how far Harry Truman would like to lead us and in what direction."[13]

If the Czech crisis prompted "jitters," the coming of war in Korea raised a more general alarm. A month after the beginning of the war in 1950, a forum on Korea attracted a large and lively audience, while many on campus again worried about the impact of war. As one student, Janet Rosenblum, put it in 1951, normal life was hard to imagine in light of the possibility of another world war; it was difficult to concentrate on studying "when the implications of the atomic bomb and full scale war constantly invade our thoughts." Fraternities, which had been hit hard by the drain on male students during World War II, began planning for more rough times, and ROTC enrollments hit new highs. The war also affected course work, as some year-long courses were offered in a single semester so students who faced the draft could complete their studies more quickly; those facing possible induction were also given the option to substitute classes relevant to military service and defer other requirements.[14]

More generally, the power of the atom and the potential for war seeped into the student consciousness. Of the generation that came of age in the 1950s, and especially for those who would later join the New Left, sixties activist and chronicler Todd Gitlin writes that "the Bomb" was perhaps the most pervasive fear. Though some appreciated the bomb's role in ending World War II, this generation was the first to fear the end of days: "Rather than feel grateful for the Bomb," Gitlin writes, "we felt menaced. The Bomb was the shadow hanging over all human endeavor. It threatened all the prizes." Just as Janet Rosenblum had expressed her fear of the implications of atomic war, another student,

William Heinz, expressed his trepidation about the arms race. Winning the arms race will be "no enviable victory," he wrote in 1950, "because it cannot be decided until a major war breaks out. All indications are that in such an event there will be few or none left who know or care who won the race." A few years later, the editors of the *Daily Cardinal* opined more broadly that students lacked a sense of normalcy. Students in the fifties had been "weaned on blitzkrieg, genocide, mass annihilation, peaceful coexistence, posture of patience, and all the isms that have been hurled at us since the turn of the century." "It's true we have all the facilities and opportunities at our disposal for living the so-called good life," the editors concluded, "but how can we enjoy it when someone is always ominously warning us about the dangers of alphabet bombs and increased draft calls?"[15]

Discussion of the bomb regularly invaded the campus. In 1948, the university scheduled an "Atomic Energy Week" to promote discussion of the consequences of the atomic age. A panel discussion titled "Will Atomic Energy Serve or Destroy Mankind?" highlighted the week, but even though it included UW chemistry professor Farrington Daniels, who had worked on developing nuclear energy during World War II and remained a proponent of its peaceful uses, the discussion was dominated by mostly pessimistic views of atomic energy. Another UW chemistry professor, Joseph Hirschfelder, gave a particularly sobering account of the potential of the atomic age just a couple of years later. At a 1950 roundtable meeting of some of the nation's leading atomic scientists in Madison, he acknowledged that it was highly improbable that Madison would be the target of a nuclear attack, but he estimated that an atomic blast over Bascom Hall, near the center of campus, could kill ten thousand students. Asked which buildings on campus would be the safest in the event of an attack, he responded that none would be safe: most of the campus would be leveled. Chemistry professor Aaron Ihde's report for the faculty and student civil defense committees on what to do in the event of a nuclear attack, described in a front-page *Cardinal* article, warned students to protect themselves in ways such as "Close your eyes and cover with arm," "Wait for heat and shock waves to pass (two minutes)," and "Avoid panic. Don't start rumors."[16]

Campus speakers also kept the Cold War in front of students. Just as General Bradley had painted a dark picture of the world for UW graduates in 1948, a succession of speakers during the late 1940s and 1950s raised the specter of the Cold War for Wisconsin audiences. Norwegian ambassador Wilhelm Morgenstierne, at a gathering of the UW International Club in March 1948, told the students that Norwegians "will die on our feet rather than live on our knees." And in a February 1950 speech on the need for a bipartisan foreign policy,

Oregon senator Wayne Morse declared that "it is most likely that our generation will witness the sunrise or sunset of peace" (Morse, a Madison native and UW graduate, would later become famous as one of only two senators to vote against the 1964 Gulf of Tonkin resolution, which authorized President Lyndon Johnson to escalate American involvement in Vietnam). Students also contributed to the regular warnings about the Cold War, with senior Dan Reich stating at the university's 1952 Honors Convocation that "the single, overpowering fact of our times is the hostility between the Soviet Union and the United States. . . . The permanence of Western Civilization and its ideals— our ideals—depends on the ability of Western man—of us—in meeting this challenge."[17]

Another commencement speech, by UW President E. B. Fred in 1951, points to the spread of Cold War militarization into the very language of the era. "Upon every citizen rests the obligation to serve his fellow men in civil life as the soldier serves his country in war," Fred declared. "*This is the age of the draft. In the final analysis, no one is exempted.* For one reason or another, some may be exempt from military service. But none of us is exempt from sacrificial service to those traditions and institutions which are the lifeblood and framework of democracy. The military draft may be selective, but the moral draft operates inexorably upon all of us." While the essence of his message had very little to do with actual military service, Fred's decision to draw on military language in order to connect with his audience highlights the deep infiltration of this language into everyday use and understanding.[18]

References to the Cold War popped up in a variety of other contexts as well. Conservative student Alan McCone wrote a regular column for the *Daily Cardinal* titled "Atom Age Campus" in the mid-1950s, while a 1951 dorm blood drive referenced the sacrifice of Americans in Korea to encourage donation. A few years earlier, another plea to support the Red Cross had used a particularly grisly image to make its point. A full-page advertisement in the *Cardinal* pictured a crowd of people, led by a mother carrying her baby, fleeing from a burning city. It was expected that readers would implicitly understand the message; all that was needed below the picture was the straightforward pitch: "Donate to Your Campus Red Cross Drive."[19]

And lest anyone think that the Cold War could not be funny, the campus humor magazine, the *Octopus*, regularly lampooned the Cold War and drew on it as a popular reference in its jokes. A 1948 article, "Fun with Atoms," encouraged the purchase of "atom-cracking kits" for home use: leftover radioactive material had lots of fun uses, like putting it in the salt and pepper shakers and watching everyone in the family glow in the dark. Drawing on Cold War language a few years later, the magazine welcomed new students as "inductees first class," while it also mocked the loyalty oath that students had to take as a part of ROTC. The mock oath printed in the magazine included directions to "Sign! Do not read! Follow Orders! Shoot if You Must! This Grey Old Head!" while students had to declare that they did not have even the "teensiest knowledge" of such potentially subversive groups as the Friends of the Kremlin, Boy Scouts of America, the Lutheran Church, Nephews of the Haymarket Rebellion, and so on. In 1955, an entire issue was devoted to making fun of ROTC, a popular pastime if not especially appreciated by some on campus. The issue mocked ROTC as well as militarism more generally, promoting a book by J.D. Salacious, *The Catcher in the ROTC*, and including a full-page cartoon of a fallout shelter and a man in uniform leaning over a woman with a tight-fitting dress, his hand on her leg. "Sergeant," the caption read, "you don't mean to say that to be absolutely safe from fall-out we'll have to stay here for another 5 days!"[20]

Writers in the *Octopus* were having fun with some of the cultural references of their day, but the regularity of these references, and the ease with which they became a part of students' consciousness in the decades after World War II, highlight the broad social and cultural impact of the Cold War in Americans' lives. Students felt the impact of Cold War militarization through mandatory ROTC and the draft even as they were reminded of the dangers in the world outside Madison by such events as the Korean War and, later, the 1956 Hungarian revolt and the Soviet Union's 1957 launching of Sputnik. Sociologist and future New Left hero C. Wright Mills (himself a UW PhD, class of 1941) was among those who put voice to these changes, commenting in 1956 on the militarization of American life. As Mills put it, Americans were living "in a nation whose elites and whose underlying population have accepted what can only be called a military definition of reality."[21]

❖

Just as student life was profoundly affected by the Cold War, the university itself underwent a deep transformation, a development that would resonate into the sixties and would focus many of the greatest clashes of that era. The battle against the Soviet Union highlighted the need for a nation united behind American values, and it also meant a marshalling of American resources for an indefinite struggle. Higher education was already important to the nation's political and cultural life, but the Cold War brought a deepening relationship between the federal government and universities, a relationship that included higher education's emerging role in providing a skilled population for the Cold War struggle but that was most explicit in the area of scientific research. With laboratory facilities, faculty scientists, and a qualified workforce of graduate students, universities offered the resources to conduct research that many believed necessary to win the Cold War, and both the federal government and many university leaders worked to cement a bond in the postwar years. In unprecedented fashion, many universities became integrated into the nation's efforts to maintain scientific and technological leadership throughout the world and, as a result, became "Cold War universities," a central component of America's national security apparatus.

Federal government support for universities had been limited before World War II, often targeted to programs like agricultural development, but the crisis brought on by the attack at Pearl Harbor signaled a new direction. Transformed relatively quickly to provide a variety of support roles for the American war effort, universities served as specialized training centers for troops, and war research was funded to the tune of $325 million from the federal government's Office of Scientific Research and Development between 1941 and 1945. The Manhattan Project in particular highlighted the potential for a new model of federal government and university collaboration: much of the research was conducted at American universities, while the crucial Los Alamos lab in New Mexico, where the first atomic bombs were built, also remained heavily dependent on university scientists. Los Alamos National Laboratory was organized by the U.S. Department of Energy, but it was run by the University of California, Berkeley; Berkeley physicist J. Robert Oppenheimer, the lab's chief administrator, recruited top scientists and engineers from the nation's universities to work on the project.[22]

In Madison, the university's contributions to the war extended across the campus. In addition to hosting programs that provided specialized training for more than ten thousand soldiers during the war, UW contributions came from such professors as chemist Farrington Daniels, who served as the scientific administrator at the Metallurgical Laboratory in Chicago, a key Manhattan Project site. Like Daniels, more than a hundred faculty members were working on national defense programs by November 1942, either in UW labs or in government labs while on leave from the university. Future university president E. B. Fred (then dean of the graduate school) and vice-president Ira Baldwin (then chair of the bacteriology department) both conducted secret government research on biological warfare, and Baldwin served as the lead scientist and administrator of the Biological Warfare Project under the War Department. A group of university scientists worked on developing new strains of penicillin for the War Production Board, and UW President Clarence Dykstra served as the first head of the Selective Service when the draft was reinstated in 1940.[23]

By 1945, this wartime experience offered an important model and a transition in the development of a much fuller relationship between universities and the federal government. While many in the federal government favored continued cooperation with universities, including then–Army Chief of Staff Dwight Eisenhower, who understood that the army had become dependent on civilian scientists, one of the foremost advocates was Vannevar Bush, head of the Office of Scientific Research and Development during the war. Bush had been in charge of coordinating the government's scientific efforts during the war, and he authored a 1945 report for President Truman that called for increasing cooperation in the postwar period between the federal government and universities on scientific and technological developments. Highlighting the importance of universities for the national defense and the many ways in which university research had helped secure victory in World War II, he argued that the nation's universities and colleges were best positioned to carry out basic research. They were "wellsprings of knowledge and understanding," he argued, where scientists could pursue the truth and develop knowledge that could be applied by both government and industry.[24]

Even as the federal government viewed universities as a resource for fighting the Cold War, so too did many in higher education. Motivated partly by practical concerns—federal dollars brought prestige, while a failure to acquire these dollars meant that reputations and top faculty might slip away— universities were also spurred forward by the self-conscious belief that they had a significant role to play in America's Cold War effort. Crucial context for this belief was the growing number of university administrators who had served in some part of the federal government, many of them during World War II. Historian Kenneth Heineman's research shows that while the presidents of many elite private universities had often worked with the federal government in some capacity before World War II, this wasn't true of the majority of public university presidents until the 1940s and 1950s. Where none of the twenty-five public university presidents Heineman surveyed had done work for a government agency involved in national security issues in 1933, 40 percent had this kind of experience in 1950, most commonly at the State Department or the Department of Defense. The number was even higher when adding in work for the federal government in areas not related to national security, and some administrators also worked for foreign-policy foundations or corporations involved in defense work.[25]

Administrators at the University of Wisconsin were among the many who recognized the importance of higher education in fighting the Cold War. For President Fred, the university's traditional goal of developing competent citizens blended easily with the nation's Cold War struggle. "I believe that four years of attendance at the University of Wisconsin," President Fred told a visiting group in 1951, "makes our young people better men and women, better citizens, and better defenders of the American way of life. . . . American education is the rock against which the wave of Communism shall inevitably break and ebb away. Such an open door to life and liberty as American education represents, no iron curtain and no bamboo curtain can long keep barred." Moreover, while Fred had worked on research for the federal government during World War II, he continued a close cooperation after the war was over. He served as the inaugural vice-chairman of the National Science Board at the National Science Foundation (NSF) in 1950 and also worked in the Departments of Agriculture; State; and Health, Education, and Welfare. Conrad Elvehjem, a biochemistry professor who would succeed Fred as UW president in 1958, worked on an important NSF committee on government-university relations in the early 1950s.[26]

Like many other leaders in higher education, Fred was reluctant to commit universities wholly to the Cold War struggle, but he also believed that universities did not and could not exist outside of that struggle. In a speech during the early days of the Korean War, while the university was busy enumerating its war-related resources and corresponding with the federal government regarding its role in the war effort, Fred ventured even further than his well-tread emphasis on training an educated citizenry. He rejected the idea of turning over the university entirely to military purposes, but he declared in stark military language that universities were "one of the basic arsenals of democracy. . . . As a community of scholars, equipped to carry on instruction and investigation in broad areas of knowledge, a university is a stockpile of specialized and highly useful manpower, information, plans, and equipment." Several months later, he expressed similar sentiments in a meeting of department chairmen. While he called for the university to continue to "carry on our unique and essential function of providing learning for the future," the national emergency raised by the Korean War meant the need to "render maximum service to the state and the nation now." Moreover, he singled out scientific research as a service the university could readily offer.[27]

There was also agreement at the other end of State Street, the mile-long avenue connecting the university and the state capitol. State officials played a crucial role in shaping the public university's budget, and as early as 1948,

Governor Oscar Rennebohm was quick to remark on the relationship between education and the national defense. Not just for business or social prestige, he said, "the proper education of all the people of the United States in this hour is our best and most effective national defense against the enemies of our way of life at home and abroad." Several years later, in 1955, the legislature's University Policies Committee stressed the need for high-quality university education in these terms: "The State of Wisconsin cannot afford to cheapen the quality of the education which she offers to her sons and daughters. This would certainly be false economy. Rather, Wisconsin must meet the competition of other states, and the United States must meet the competition of foreign nations." In the report's section on university research, the committee was even more candid, declaring that scholarly research was vital to "our survival as a nation."[28]

Still, the increasingly close ties between universities and the federal government did not go without some scrutiny. UW business manager Alfred Walter (A. W.) Peterson had expressed concern over "long-distance management" by the federal government as early as 1935, and this fear was echoed in the immediate postwar years by a number of university as well as government officials. Even Vannevar Bush, a key advocate of cooperation between universities and the federal government, was cautious; a Republican, he was especially concerned about the size of government and the effects of politics on research. In 1950, *Time* magazine reported on the worries among many in higher education about the "federalization" of universities and the possibility for imbalance between research and teaching and between the sciences and humanities, imbalances already present on some campuses. Others worried about the shift from basic to applied research and the preponderance of money that was coming from military agencies in particular. At Wisconsin, UW administrators told a committee of the state legislature in 1954 that they remained cautious in their approach to federal funding. Concerned about possible federal control, they were also worried about depending too much on a source of funds that might dry up if Congress decided to reduce research appropriations.[29]

Despite these misgivings, however, federal government appropriations for university-based research, as a central component of the relationship between the federal government and higher education, increased quickly. Just as the Depression had convinced many Americans of the need for federal government involvement in the nation's economic policies, the twin crises of World War II and the Cold War led many in government and in higher education to recognize the increased importance of scientific research and the need for a federal government role in funding and directing that research. The process was often decentralized and haphazard, which helped it avoid the attention of those who might have made more of an effort to halt it, but the trend itself was unmistakable. Government support flowed through a number of agencies and created such a complicated web of relationships that one historian has labeled the result the "federal research economy." Some government agencies funding campus research were closely tied to military interests, like the Department of Defense, the Office of Naval Research (established 1946), the Atomic Energy Commission (1946), and the National Aeronautics and Space Administration (1958), while such agencies as the National Institutes of Health (1887) and the National Science Foundation (1950) reflected a broader interest in scientific research that sometimes, but not always, correlated with the Cold War.[30]

Following the dollars highlights the rapid growth of government-funded research in the postwar years. In the 1950s, federal agencies doled out hundreds of millions annually, and by the early 1960s, the federal government was spending about $1 billion a year on university-based research (this was in addition to the billions more spent on research and development outside of higher education). The National Science Foundation's budget, for example, grew from a modest $100,000 in 1950, its first year in operation, to $100 million just ten years later, most of it flowing to universities and university-based research centers. By the late 1960s, the numbers were even more dramatic, with universities spending $3 billion on research in 1968, 70 percent of it funded by the federal government and much of that coming from defense-related agencies.[31]

Research funding was spread among many universities, but it was concentrated especially in the nation's leading schools. At Michigan, for example, university president Harlan Hatcher emphasized the need for continued research to stay ahead of the Soviets and supported close Cold War ties with the federal government, with the university increasing its federal government contracts from $4 million in 1951 to $10 million in 1957. Several years later, in 1966, Michigan was the nation's largest recipient of federal dollars (research contracts and other funds), receiving more than $65 million from the federal government in just that one year. Like Hatcher, University of California president Clark Kerr was also a booster of a close partnership between the federal government and higher education. Berkeley's Lawrence Radiation Laboratory, named after physics professor Ernest Lawrence and established in the 1930s, helped stake out Berkeley's position as a leader in the field, and the laboratory and a number of Berkeley physicists, including J. Robert Oppenheimer, played a crucial role in the Manhattan Project during World War II. The Atomic Energy Commission worked closely with the Radiation Lab after the war, and Berkeley, benefiting as well from California's growing industry and population, became a leading destination for federal funds.[32]

Wisconsin, meanwhile, was also active in seeking federal dollars during these years. The university's Board of Regents approved a campus expansion and construction plan in 1946 based partly on the expectation of continued funds from the federal government, and the three presidents who guided the university from 1945 until 1970 were all avid promoters of university-government cooperation (as were the presidents that followed). With its large size and its prominent faculty, it quickly became a leading destination for federal dollars, its federally funded research jumping from $661,000 in 1950 to $8,872,000 in 1960, a thirteenfold increase. Seen from another perspective, the percentage of the university's overall research budget that was supported by federal government dollars grew from about 15 percent to more than 45 percent over the same period. Moreover, most of these funds came from a small number of government agencies. Between 1950 and 1960, for example, funds from the Atomic Energy Commission (AEC) grew from $181,000 to $904,000; funding from National Institutes of Health (NIH) jumped even further, from $222,000 in 1950 to more than $4 million in 1960; and the National Science Foundation (NSF), which had only come into being in 1950, was funneling $2.6 million to the university only ten years later. In all, the university had 957 government contracts and grants in 1960, thirty-three of them bringing in over $50,000 annually and thirteen calling for more than $100,000. Some of the largest projects included the university's Nuclear Engineering and Nuclear Physics Program (AEC), its Primate Center (NIH), and the Geophysics Research Program (NSF).[33]

Federal dollars directed to university research were already increasing rapidly in the 1950s, but they gained even more speed after the Soviet Union's October 1957 launch of Sputnik, the first human-made satellite to orbit the earth. President Eisenhower tried to downplay Sputnik as a crisis of the Cold War, hoping to minimize the political fallout from the event, but for many, the fact that the Soviets had beaten the United States into space was a blow to American notions of technological superiority. As the news hit the front pages of the country's newspapers, it immediately crystallized already growing concerns that American education was lagging behind the Soviets. Sputnik's influence on higher education would extend beyond scientific research, but the rapid increase in research dollars is particularly clear, with total federal spending on academic research increasing from $456 million in 1958 to more than $1.2 billion in 1964. Funds from the Department of Defense (DOD) and AEC more than doubled, while funds from the NSF rose from $16 million to $126 million, and the National Aeronautics and Space Administration (NASA), which was created in 1958 to lead America's space program, would spend $44 million to fund academic research just six years later.[34]

With the newly available funds, the numbers at Wisconsin were even more remarkable in the 1960s. Overall federal research spending increased from $8.4 million in 1960 to $20.6 million in 1964, and by 1970, the federal government was sending more than $30 million in research dollars to Wisconsin, well more than half of the university's entire research budget. NIH and NSF provided the most funds, while other significant agencies included the State Department, the Department of Housing, Education, and Welfare, NASA, and the DOD. Compared to other universities, Wisconsin ranked eleventh in 1965 in federal research and development spending; a few years later, it had moved up to seventh as a destination for federal research funds.[35]

Signs of the changes brought by this flood of federal money were evident throughout the campus. Research dollars reverberated broadly and helped spur graduate school enrollment, which doubled between 1955 and 1963, underwrite new construction, and, in some cases, fund the dramatic growth of entire departments. The expansion of Wisconsin's meteorology department, for example, was fueled largely by Cold War research funds. Starting in 1948 with two faculty and a $9,500 equipment grant from the Wisconsin Alumni Research Foundation, federal grants and contracts funded changes that were so rapid that by 1970, just over two decades after the department was established, it employed nineteen faculty members and its graduate program was considered one of the best in the nation. By that time, it was receiving more than a million dollars a year in research grants, the bulk coming from NSF, NASA, the U.S. Army, Office of Naval Research (ONR), and the Weather Bureau. In the late 1960s, it moved into a new fifteen-story Meteorology and Space Science Building, courtesy of grants from NSF, NASA, and the state of Wisconsin.[36]

Within this complex web of contracts, perhaps the most prominent of the many links between Wisconsin and the Cold War was the university's Army Mathematics Research Center (AMRC). Most research in higher education before World War II had been closely related to universities' basic teaching mission, with researchers carrying on normal teaching duties, but the Cold War saw a proliferation of institutes, labs, centers, and other campus units that operated with varying degrees of autonomy. Some of the most famous examples include the California Institute of Technology's Jet Propulsion Lab, Michigan's Institute for Social Research, Johns Hopkins's Applied Physics Lab, and Berkeley's Radiation Lab; each of these, like the AMRC, stood at the nexus of the government–higher education relationship, sites where federal government and university funding, staff, and interests overlapped. At Wisconsin, some of the researchers at the AMRC were regular faculty members and were affiliated with other departments on campus, while some were visiting researchers who were on campus for a semester or a year and had no connection with other parts of the university.[37]

Both the U.S. Army and the university recognized the defense-related significance of the AMRC. President Fred saw the center's establishment in 1956 as both an opportunity and a responsibility for the university, "an opportunity to make Wisconsin one of the great mathematical centers of America, a responsibility to do so in the interest of our national strength both military and scientific," while the center published a brochure in 1959 that testified to the army's interest in high-level mathematics. "In its day-to-day operations," the brochure explained, "the Army leans upon mathematics as a ubiquitously necessary tool for the design of weapons and structures, for the compilation of maps and tables, for the organization and analysis of systems of communication, transportation, logistics, etc." The AMRC, then, was intended as a general source of research in mathematics as well as a resource for the army's specific mathematics-related issues; it was a mix of basic research that had no direct application to the immediate concerns of the army and applied research that possessed a more explicit link to current national security issues. The work of faculty members at the center was not classified, and most of the research was done at the discretion of the faculty and not the army, yet many members still maintained security clearances so they could consult with the army on issues relating to national security.[38]

The existence of AMRC testified to the U.S. military's reliance on scientific knowledge for the nation's defenses as well as the university's willingness, perhaps even eagerness, to deepen its ties with the federal government. From its inception in 1956, the center brought the university prestige, a steady stream of visiting researchers, and a budget—about $1.3 million a year by the late sixties—that was funded almost entirely by the U.S. Army. For the army, the center provided an important foundation of mathematics knowledge as well as easy access to highly skilled scientists. From the vantage point of the late sixties, it is remarkable that the center's arrival on campus in the mid-1950s occasioned no protest; even at the time of the draft sit-in in 1966, the center received little notice. Within just a few years, however, as the pace of student protest quickened and the issue of the university's relationship with the federal government and the Cold War moved to the center of radical concerns, the AMRC would come to symbolize one of the worst excesses of university-government cooperation. In 1970, it would become the site of one of the most notorious events in the university's history.[39]

❖

Although Cold War–related scientific research at Wisconsin and other major American universities provides perhaps the most direct link in the relationship between government and higher education, leaving as it did a particularly clear trail in the form of billions of dollars that were shifted from government to university budgets, it was only part of the federal government's wide investment in Cold War universities. As the United States engaged in what was much more than a struggle for battlefield supremacy, universities contributed on a wide variety of fronts. Famously put by University of California president Clark Kerr in his 1963 lectures at Harvard, universities—"multiversities," he called them—had become producers of knowledge, crucial to the development of a modern nation. That same year, UW president Fred Harvey Harrington argued that universities can, and often do, change the world. "The University is a central unit in our modern culture," Harrington wrote. "It is the gate to life and leadership in this country."[40]

Many others concurred that universities provided a broad foundation for America's future, including its success in the Cold War. President Eisenhower's Committee on Education Beyond the High School issued a report in August 1957 (before the Soviet Union launched Sputnik) that remarked on the "dramatic strides" in higher education in the Soviet Union. "[America] would be inexcusably blind," the report read, "if she failed to see that the challenge for the next twenty years will require leaders not only in science and engineering, but in government and politics, in foreign affairs and diplomacy, in education and civic affairs." Likewise, Dean of Students LeRoy Luberg, in assessing the relationship between the University of Wisconsin and the federal government for an administration report issued in 1964, commented that "the growing partnership between the federal government and higher education has become a major social, educational, economic, governmental, and military phenomenon of America's twentieth century." Noting that the relationship had developed mostly ad hoc, he concluded with a nod to the benefits of a strong partnership. While the education of undergraduate and graduate students at the nation's universities would "require the help of our federal government," such a partnership would also help the nation "meet its demands for defense and welfare." Universities, then, were important not just to scientific development, but to development in all areas. Producing teachers, businesspeople, technicians— these had long been essential functions of universities, yet the expansion and shifts in higher education during the Cold War, and often *because of the Cold War*, meant a significant transformation of universities that went well beyond the swell in research budgets.[41]

A significant milestone in the federal government's broad support of higher education was the 1958 National Defense Education Act (NDEA). The 1944 GI

Bill had provided the means for millions of war veterans to attend college, but the NDEA, a reaction to the success of the Soviet Union's space program and their launch of Sputnik a year earlier, was a specific outgrowth of the Cold War. The legislation's title directly linked education and the nation's defense, and it included a number of provisions to boost all levels of education. Among others, it created a loan fund to help students specializing in science, math, and foreign languages, provided matching funds for the purchase of equipment related to those same fields, funded graduate fellowships, and set aside money for the development of area studies programs.[42]

Money from the federal government flowed throughout the University of Wisconsin in these years and helped to underwrite its dramatic expansion. Almost two thousand UW students benefited from more than a million dollars of NDEA loans in the program's first several years, and while research contracts remained a key funding tool, other kinds of support also widened. In 1960, for example, research funds accounted for nearly $9 million of support, while other federal government funds totaled nearly $5 million, helping to subsidize a variety of academic programs, faculty salaries, and building construction. And while funds were certainly concentrated in select parts of the university, their effect was felt much more broadly: in 1961, more than $11 million were distributed to the physical sciences (49 percent), medical sciences (26 percent), biological sciences (13 percent), and the social sciences (10 percent). Seventy-seven of the university's ninety departments were participating in one or more programs funded by federal government dollars.[43]

Among the many parts of the university affected by the Cold War and NDEA funding, one of the most significant was international studies. As the Cold War spread into the third world, area studies programs developed quickly in the late 1950s and early 1960s in order to fill the need for American knowledge of languages and cultures around the world, with the Central Intelligence Agency (CIA) just one group that saw area studies as a crucial means for gathering intelligence related to the Cold War. Historian Fred Harvey Harrington was perhaps the key proponent of area studies in Madison, and by the time of his resignation from the presidency in 1970—he had joined the university's administration in 1955 as a special assistant to President Fred—the university was offering instruction in fifty-four languages, most of them added to the curriculum since World War II. One of Harrington's first moves was the creation of a Center for Luso-Brazilian Studies in 1959, which qualified for one of the first NDEA area studies grants, while NDEA grants also supported an Indian Studies Program established in 1960 and an African Studies Program established a few years later. Some of the funds for these and other area studies programs also came from large foundations, like the Ford Foundation and Carnegie Corporation, though these foundations often worked closely with the federal government and were deeply involved in America's Cold War effort as well.[44]

Finally, business education at the university expanded rapidly in the early years of the Cold War, the result of increasing specialization in the business world as well as the importance of economic growth to the Cold War (not to mention the massive Cold War–related government spending that fueled the American economy in the 1950s and 1960s). Economic growth had always been a national priority, but it too took on new meaning and urgency in the postwar years. Which system, American or Soviet, could produce more goods and a better life for its citizens? While influential journalist Walter Lippmann warned in 1960 that "the prevailing picture of the Soviet economy as primitive and grossly inefficient was false," Soviet Premier Nikita Khrushchev often took to posturing about the strength of Soviet production. The Soviets would "soon catch up to the U.S. level of per capita output of meat, milk, and butter," Khrushchev pontificated in May 1957. "Then, we shall have shot a highly powerful torpedo at the underpinnings of capitalism. . . . Growth of industrial and agricultural production is the battering ram with which we shall smash the capitalist system." Of course, economic productivity was also at stake during Nixon and Khrushchev's famous Kitchen Debate in 1959. Even liberals who had criticized monopoly at the beginning of the century and had railed against "economic royalists" during the New Deal understood that criticism of capitalism was no longer tenable during the Cold War. Led by economist Leon Keyserling of Americans for Democratic Action, liberals helped make economic growth, which held the promise of lifting all boats, part of America's Cold War faith.[45]

While business education expanded across the country, the postwar mood at the University of Wisconsin was in sharp contrast to the mistrust of capital that had held sway for much of the early twentieth century Progressive Era and the years between the world wars. The School of Commerce initiated an MBA program in 1945 and offered a PhD beginning in 1947, while the school really came of age with the opening of the Commerce Building in 1956, the first time the entire department had been housed in one building. Ties with the corporate world also expanded, with corporations contributing more than one million dollars to the university's research budget in 1960. In essence, the Cold War contributed to changes already underway in the business world, supporting the effort to educate a skilled workforce and helping to cement the relationship between government, higher education, and the corporate world. It was certainly no coincidence that the Commerce Building, which provided a physical symbol of this development, would be the scene of some of the most violent eruptions of student protest in the sixties. The 1967 protests against representatives of Dow Chemical Company, on campus to conduct job interviews, struck at the heart of these changes in the university and forever established the Commerce Building's place in Wisconsin lore.[46]

Confirming the transformation of the university during the early years of the Cold War were the variety of efforts to maintain academic balance as some parts of the university benefited more than others from Cold War priorities. In 1955, for example, President Fred appointed history professor Fred Harvey Harrington a special assistant to seek research funds in areas outside the natural sciences, while the administration also tried to convince the university's Wisconsin Alumni Research Foundation, a group that funded research in the natural sciences, to broaden its support to the humanities and social sciences as well. In 1958, the UW system's Coordinating Committee for Higher Education issued a "Blueprint for Educational Planning in Wisconsin" that called for more attention to research in the humanities and social sciences and insisted on the importance of educating the "complete man"; a few years later, a Board of Regents report came to many of the same conclusions, noting a serious imbalance between the scholarly opportunities available in the physical and biological sciences versus other fields. As universities across the nation grappled with the effects of federal government involvement on academic research, the regents decried the trend toward research with practical application, rather than basic knowledge, that characterized many government grants.[47]

One of the most distinguished voices that rose in opposition to the shift in the university's underlying direction was that of historian Merle Curti. A Pulitzer Prize winner and president of the American Historical Association in 1954, Curti dissented from the congratulatory tone at the 1958 opening of the Wisconsin Center, a new building that would house the university's extension division. Contrasting the state of the social sciences at Wisconsin with the university's proud tradition in the field, Curti argued that Wisconsin had lost ground. At the turn of the century, Wisconsin's social sciences had been among the best in the nation, led by such figures as John Commons, Edward Ross, and Richard Ely, but no longer. As Curti noted, it was the natural sciences that had benefited most from the leadership of E. B. Fred, who had then been president of the university for more than a decade. And yet, Curti argued, it was the humanities and the social sciences that were most necessary in order to navigate the complexities of the emerging world order.[48]

Despite the misgivings of Curti and others during these years, a fundamental shift was underway, and the emergence of Cold War universities at Wisconsin and elsewhere across the nation was unmistakable. As universities became increasingly crucial institutions in the nation's struggle with communism, Cold War militarization crept into students' lives, and universities undertook significant changes in direction and mission. Some of these changes were the result of the federal government's unprecedented financial investment in higher education, and some changes developed more organically from administrators, faculty, and even students who believed in the role that higher education could play in the fight with the Soviet Union. The concerns that accompanied these changes, however, would not disappear. Expressed sporadically in the fifties, they would grow in number and intensity in the sixties. The expansion of higher education was a Cold War imperative, crucial to economic growth, scientific manpower, and the production of knowledge, but that same expansion, when mixed with increasing unease about the direction of higher education and discontent over the policies of the federal government, especially the escalating war in Vietnam, would be explosive.

❖

A crucial piece of the transformation of universities in the Cold War era, and one that would have enormous consequences for the New Left in the 1960s, was the massive expansion of student enrollment at colleges and universities throughout the nation. There were many reasons for this growth, which began in the early and middle 1950s and lasted into the early 1970s, but at least one key cause was the Cold War. Indeed, it is one of the great ironies of the era that as Cold War universities expanded in size to match their increased importance to American society, culture, and defense, these swollen institutions would became centers of opposition to the very forces that built them. As the Vietnam War exposed the cracks in Cold War orthodoxy in the middle and late 1960s, this contradiction of Cold War–era higher education would have dramatic consequences for the New Left and its ability to present a serious challenge to America's institutions.

Enrollment at institutions of higher education has increased throughout much of American history, as the overall population has grown and a university education has become an increasingly important stepping stone to prosperity, yet the expansion of enrollment in the two decades between the early 1950s and early 1970s was nonetheless remarkable. University enrollment in the United States fluctuated in the years immediately following World War II, as the flow of veterans going to college on the GI Bill came and went, but after hitting a national low of 2.1 million in 1951, enrollment increased every year into the early 1970s. By 1959, enrollment was more than 3.6 million; by 1963, more than 4.7 million. Just a few years later, in the fall of 1966, as the Vietnam War was escalating rapidly and the number of American troops on the ground there surpassed three hundred thousand, college enrollment had tripled from its 1951 low and was now nearly 6.4 million. It continued to grow even then, reaching nearly 8.6 million by 1970.[49]

The story at the University of Wisconsin and at comparable universities like Michigan and Berkeley mirrored the national trends. At Michigan, enrollment grew from seventeen thousand in the fall of 1952 to more than thirty-six thousand in the fall of 1966, while Berkeley saw growth from less than nineteen thousand students in 1960 to almost twenty-six thousand in 1966. At Wisconsin, after spiking in the immediate postwar years and then hitting a postwar low of 13,346 students in 1953, enrollment began to grow rapidly, increasing every year between 1954 and 1969, when it hit a high of 35,549. The College of Letters and Sciences and the university's Graduate School, which were two of the largest parts of the university to begin with, experienced especially strong growth. While the university's overall student population doubled from 1953 to 1965, for example, enrollment in the College of Letters and Sciences increased 150 percent during these years; the number of students in the Graduate School increased 190 percent.[50]

There are many reasons for the rise in university enrollments starting in the early 1950s. The 1944 GI Bill, which had offered education benefits to millions of World War II veterans (later GI Bills would provide similar benefit programs for veterans of future conflicts), had mostly run its course by the time enrollments started their two decade climb, but it had raised expectations for future generations of young men who might not otherwise have anticipated a college education. Women, too, saw increased educational opportunities in the postwar years, with women's enrollment in higher education rising at a faster rate than men's during much of this period. More broadly, workers in the postwar years needed more technical training than they had in the past, the result of a rapidly expanding economy and increasing specialization in the business world—"needed today are college-trained men," *Fortune* writer Herrymon Maurer wrote of the shortage in business workers in 1953—and this increased demand certainly influenced supply. Finally, the baby boom, the rise in birth rates that is generally recognized as starting in 1946 and ending in 1964, helped propel university enrollment, though not until the middle and later sixties when the first children of the baby boom began to reach college age.[51]

Despite these various factors, none of them, or even all of them together, fully make sense of the expansion of enrollment that started in the early 1950s and lasted for almost twenty years. There were a variety of reasons that more and more young Americans wanted to go to college, even before the baby boom meant that there were simply many more men and women of college age, but the Cold War cannot be discounted as a key factor. The NDEA embodied the federal government's interest in supporting higher education, while the federal government's role is especially evident in the hundreds of millions of dollars it distributed annually to universities and colleges across the nation. It supported student scholarships, underwrote a variety of programs, and contributed a steadily increasing amount of research dollars, all in the context of the escalating importance of higher education to the nation's security. The growth in the graduate school is especially linked to federal dollars, as the federal government was providing almost 50 percent of the university's research budget by 1960 while the number of graduate students tripled in size by 1966, before the first of the baby boom generation even finished their undergraduate education. Seen from another perspective, federal dollars helped underwrite much of the staff and physical plant expansion—classrooms, dormitories, labs, faculty, staff, and so on—that simply did not exist in 1945 but that would be necessary in order to educate the number of students who would enter higher education in the following decades.[52]

Though there was some concern over the rapid expansion of the university and its effect on education—concern that emerged as early as the late 1940s, when one student commented in the *Daily Cardinal* on the militarization of the campus and of American life more generally—most leaders at Wisconsin were proponents of a large university. These leaders embraced the university's lucrative relationship with the federal government, believing that universities served an important function and that the great centers of American higher education were those that attracted ever-growing numbers of faculty and students as well as federal dollars. In the middle 1950s, a few years after the expansion had begun, President Fred made explicit his support for growth, suggesting that higher enrollments offered a number of advantages, including stronger national defense. "The increased number of college and university graduates," he wrote in the university's alumni magazine in 1955, "will provide a large reservoir of talent in the arts, sciences, and professions—thus adding to our nation's cultural, economic, and, if you please, military strength." Nor was Fred alone, as his view closely echoed that of the National Manpower Council (founded at Columbia University in 1951 and supported by a grant from the Ford Foundation). "Great care must be taken to insure that the universities can continue to meet their major responsibilities of discovering new knowledge and training tomorrow's scientists and scholars," the council declared in 1953. "Only if this is done will the nation be able to reap the full benefits of science and technology for defense and for its expanding welfare."[53]

By the end of the 1950s and into the 1960s, with federal dollars reaching into all parts of the university and subsidizing the incredible expansion in enrollment that had started in the early 1950s, the University of Wisconsin, like many other universities throughout the nation, had become a Cold War university. As the nation's university population ballooned from a little more than two million in 1951 to more than six million in 1966, however, neither the federal government nor universities could foresee the unintended consequences of their deepening partnership. The relatively isolated voices that had questioned the shifts in higher education would become much more powerful in the coming years, as the contradictions of Cold War–era higher education would be laid bare. As young people in the sixties became disillusioned with the society around them, especially with the Cold War both at home and abroad, universities would become centers of dissent, often even targets of dissent, and would provide a growing base for the New Left. The 1966 draft sit-in was the first major confrontation over the partnership between the federal government and the University of Wisconsin, but it would not be the last.

2

"Let the rascal speak"

McCarthyism and Student Political Activity
in the Fifties

When Jeffry Kaplow arrived at the University of Wisconsin in September 1952, he was a freshman from Brooklyn, one of several hundred students from New York at the university that year. Like many of those students, he also had an interest in politics; his mother, a seamstress and Communist Party sympathizer, was just one of many relatives involved in one way or another with the Old Left, the constellation of socialist, communist, and other radical groups that had been politically influential earlier in the century but had declined rapidly with the onset of the Cold War. Kaplow himself had been a member of the Brooklyn chapter of the Labor Youth League (LYL), which had been formed in 1949 as the youth group of the Communist Party; when he arrived at Wisconsin, he found a chapter of the same organization, by then the only LYL chapter in the country that was recognized by a university as a legitimate student group. Despite the risks that went along with membership in an avowedly Marxist organization in the 1950s, during the height of the anticommunist fervor named after Wisconsin's own junior senator, Joe McCarthy, he quickly joined.

Kaplow and his fellows in the league enjoyed the benefits of Wisconsin's relative commitment to civil liberties, at least in the context of the McCarthy era, but the operations of an organization like the Labor Youth League, officially labeled "subversive" by the federal government, were still severely limited. "There was a great deal of talk and a certain amount of show in our Madison days," Kaplow remembers, but "if Madison in the 1950s was quasiunique in being the only university community not to brand us young Reds as pariahs, we were nonetheless constrained to work quietly." Often on the defensive, members spent a good deal of their time trying to prove to the rest of the campus "that we were not conspirators bent on destroying all that was holy in the American republic." In practice, this often meant that members applied much of their energy and ideas working within more mainstream campus organizations. Though condemned by some as an effort to infiltrate and take over these groups, Kaplow suggests that this practice was a way for members to work on issues that they genuinely believed in, like civil rights, peace, or academic freedom.[1]

There was also a certain level of secrecy that went along with membership in the LYL, some of it almost comical decades later. Kaplow recalls that league members were assigned to teams, and even among other students he socialized with and suspected of LYL membership, it was understood that he should not ask for confirmation. Another LYL member, Saul Landau, also remembers that members were divided into groups, or cells, as a result of the Communist Party's fear that a severe government crackdown was right around the corner. Landau was recruited into the league in the early fifties by a housemate, Henry Wortis, who would leave copies of communist newspapers and magazines in the bathroom—an "obvious but effective" ploy, according to Landau. The league's secrecy also held a particular allure: on Sunday mornings, as Landau describes it, "Henry would put on his trench coat, ask me to feed his dog if, for some reason, he didn't get back in time, and then mysteriously leave the house, often turning his head several times to check that no one was following him."[2]

In many ways, the league's existence in Madison highlights the conflicting trends at the University of Wisconsin. Throughout the country, the domestic anticommunism of these years had a powerful impact on student activism and politics; many observers noted that young Americans seemed more risk-averse, while campus politics was a generally quiet affair. Still, the Labor Youth League and a few other groups in the late 1940s and 1950s maintained a politics that defied the era's currents. Kaplow bemoans the amount of time that the league spent defending itself rather than pushing a more positive program, but it is an accomplishment in itself that the group persevered throughout some of the most difficult postwar years. Read against the context of McCarthyism, Kaplow's statement that the LYL "was a holding operation against consensus and conformity, and the silence to which they gave rise" indicates a certain degree of success. While much of the nation, including the overwhelming majority of university students, moved closer to the political center during the postwar decades, Kaplow and others like him served as a powerful reminder of an alternative perspective to the increasingly entrenched Cold War consensus.[3]

The university, too, played an important role in the political activism of the Labor Youth League, and a few years later such campus groups as the Madison-based Student Peace Center and Socialist Club. Though the university ultimately produced a mixed record when it came to protecting the rights of radical student groups and allowing controversial speakers to use campus facilities, Wisconsin remained committed to at least a partial defense of civil liberties, free speech, and free student association. Again and again in the late 1940s and 1950s, even as many other universities were bowing to the substantial pressures of domestic anticommunism, pressures that were even more intense for public institutions, Wisconsin affirmed the rights of politically unpopular student organizations. In doing so, it drew on a long tradition, dating back at least to the late nineteenth century, of campus support for academic freedom and critical inquiry. While Cold War–era administrators had little sympathy for communism or other radical political ideas, they believed that the best way to combat radicalism was to bring it in the open, to let it compete (and lose, they believed) in the marketplace of ideas.

The institutional space in Madison and in scattered other universities meant that even as higher education played an increasingly important role in the nation's struggle with the Soviet Union, universities were also emerging as centers of dissent against the Cold War. In 1950s Madison, one of the most important developments within the small community of radical students was the break from the Old Left and the anticipation of something new, even if the development of the New Left was still a few years away. Jeffry Kaplow, like Saul Landau and Henry Wortis, represented an important stream of students that fed into the Madison political left—East Coast, Jewish, and with connections to older organizations that provided a conduit of radicalism when oppositional politics were in sharp decline—and these students mixed with Wisconsin's political traditions and many of the state's own best students to explore new directions. While the Labor Youth League in particular remained closely tied to the Communist Party in the early 1950s, students in Madison would create organizations in the middle and later years of the decade that were independent of any national organizations and that embraced ideological diversity as well as fledgling efforts toward direct action and a cultural politics that pointed toward the future. It would be a few more years before there existed a recognizable new left, but the developments in Madison in the middle and late fifties, in addition to the more general critique of the Cold War that persevered even at the height of McCarthyism, laid an important foundation for the more powerful movement to come.[4]

❖

The Cold War had important consequences for the political and cultural climate of higher education in the fifties. Despite significant opposition, many American campuses had been politically active in the years before World War II, especially in the 1930s. The socialist Student League for Industrial Democracy and the communist National Student League represented much of the nationwide campus left during the early 1930s, and the two organizations merged in 1935 to form the American Student Union, which claimed twenty thousand members at its 1939 peak even as it faced investigation by the House Un-American Activities Committee (HUAC, then known as the Dies Committee for its leader, Texas representative Martin Dies Jr.). A variety of youth groups on and off campus were involved in coordinating antiwar rallies, including the 1935 National Student Strike Against War that drew 175,000 people across the country to protest militarism and to mark the anniversary of America's entry into World War I, and Madison, too, saw peace rallies throughout the middle and late 1930s. A group called the Peace Federation sponsored a 1940 antiwar rally in Madison that drew eight hundred students, while one of the era's most important campus groups was the University League for Liberal Action, which was affiliated with the American Student Union. The group's suspected communist ties drew considerable concern in Madison and throughout the state, but the university resisted calls to crack down, even when the group hosted the American Student Union's national convention in 1939 and invited Communist Party leader Earl Browder to speak.[5]

After the lull in campus activity brought on by the war, the emergence of the Cold War in the late 1940s had a deadening effect on all kinds of campus political activity, especially activity on the left. Americans had always viewed communism with suspicion, and the investigations by HUAC and President Truman's 1947 government loyalty program further established domestic anti-communism as a powerful force in American life. Wielded by many, but perhaps most adeptly by Wisconsin's junior senator, Joseph McCarthy, whose name became synonymous with the virulence of the period after his 1950 emergence onto the national stage, domestic anti-communism meant a significant narrowing of the political and cultural spectrum. In a sense, many Americans hunkered down in the face of the perceived threat from the Soviet Union, rallying around traditional American values and norms and agreeing that it was no longer acceptable to question the fundamental truth of American principles, including capitalism and the righteousness of American foreign policy. While the Cold War overlay the era's politics, culture, and even family life, those who challenged the emerging consensus were shunted to the margins and viewed with increasing suspicion.[6]

During these years, many Americans noted that university students were more conformist than they had been in the past and were less willing to challenge the status quo. In a lengthy 1951 article, the *New York Times* surveyed seventy-two major colleges and found that "a subtle, creeping paralysis of freedom of thought and speech is attacking college campuses in many parts of the country, limiting both students and faculty in the area traditionally reserved for the free exploration of knowledge and truth." In addition to the general fear and uncertainty in American life at the time, the *Times* noted that many students feared being labeled a communist, a label that could carry social disapproval as well as rejection for further study or employment. Some analysts also found that students seemed more interested in earning a living than in rocking the boat. A 1949 poll of graduating seniors by *Fortune* magazine led to the conclusion that "forty-nine is taking no chances." Above all else, the poll found that students prized security and abhorred risk, remarking that "they seem, to a stranger from another generation, somehow curiously old before their time." *Fortune* especially decried the lack of entrepreneurial spirit: security meant working for other people, and the good life, as these graduating seniors saw it, was calm and ordered: a comfortable home, a good wife, three children, one or two cars.[7]

Other writers in the 1950s highlighted similar trends. William Whyte and Paul Goodman both wrote much-discussed works on conformity (Goodman's book was actually published in 1960), and sociologist David Riesman became instantly famous for his 1950 book, *The Lonely Crowd*, cowritten with Nathan Glazer and Reuel Denney. Reisman postulated the existence of different character types and argued that, in the late 1940s, the "other-directed person"—flexible and accommodating, wanting to be loved rather than esteemed—was coming to dominate American society. Considering young people in particular, Riesman came to many of the same conclusions as *Fortune* when he analyzed interviews of graduating seniors done by *Time* magazine in 1955: students, Riesman suggested, were in a hurry, not because of ambition, but because they had already made up their minds where they were heading. Often self-consciously contrasting themselves with their fathers, who had gone out on their own, seniors going into business indicated their preference for going to work for a large corporation. Moreover, their lack of ambition in work mirrored their already laid plans for marriage, family, and home.[8]

At Wisconsin, there were clear signs that some of the vitality that had marked the campus in the 1930s was missing. Heightened anticommunism meant that the act of participating in a demonstration or joining an organization like the Labor Youth League brought with it a clear set of risks, and some members of radical groups even reported harassment and intimidation from their fellow students. Some examples of activism akin to that of the 1930s or 1960s stand out, but these were few and far between. Testifying to the changed campus mood, all nineteen of the students who staged a relatively tame protest at a 1950 ROTC event, holding signs opposing militarism and compulsory ROTC, were officially disciplined by the university. The university's Committee on Student Conduct concluded that while students had rights to free speech and protest, these did not extend to the disruption of official campus events. Dave Trubek, a student in Madison from 1953 until 1957 and active in liberal, though not leftist, politics, also experienced the consequences of even casual associations with radical campus groups. He found himself in especially hot water when he signed up for a military commission and indicated on his loyalty oath that he had attended a campus concert sponsored by the Labor Youth League and featuring Pete Seeger, the popular leftist folk singer. For this he faced hours of interrogation with military intelligence officials from Washington, D.C.; they asked him "about every possible person I'd ever met," including his father, who was active in Democratic Party politics.[9]

University observers regularly commented on the lack of campus political activism during these years. For *Cardinal* writer Karl Meyer, the late 1940s decline of the campus chapter of American Youth for Democracy, a group that had come under attack locally and nationally for its communist ties, indicated the "withering campus left," while the editors of the *Wisconsin Athenaean*, the campus literary magazine, offered one of the most scathing critiques of UW students and their lack of political involvement. In a 1951 editorial titled "Generation of Jellyfish," they catalogued some of the symptoms of conformity on campus, including the lack of attendance for important campus speakers, a general lack of knowledge about international issues, and a "hapless" student government. "The worst part of it is that we aren't even curious," the editors bemoaned. Describing a theoretical graduation ceremony, they directed their frustration at "future leaders": "For the most part, they are a sterile assemblage of prisoners of orthodoxy. A group with little curiosity, content to munch chocolates and watch a television set while the rest of the world staggers blindly to destruction, a group hungry for a rut to cower in, a collection of youngsters already middle-aged, lulled by life into a state of vegetative smugness."[10]

The editors at the *Daily Cardinal* often echoed the same sentiments. A 1953 editorial noted the "deadening" silence at the beginning of the school year: students continued to complain about "the inequities of existence," but fewer were willing to do anything about it, a trend the paper suggested had been growing since the end of World War II. In 1957, the *Cardinal* noted that "students attending university today are primarily interested in security and little else. . . . The vast majority has not ventured out of its protective shell since the beginning of the year." It did not go unnoticed, moreover, that campus politics excited very little attention; in 1955, almost three times as many students cast ballots in the election for prom queen than in the election for student government. And indicative of the times, perhaps the most significant problems that administrators faced in terms of student behavior were springtime panty raids and water fights. In 1958, a particularly bad year, two days of water fights and panty raids resulted in numerous students arrested for unlawful assembly. The police used tear gas to break up the crowd—a sign, perhaps, of things to come.[11]

Ironically, even as the Cold War was often blamed for the absence of youthful activism, one of the criticisms aimed at students was that they lacked interest in Cold War issues. Observers at the University of Wisconsin were often critical of their fellow students for not being informed about international events, and David Riesman's mid-1950s analysis concluded that America's graduating seniors showed little concern over the international situation. Yet even as students were not always well versed in the details of the Cold War—the status of the NATO alliance or the ratio of U.S. to Soviet Union gross national product—this does not mean that the Cold War was unimportant to them. The immediacy of the threat of war and atomic destruction faded some with time, but many youth still recognized the possibility of nuclear war and the threat of destruction that continued to loom. The war scares of the late 1940s and the fears of nuclear fallout in the 1950s; the pervasiveness of the Cold War in popular culture, as in movies like *Them!*, *Invasion of the Body Snatchers*, and *The Blob*; the regular discussion of civil liberties and academic freedom in the context of McCarthyism—these were just some of the ways in which the Cold War penetrated youth's consciousness.[12]

Certainly the concern among youth for security was a close corollary to the international insecurity of these years. In 1957, Dave Trubek, then editor of the campus literary magazine, made a direct connection between McCarthyism and students' desire to "play it smart," to stick to opinions that "are safe and wholesome, to say nothing that isn't already a cliché." The root of campus conformity, he suggested, was fear: "The main trouble with us is we're just plain scared. We are scared of the world we are entering and we have crawled into conformity to avoid meeting it." The questions surrounding war and the future of the world weighed particularly heavy: "We have nothing but the specter of a world on the brink of disaster, a world frequently too complex for us to understand. . . . Our past has become an academic question, our present a visceral reaction to too much reality, our future only a wavering, inconstant question mark."[13]

Finally, in a particularly perceptive analysis, prominent UW political science professor David Fellman highlighted the broad pressures exerted by the Cold War and their equally expansive impact on college youth. In a 1958 radio conversation between Fellman, sociology professor Howard Becker, and English professor Frederick Hoffman, the three agreed that the campus was more conformist than it had been in the past. While Becker suggested that many of the fights of the 1920s and 1930s had little substance and that there remained few issues of consequence to excite student political activism, Fellman, an expert on civil liberties and chair of the American Association of University Professors from 1959 to 1964, attributed the lack of campus political activity directly to the Cold War. Whether the result of a real shift in opinions or merely students' prudence in avoiding the consequences of unorthodox political activity, Fellman argued, the Cold War had significantly shaped campus life. Some students were more likely to moderate their views in recognition of the possible consequences, while the tensions and insecurities of the Cold War meant a kind of closing of ranks that precluded certain kinds of political thought and behavior. "As a society feels insecurity," he declared, "it tends to close ranks and tighten up its discipline and simply will not put up with certain marginal forms of political behavior." As Fellman understood, the Cold War was much more than readying soldiers for combat; for most Americans it was a clash of civilizations, and with so much at stake, there was little room for dissent at home.[14]

❖

There was more than a little truth to all of the reports about student conformity, in Wisconsin and across the nation, but despite the deadening effect of domestic anticommunism, there were at least some corners of the nation, and some parts of the University of Wisconsin, where student activism remained alive, if perhaps subdued. Even with all of the handwringing over the so-called silent generation, a small group of Wisconsin students made quite a bit of "noise" in the context of the McCarthy period. There were few of the protests that had marked the

1930s and would re-emerge with even more force in the 1960s, but students in the 1950s challenged the status quo with a politics that was often unorthodox and was sometimes even radical. Belying the notion of a sharp break between the politics of the fifties and sixties, this activism helps to explain why Madison was one of the first places where a recognizable new left emerged in the early 1960s and why the campus continued to be on the leading edge of radical politics throughout much of the era.

Between 1945, the year that World War II ended, and 1965, when Madison's New Left broke into a full-fledged campus movement, a large number of student organizations offered a counter to the political narrowing brought on by domestic anticommunism. Some of these were outright communist in their orientation, others claimed a socialist, noncommunist ideology, and still others stood in various places from liberal to left. They reflected in some ways the status of the political left throughout the country, which had experienced significant success in the 1930s and during World War II but faced increasingly difficult times as the nation sank into the Cold War. On the national level in the 1950s, the left consisted of a number of organizations, like the American Communist Party and the Committee for Non-Violent Action (a pacifist organization), that were battered by the forces of McCarthyism. In Madison, the most important groups included two that were affiliated with the Communist Party, American Youth for Democracy (AYD), which existed from 1945 to 1949, and the Labor Youth League (LYL), from 1950 to 1956, as well as two groups that were independent of any national organizations and that would last into the middle 1960s, the Student Peace Center (SPC), established in 1955, and the Socialist Club, established in 1957. Like national groups on the political left, these organizations were often embroiled in controversy, but they still managed to stand at the center of a meaningful discourse over American foreign policy, civil liberties, and civil rights that emerged well before the 1960s and before the Vietnam War highlighted the cracks in the Cold War.[15]

In terms of actual numbers, radical campus organizations were relatively small; on a campus with between ten and twenty thousand students in the 1950s, and more than thirty thousand by the middle 1960s, leftist students remained a considerable minority. American Youth for Democracy listed more than sixty students in its 1945 application for university registration, a respectable membership for a campus organization, but this was the exception and was before the emergence of McCarthyism as a powerful force in American politics and on campus. In most instances, leftist groups claimed no more than a few dozen members, and the number of *active* members was sometimes even smaller. When the Student Peace Center was established in 1955, it listed eight members in its application; the Socialist Club claimed twenty-one at its beginning a couple of years later. The most controversial of all these groups, the Labor Youth League, was also small. While the Peace Center and Socialist Club grew over time, the Labor Youth League's membership, hard to pin down because of the group's secrecy, seems to have been in the range of fifteen to twenty-five students for most of its existence. Needless to say, these groups were influential despite, rather than because of, their numbers.[16]

While each of these groups possessed an individual outlook, all of them were drawn together in their commitment to a fundamental rethinking of American society and politics and especially in their challenge to America's Cold War policies. Other campus groups came and went throughout these years, sometimes in the course of a year or two, but even as groups like Students for Democratic Action, a student chapter of the liberal Americans for Democratic Action; Robin Hood's Merry Men, an anti-McCarthy organization; and occasionally even the Young Democrats worked on a variety of liberal issues and sometimes bucked the political conventions of the postwar decades, these groups rarely went so far as to challenge the accepted truths of the Cold War. More radical groups, in contrast, defied the prevailing winds of domestic anti-communism, which sometimes blew strongly even in relatively liberal Madison. Rarely backing away from controversy, and perhaps even inviting it at times, they pushed a persistent critique of the Cold War at home and abroad.

Reflecting the course of events in the postwar decades, students at Wisconsin highlighted an alternate view of the Cold War's beginnings and a critical assessment of America's continuing role in the world. For American Youth for Democracy, this meant calling on the Truman administration to halt its gradual but unmistakable drift into the Cold War as well as challenging the widespread belief that it was the Soviet Union that was poisoning international relations. In the first couple of years after the end of World War II, the group supported "Big Three" unity (United States, Great Britain, and the Soviet Union), and in 1946, it condemned as "war-mongering" Winston Churchill's bellicose rhetoric against the Soviet Union. As the reality of the Cold War set in, AYD pointed more and more to the United Nations as a solution to worsening East-West relations, and in 1948, it enthusiastically supported the campaign of former vice-president and third-party presidential candidate Henry Wallace.[17]

AYD's positions became increasingly out of step with mainstream American opinion in the late 1940s, but the Labor Youth League took an even more critical perspective on U.S. foreign policy. Though its program was sometimes limited to publishing broadsides and hosting controversial speakers, this was more than enough to stir the generally calm waters of campus politics, with the group's speakers sometimes attracting large crowds and usually generating coverage in the campus newspaper. In the early 1950s, the league waded into the Korean crisis, denying Soviet involvement and criticizing the United States for raising the threat of atomic war on the Korean peninsula. The LYL also pointed a finger squarely at the United States for starting and maintaining the Cold War: "The great danger of a 3rd world war comes not from the Soviet Union—but from American imperialism," a league publication declared. "[American] provocation of armed conflict in Korea is the most brutal and vicious attempt to make the Soviet Union appear guilty for the Cold War."[18]

Following the dissolution of the Labor Youth League in 1956, which coincided with Nikita Khrushchev's revelations of Stalin-era atrocities and the shockwaves this news sent through the Communist Party worldwide, the newly formed Socialist Club remained critical of American foreign policy even as it avoided the reflexive criticism of the United States and support for the Soviet Union that had often animated the league. In 1958, the group was active in its opposition to U.S. intervention in Lebanon, and when Venezuelans demonstrated in massive numbers upon Vice-President Richard Nixon's visit to Venezuela that same year, the club pointed to the protests as a direct result of flawed U.S. policy in Latin America. A few years later, in 1961, the group endured considerable harassment from anti-Castro students when it led the campus opposition to U.S. policy on Cuba, circulating a petition critical of American policy and holding a protest rally against America's role in the Bay of Pigs invasion. Finally, in October 1963, the Socialist Club was one of the key groups to put together a campus demonstration against the U.S. role in Vietnam, the first Madison protest to raise the issue of Vietnam and part of a nationwide campaign that fall.[19]

Another group that sponsored the 1963 anti-Vietnam rally was the Student Peace Center. Generally avoiding the controversy that avowedly Marxist organizations attracted, the group's activities highlighted its opposition to militarism and, more specifically, to an American foreign policy that emphasized the buildup of arms and the willingness to use military power throughout the world. It would be active in campus protests against nuclear testing and civil defense in the early 1960s, often teaming with another group, Students for Peace and Disarmament, that had ties to the national Committee for a Sane Nuclear Policy (SANE), and it was perhaps most famous for its Anti-Military Balls, held annually beginning in 1957. On the night following the Military Ball, traditionally one of the university's most important social functions of the year, the Anti-Military Ball was meant to counter what the SPC saw as the glorification of the military on campus. With skits and antiwar songs, the dance drew hundreds of students by the end of the 1950s and became a campus event in its own right.[20]

The group also played an important role in continuing the fight against compulsory ROTC. ROTC had long been an issue on campus, but despite regular discussions in the campus newspaper, debate within the student government, and occasional student referenda on the issue (one such referendum, in 1958, had to be thrown out because campus women had accidentally been allowed to vote at some polling places), it was not until the late 1950s that the move to shift ROTC from a compulsory to a voluntary system gained any traction with the university's administration. While universities had long worked closely with the military on ROTC, with higher education officials recognizing their role in the Cold War as well as the potential of ROTC to provide a civilian "check" on military power, a compulsory system no longer seemed necessary to many. When the Peace Center held a 1957 protest against compulsory ROTC, it generated little of the controversy that a similar protest had engendered in 1950, and when the military made it clear in the late 1950s that it did not believe a compulsory system necessary for national defense, this opened the door to changes at many universities, including Wisconsin. The state legislature, the faculty, and the Board of Regents all agreed to move to a voluntary system in 1960, with the issue largely disappearing, at least until the late 1960s. At that time, activists would call for the complete removal of ROTC from the Madison campus, arguing that ROTC was one more link between the university and the government's engagement in the war in Vietnam.[21]

In addition to these groups providing a source of political dissent during the years that McCarthyism held powerful sway in America, another outstanding feature of each of the organizations, and one that did not go unnoticed by their critics, was that their membership included a large number of Jewish students, with many coming from New York and, to a lesser extent, other parts of the East Coast. Of the sixty members whose home towns were listed on AYD's 1945 registration form, for example, thirty-seven were from New York, five from New Jersey, and four from Illinois; six were from Wisconsin. Two years later, the newly elected officers included Henry Elson, Bronx; Elaine Utahl, New York City; Anita Kaufman, Wisconsin Rapids; and Laura Parmet, Brooklyn. In the Labor Youth League and Socialist Club, too, a similar pattern held true. Based on the university's compilation of the known members of LYL between 1950 and 1953 (the group was only required to list its officers on its registration form and many members continued to keep their identity secret), seven of the ten members were from New York, including four from Brooklyn, while the other three were from Wisconsin. And though the 1950 campus protest against ROTC was not sponsored by any particular organization, it also included many out-of-state students: of the twenty students listed in one university document, seven were from Wisconsin, six from New York, two from New Jersey, two from Illinois, and one each from Kansas, Iowa, and Ontario, Canada.[22]

While not all East Coast students were Jewish, many were, with their presence on campus and their involvement in radical student politics continuing a pattern that had started near the beginning of the twentieth century. Drawn to Wisconsin because it lacked the quotas and admission restrictions in place at many other universities, Jews made up as much as 10 percent of the student body in the 1920s and 1930s, and they continued to come to Madison even after many East Coast universities removed their admission restrictions in the 1940s and 1950s. Official enrollment figures from these years show that New York was the source of the second greatest number of out-of-state students in Madison, after Illinois, and many students were encouraged by friends or relatives who had attended in earlier decades or were attracted by Wisconsin's reputation as a first-rate and politically active school. Buttressed also by a growing number of Jews who came from Wisconsin and other parts of the country, Madison had an active Jewish student community. The campus chapter of the national Menorah Society was established in 1911, while Jewish fraternities and sororities thrived. In 1925, Wisconsin was the second campus in the nation to establish a chapter of Hillel, an organization that provided a social and religious center for Jewish students who were far from their home communities and that is still active on campus today.[23]

Yet even as the lack of restrictive admission policies contributed to a growing Jewish population at Wisconsin, anti-Semitism was still commonplace, and the campus divide between non-Jews and Jews became a significant cleavage for many years. Housing restrictions were pervasive and Greek life was divided, but it was the association with radical student politics that received particular attention, with anti-Semitism and anti-radicalism often blending together easily. While there were some contrasting voices, including that of UW business manager A. W. Peterson, who argued in 1948 that the university's greatness depended on its cosmopolitan student body, many believed that the campus would be a better place if there were fewer "New Yorkers" (a common euphemism). Some of this emerged during student protests—Dave Trubek and Paul Breines recall being told that they should "go back to New York" during protests against Joe McCarthy and lunch counter segregation, respectively—but it also came from university and, especially, state government officials. In 1940, as controversy over campus radicals was at a high point, campus Dean of Men

Scott Goodnight assured listeners on a local radio station that only a tiny fraction of the student body were communists, so few that they "could be put in one end of a box car for convenient shipment back to New York." Various other efforts to restrict out-of-state student enrollment were also tinged with anti-Semitism. Governor Oscar Rennebohm slammed New York and New Jersey students after the 1950 ROTC protest (though he later backtracked on his statement), while Republican state assemblyman Nile Soik angrily drew public attention to the high number of out-of-state students who had signed a 1961 petition calling for the dissolution of the House Un-American Activities Committee. A few years later, Republican assemblyman Harold Froehlich would draw on this same tradition as he called for more restrictive admission policies for out-of-state students after the 1966 draft sit-in.[24]

While Jews were prominent in many radical student groups, the Student Peace Center provides at least one partial exception to the pattern. Established in 1955, the SPC was founded not by Jews from out-of-state, but by a group of avowedly Christian students, most of them from Wisconsin, whose early meetings were held in the campus's Baptist Student Center. At least some of them were pacifists, and they affiliated from the beginning with the American Friends Service Committee (AFSC), a Quaker organization that was committed to working for peace and social justice. Indeed, the SPC highlights the involvement of committed Christian students in liberal and sometimes even radical causes. The campus YMCA and Baptist Club were among those involved in human rights and civil liberties issues in the 1950s, and one 1956 gathering at the campus YMCA in support of the Montgomery bus boycott included members of the Baptist Club, the Student Peace Center, the campus NAACP, and even a few students, according to the *Daily Cardinal*, "from left-wing reformist groups not usually associated with a meeting of prayer." More broadly, adult religious leaders on campus were often supportive of civil liberties and racial equality, a trend that continued into the 1960s despite being overshadowed by that era's more activist students. Reverend George Collins, of the Student Baptist Center, was a founding member of the Madison NAACP in 1943 and declared in 1955 that "the Christian gospel demands the practice of brotherly relations in every area of life."[25]

Despite the SPC's origins, however, it was only a few years later that the group's membership more closely resembled that of other radical campus groups. Ellamae Calvert, a Methodist student from Benton, Wisconsin, who had established the SPC, was among the early members who graduated and moved on, while the new students who joined the Peace Center and carried it into the late fifties and sixties often came from different backgrounds. In the mid-fifties, Jim Sipple and Ned Cochrane, both SPC members, had applied for conscientious objector status based on their Christian beliefs, but when another SPC member, Ken Knudson, applied for the same status in 1959, his objections were moral and political, not religious (though Knudson was from Sturgeon Bay, Wisconsin, and not from the East Coast).

Another sign of the change was the election of Nina Serrano to chair the SPC in 1957. A New York Jew, she was friends with some of the early members of SPC and remembers being elected despite rejecting the pacifism of many of the other members. She was typical of the new members in that she belonged to other radical campus groups, and by the end of the 1950s, there would be considerable overlap between the Peace Center and the Socialist Club in particular. Serrano, Martin Pierce (Huntington, New York), Edward Beals (Wichita), Arthur Hack (Brooklyn), Saul Landau (Bronx), Matt Chapperon (Roslyn Heights, New York), and Marshall Brickman (Brooklyn) were just some of those who were involved in both groups in the late fifties, while some of them had also been members of LYL before it dissolved in 1956. The connections were so transparent that the Peace Center's faculty adviser, soils science professor and Quaker activist Francis Hole, considered withdrawing from his advising role in 1960. In a letter to then-chairman Dick Lerner (Brooklyn), Hole acknowledged the hard work put into the organization by members of the Socialist Club, but he expressed concern that the SPC lacked participation by students from campus religious centers and from AFSC, with which the Peace Center was still technically affiliated. As he saw it, the SPC had an increasingly narrow outlook, and its continued affiliation with AFSC was a convenience rather than a genuine commitment to the Friends' principles.[26]

East Coast Jews were undoubtedly overrepresented in radical student groups, but this does not mean that these organizations should be dismissed as the sole creation of New Yorkers or as the tools of Old Left groups that continued to operate in New York and some of the country's other urban centers. Although this was exactly the view taken by many of these groups' critics, Wisconsin had its own radical traditions, based in turn-of-the-century Progressivism as well as the continuing strength of the Socialist Party in Milwaukee. It was these traditions, in part, that attracted many out-of-state students in the first place. Moreover, there were always a number of students who did not fit the profile of the radical New York Jew; there were many campus leftists who came from Wisconsin—such as Ted and Andrea Cloak, Franklynn Peterson, Lee Baxandall, and Ken Knudson, to name just a few—and there were many others who came from Illinois or other parts of the Midwest. Finally, there were always many more New York and East Coast Jews who were *not* involved in radical campus politics than those who were. Suggesting the tension that sometimes emerged between Jews involved in radical politics and those who were not, Henry Wortis, a well-known member of LYL in the middle fifties, remembers finding himself in the doorway of a store near campus with another Jewish student from New York. After a few minutes of silence, the other student, a member of the UW Young Democrats, turned to Wortis: it was students like Wortis, he said, that gave all New York Jews a bad reputation.[27]

Moreover, even for the many Jews involved in radical politics in Madison, the role of Jewishness is complex and difficult to unravel. For most Jews on the left, being Jewish had more cultural than religious content, an outgrowth of a specific social and political environment that was more closely identified with the union hall than the synagogue. As immigrants in the late nineteenth and early twentieth centuries who had settled in New York City, Chicago, Philadelphia, and other large cities, Jews had joined the American working class and had taken prominent roles in the developing labor union movement, including its sometimes radical politics. As many second- and third-generation Jews in particular replaced the religious devotion of their immigrant parents and grandparents with an activist politics, the Jewish community was often bound together by unions, newspapers, and even summer camps that supported a kind of cultural or ethnic Judaism. Many Jews who grew up in the post–World War II decades had community and often family ties to leftist politics; at least some had seen the effects of McCarthyism close up and had come of age with a lasting distrust of mainstream American politics.[28]

The complex meanings of Jewish identity and its relationship to leftist politics emerges in the memories of Wisconsin students from this era. For Paul Breines, who grew up in New York but with few leftist connections, it was in Madison where he first felt Jewish. Of becoming active in the UW Socialist Club, he recalls that, "becoming a leftist, that was becoming a Jew for me." Roz Baxandall (then Roz Fraad), on the other hand, remembers that her Jewish identity, a product of her leftist upbringing in New York, was challenged by other Jewish students in Madison. Rooming with two girls from Chicago who observed traditional Jewish holidays and understood their Jewish identity in religious rather than political terms, "these Midwestern, *nouveau riche* gals were my introduction to American Judaism." "I'd assumed I was Jewish" she remembers, but it was only at this time that she became conscious that her parents were actually atheists.[29]

Franklynn Peterson's story offers another interesting twist on the ways that Jewishness played in the New Left's radical politics. Raised in a small Wisconsin mill town, Peterson quickly found his way to radical campus politics after he arrived in Madison in the fall of 1956. Even as he was elected to lead the Socialist Club in 1960, however, a fact that he credits to his working-class background and, as he tells it, his "straight nose" (qualities that were prized by a group that was self-conscious about its largely middle-class background and eager to have a non-Jew as its public face), he was also in the process of leaving behind his Lutheran background. In a development that he says "amused" the friends he was making on the left, he started to hang around the campus Hillel chapter, a place where many Jewish students gathered but that most leftist Jews either ignored or scorned. Peterson would continue to explore Judaism while he was a student, converting later in life, and he would marry Gail Bernstein, a New Jersey Jew and another member of the Socialist Club. Interestingly, it would be Bernstein's Orthodox grandparents, rather than Bernstein or her likewise secular parents, who introduced him to a variety of Jewish religious traditions.[30]

Without oversimplifying the complexities of Jewish involvement in radical movements, many Jews understood their Jewishness as rooted in an activist, and usually leftist, politics. Investigating the differences in post–World War II political culture among New York City's Jewish and Catholic populations, historian Joshua Zeitz suggests that although Catholics often promoted obedience to authority, many Jews grew up in homes that prized intellectual freedom, with dissent identified as a core element of Jewishness. Sociologist Rebecca Klatch makes similar observations about the role of Jewishness in sixties-era activist politics. In interviews with Jewish members of Students for a Democratic Society, the largest of the New Left organizations, she found that while few Jewish activists had a religious upbringing, they still had a strong cultural Jewish identity. The Holocaust sometimes shaped their politics, a recent and powerful reminder of the effects of oppression, and anti-Semitism also reinforced their position outside of the American mainstream. Jews were active in New Left politics around the country: they played an important role in the development of Students for a Democratic Society in the early 1960s and made up perhaps a third of the students who were involved in Berkeley's Free Speech Movement in 1964. In Madison, Jews were crucial to a radical community that blended East and West, Jew and non-Jew, and that provided a crucial conduit of radicalism, especially in the early development of the New Left.[31]

❖

The emergence in Madison of a potent critique of the Cold War owed much to the dynamic mix of students who came to Madison in the 1950s and 1960s, but it must also be recognized as a legacy of the University of Wisconsin's commitment to free speech and its relatively broad tolerance of dissent. Even as there was an individual component to the unorthodox campus politics of the 1950s and early 1960s, then, there was also an institutional context to the maintenance of a radical campus politics during the height of the McCarthy years. Universities across the nation faced scrutiny from domestic anticommunists, especially as higher education became increasingly central to the nation's security, and public universities like Wisconsin, dependent for much of their funding on the goodwill of state legislatures, were especially affected. At the UW, postwar presidents E. B. Fred, Conrad Elvehjem, and Fred Harvey Harrington could not ignore the potential backlash over radical student activity in Madison, and they ultimately produced a mixed record, balancing an institutional commitment to civil liberties and academic freedom with the realities of the Cold War era. Still, while many other universities were seriously narrowing or eliminating the opportunities for radical or even unorthodox student activity, Wisconsin stands out for its relative tolerance of radical student groups and speakers, maintaining a space for serious and open discussion that defied mainstream political currents.

In the postwar years, the university was already drawing on a long tradition of vigorous and open debate, even in the face of public controversy. This tradition dated back at least to 1894 and the controversy surrounding economics professor Richard T. Ely, who had been hired two years earlier as director of the School of Economics, Politics, and History. Ely was accused of supporting strikes and boycotts, an incendiary charge in the late nineteenth century and one that received national coverage in the *Nation*, New York's *Evening Post*, and other publications. The accusation from Wisconsin superintendent of public instruction Oliver Wells led to a thorough investigation, and even though it soon became clear that Ely would be exonerated, the university's Board of Regents decided to use the opportunity to make public its broad support for free inquiry in the university community. "Whatever may be the limitations which trammel inquiry elsewhere," the regents declared that year, "we believe the great state University of Wisconsin should ever encourage that continual and fearless sifting and winnowing by which alone the truth can be found." This support for "sifting and winnowing" would quickly become a source of pride for the university, captured on a plaque attached to the university's main building, Bascom Hall, in 1910, featured prominently in every issue of the *Daily Cardinal*, and still referenced by many on the campus today.[32]

More importantly, the university's commitment would be affirmed in practice during the first half of the twentieth century. As early as 1922, when controversy arose over the use of university facilities by several well-known

radical speakers, the Board of Regents repeated its 1894 statement and specifically approved the campus invitation of socialist writer Upton Sinclair and
former Socialist Party presidential candidate Eugene Debs (Debs had also
been incarcerated for two years after the end of World War I for violating the
Espionage Act). Several years later, UW President Glenn Frank issued a strong
statement in favor of the faculty's right to academic freedom, while his successor,
Clarence Dykstra, would similarly defend the rights of student groups as scrutiny
of radical student organizations developed in the late 1930s. With some in
Madison and throughout the state criticizing the communist leanings of the
University League for Liberal Action, Dykstra was among those who came to
the group's defense, issuing a statement to the American Legion, a regular critic
of campus radicals, that "intolerance is like an epidemic." Dykstra would also
be involved in several controversies in the late 1940s after he left Wisconsin and
took over as the provost at the University of California, Los Angeles; because of
his willingness to allow controversial speakers on the UCLA campus, he became
a regular target of domestic anticommunists.[33]

These events in Madison's history set the tone for later confrontations,
but the Cold War era placed even greater pressure on higher education, with
the first salvo in the struggle over the reach of domestic anticommunism at
Wisconsin coming just a few years after the end of World War II. Even though
the term "McCarthyism" had not yet been coined, its champions in Wisconsin
were already gathering force, and at the center of the controversy was Madison's
chapter of American Youth for Democracy, a group that had been established
nationally in 1945 as the youth group of the Communist Party. The Wisconsin
chapter, for its part, claimed publicly that it was a "progressive" organization
and was open to anyone accepting its program, but the group's postwar criticisms of U.S. foreign policy were more than enough to arouse suspicion. HUAC
had already accused the national organization of being a communist front, and
when U.S. attorney general Tom Clark included AYD on the government's list
of subversive organizations in December 1947, the same month the campus
chapter invited suspected communists Gerhard Eisler and Carl Marzani to
speak, suspicion turned into outright condemnation. Though UW administrators denied that politics was involved, they quickly turned down the requests
for the speakers, citing the fact that both were under criminal investigation:
Eisler was facing charges for contempt of Congress and perjury while Marzani
was appealing a conviction for lying about his association with the Communist
Party while an employee of the federal government during World War II.[34]

Wisconsin was not the only university to struggle with its chapter of AYD
and the question of controversial speakers. Many universities, including the

University of Colorado, Brooklyn College, Temple University, and the University of Michigan, simply banned the group altogether, while Michigan also joined others in keeping controversial speakers off campus. Berkeley had already severely limited student political activity in the 1930s in response to the emergence of communist-influenced groups, but many universities tightened their policies in the immediate postwar years. Some used membership list requirements, a tactic specifically recommended by the House Un-American Activities Committee, as a way to pressure student organizations; groups at many campuses simply folded under the requirement to publicly disclose all of their members. According to Ellen Schrecker, a historian of the McCarthy era's effect on higher education, the result of many universities' efforts was that, by the early 1950s, 'the student left was all but extinct on American campuses.'[35]

At the UW, a state-supported institution and the pride of Wisconsin's system of higher education, the possibility that there were communists on campus drew significant attention throughout the state. Alumni, parents, and newspaper editorial boards voiced their opinions, while some state legislators, who regularly wrangled over university budgets and policies, were particularly critical of any sign of campus radicalism. Indeed, even before the invitations to Marzani and Eisler, at least one state legislator was in contact with the university concerning the AYD chapter, highlighting again the concern about the role of out-of-state students in campus radicalism. Just as the state legislature was discussing the postwar enrollment crunch and a push by some lawmakers to restrict out-of-state students, Republican state senator Bernard Gettelman wrote to university officials in 1947 asking for information about AYD members. Dean of Students Paul Trump responded with a list of members, including their hometowns, and he noted that the status of AYD was currently under consideration by the UW's administration and faculty.[36]

As in other controversies, students made known their own opinions on the status of AYD and its efforts to bring radical speakers to campus. In a letter to the *Daily Cardinal*, one student slammed AYD for its suspected communist affiliations and, unsatisfied with the university's denial that its decision to keep Eisler off campus had anything to do with his politics, argued that Eisler's communist ties were more enough to ban him from campus. "Does a democrat have freedom of speech in a communist state?" he asked, repeating a refrain that would be used again and again by those opposing the use of university facilities by communists or suspected communists. According to this line of argument, there was no reason to provide the benefits and liberties of the American system to those who would plot to destroy that system. Two other UW students proposed a more straightforward solution to AYD's invitation that winter: "Let AYD and Eisler convene out in the middle of Lake Mendota [bordering the campus], and if the lake is not frozen over so much the better."[37]

But even as some lined up with the administration during the controversy over Eisler and Marzani, including the *Cardinal*'s editors and the majority of those who wrote letters to the paper, a number supported the rights of AYD. Bob Sollen, a *Cardinal* columnist and political science major from Michigan, accused AYD of creating controversy for the purpose of stirring up trouble, but he argued that it made no sense to fight AYD with its own methods: free speech was the only way to combat communism. Others expressing their dismay over the Eisler decision included the student government, which protested the university's ruling, and at least two campus political organizations, Students for Democratic Action, a student affiliate of the liberal Americans for Democratic Action, and Young Progressive Citizens of America, which charged the university with setting a dangerous precedent in its denial of free speech for AYD.[38]

Ultimately, the university's record on AYD, like its record during much of this period, was mixed. In addition to turning down the speaker requests for Eisler and Marzani, the university also initiated efforts to impose a membership list requirement on student organizations. Like other universities, Wisconsin denied that the requirement, which would force student groups to list all of their members instead of just their officers on annual registration forms, was politically motivated, but few believed this claim. Predictably, groups like AYD and the John Cookson Marxist Discussion Club (formed in 1947) protested the new rule, with AYD president Bernard Herschel writing to Dean Trump that it was a matter of principle that students should be able to keep political affiliations private. Herschel also questioned the ways in which such a list might be used; in the context of the "witch-hunts and hysterical investigations [that] have become the order of the day," he wrote, there was good reason for concern. Perhaps more importantly, other campus groups also raised their voices against the policy. In the weeks just prior to and after the deadline for submitting lists of members, Students for Democratic Action and the campus chapter of the liberal-leaning American Veterans Committee (AVC) criticized the policy, while the student government and the *Cardinal* expressed their opposition as well. In a letter to Trump, Ivan Nestingen, chair of AVC and later the mayor of Madison and undersecretary of Health, Education, and Welfare in the Kennedy and Johnson administrations, cited the policy's detrimental effect on student freedom and asked the university to reconsider its position. Remarkably, the university did just that; although its precise reasoning remains unclear, the university reversed itself just a few weeks after the new policy was supposed to go into effect.[39]

The university also took a lenient approach when it came to the broader question of AYD's status as an officially recognized student organization. In a March 1947 letter to a colleague at the University of Colorado (where AYD was later banned), Dean Trump remarked that despite the uproar over the national organization, Wisconsin AYD followed the university's regulations and was generally accepted by students and faculty as just another student political organization. Later that year, a proposed statement from the Student Life and Interests Committee (SLIC), which governed student organizations, declared that "freedom of choice on the basis of the interchange of student opinion is, the committee feels, symptomatic of democratic health and vitality on the campus." Though declaring that university recognition did not imply approval and expressing concern that students understand the future implications of joining a group like AYD, the committee suggested that the best way to combat communism was not to censor it: "The committee has faith in the ability of the American form of government to prove its value through unlicensed competition in the free market of ideas—on the university campus, as well as elsewhere."[40]

Madison's chapter of AYD closed its doors in 1949, along with the national organization, but the template that it established in the struggle over student political freedoms would play out with even more fervor in the controversy over the Labor Youth League, a group established in 1950 near the height of the hysteria over communism. The league replaced AYD as the youth group of the Communist Party (radical groups were often short-lived during these years, the result of repression as well as regular attempts by communists and others to reenergize their organizations), but it received the same kind of scrutiny from government officials as well as university administrators. Listed as a subversive organization by the U.S. attorney general and directed to register as a communist front organization by the Subversive Activities Control Board, a committee created by the 1950 McCarran Internal Security Act, the group was pressed around the country and, like AYD, banned on many campuses. Still, even as Wisconsin's Joe McCarthy was making a name for himself as America's leading anticommunist, Madison avoided the worst effects of the anticommunist fervor. The LYL's existence in Madison was always precarious, but it still managed to maintain its university recognition throughout the early and middle 1950s; indeed, for a few years in the middle 1950s it was the *only* university-recognized Labor Youth League chapter in the entire country.

The LYL in Madison was a relatively small group, and though it occasionally attracted attention for its broadsides against American foreign policy and the controversial speakers it invited to campus, it wasn't until January 1953, when it hosted Abner Berry, Negro affairs editor of the Communist Party's *Daily Worker* newspaper, that it generated sustained controversy. While other speakers had prompted debate in the several years since Eisler and Marzani's cancelled appearances, including former State Department adviser Owen Lattimore, who was invited by the university's Union Forum Committee despite accusations by McCarthy and other anticommunists that he was a Soviet agent, Berry's appearance hit a particularly sensitive chord. Republican state senator Gordon Bubolz, a conservative who represented McCarthy's hometown of Appleton, took up the issue the day before Berry was to speak, pouncing on the university for harboring radicals and promising to investigate the presence of LYL on campus, a serious claim in the context of the early 1950s. His public attack set off a flurry of activity. President Fred responded the next day, explaining the university's policies on student organizations and speakers and defending the rights of student organizations and their "freedom of inquiry," while the Wisconsin Legislative Council, an arm of the state legislature, officially requested materials relating to the university's rules on student organizations and speakers. What followed was a nearly year-long reevaluation of university policies that would test the resilience of state and university support for the student political freedoms that had existed in Madison for decades.[41]

As the university and the state legislature began their deliberations, Berry's speech brought intensified discussion among students, too, with the campus Young Republicans (YGOP) initially leading the charge against the LYL. In the run up to Berry's January speech, the group had resolved that the university should deny "university recognition and facilities to subversive organizations," and in March, as the fallout from the speech continued, they called directly for a ban on the LYL. Writing for the group, John Fritschler, a law student from Superior, Wisconsin, and also chairman of the Midwest Federation of College YGOP Clubs, argued that free speech was a "responsibility," one that the league abused. The Bill of Rights was not a "suicide pact," Fritschler argued, and the civil liberties that the league clung to would not exist if communism were to triumph. The university should ban subversive groups because, as he put it, "one more Alger Hiss or Harry Gold is too much." Later that year, as another controversial speaker appeared at the invitation of the LYL—Joseph Starobin, a former foreign editor of the *Daily Worker* who, among other things, warned students against U.S. involvement in Vietnam—a group of several student leaders sent a letter to President Fred again opposing the university's sanctioning of communist groups and speakers. Signers of the letter included members of Wisconsin's student government as well as leaders of such groups as the Young Republicans, the Badger Veterans Organization, and the Concerned League of Women Voters.[42]

This controversy also points to the assertiveness of conservative students in campus politics. The YGOP was in the forefront of early efforts against potentially subversive speakers and organizations in Madison, but other groups often took up the conservative torch in later years, with the YGOP sometimes split between conservative and moderate or even liberal members. In a pamphlet distributed to new students in the fall of 1949, for example, the YGOP emphasized its role in the campus's "progressive" politics; while it declared its commitment to smaller government, it also highlighted its support for eliminating compulsory ROTC and its efforts to fight campus discrimination. Moreover, even in the midst of the fight over the LYL, at least one member of the YGOP, future U.S. secretary of state Lawrence Eagleburger, declared in the campus newspaper that "the leaders of the Young Republicans are, in effect, attempting to destroy . . . liberties in just as insidious a manner as any communist." The mantle of anticommunism, then, was often taken up by other organizations, including, in 1953, a group called Students for America. The group's charter called for it to "uncover and eradicate organized subversive elements" on campus, and though it only lasted for a year, it suggested a new direction among conservative students, one that mirrored changes among state Republicans, as the LaFollette family dynasty and its commitment to Progressivism largely ended in the 1940s. Many national Republicans were also moving in this direction, with the party nominating the conservative Barry Goldwater for the 1964 presidential contest after a long struggle between the moderate and conservative wings of the party.[43]

In another twist, conservative students' position on the league found some sympathizers on the left as well, though no leftist groups advocated banning LYL from campus. While some on the left avoided communists because of the practical repercussions of associating with them, others were highly critical of the league's positions, especially its support for the Soviet Union, with the divisions on campus reflecting a long history of infighting on the American left between various factions of socialists and communists. Future historian Gabriel Kolko, then a graduate student and leader of Madison's Student League for Industrial Democracy (SLID), a socialist and anticommunist group that existed on campus for a few years in the middle 1950s, criticized the LYL in 1955 for its double talk and hypocrisy. In particular, he hit the league's defense of free speech, citing the lack of democratic protections within the Soviet Union. Another SLID leader, Bertell Ollman, was a persistent critic as well. Like Kolko, he criticized LYL for hypocrisy in their support of civil liberties, and he called out league members in 1955 for what he saw as their efforts to infiltrate other campus groups or, as he put it, to "crawl under the skirts of the campus liberal movements."

He suggested that SLID would like to "sweep them back out under the sun, where their spots can be better observed."[44]

Despite the many attacks, members of the Labor Youth League, no strangers to adversity, responded loudly. The league had been defending civil liberties since its founding, and in response to the March 1953 call by the campus Young Republicans for a ban on "subversive" groups, league president Alita Letwin argued in the *Daily Cardinal* for the need to preserve free speech. LYL should be on campus because there are students who believe in its principles and want to belong, she declared, while, more generally, "freedom of thought and action is the most elementary right of students." Suggesting that efforts to ban the league were akin to imposing a kind of thought conformity, she also sought to highlight the group's work on issues other than its support for Marxism, pointing to the group's efforts in fighting campus discrimination and working for lower tuition and higher state funding for university education. Other members of the LYL also spoke out in the pages of the *Cardinal*, though some of them did not openly reveal their membership in the league. Henry Wortis, who would testify before the U.S. Senate's Subversive Activities Control Board in 1954 on the status of the league, wrote an opinion piece denying that communists sought a violent overthrow of American democracy, while Marty Sklar, who would continue to play an important role on the campus left into the 1960s, authored a more general defense of academic freedom.[45]

It also helped the league that Senator McCarthy's lack of popularity on campus seemed to color many students' view of the recurrent controversies over domestic anticommunism. One of McCarthy's few campus appearances, in 1951, devolved into chaos when he responded to a hostile audience by calling the students "braying jackasses," and when the university reevaluated its group and speaker policies in 1953, several organizations raised objections to McCarthyism, including the Baptist Student Center and the Young Democrats. A debate on McCarthyism that July drew an audience of three hundred, most of them anti-McCarthy, while more broadly, there were a number of campus groups committed to fighting McCarthyism throughout the early and middle 1950s, including the short-lived Stick Your Neck Out Club, formed in 1952 by a group of professors and students to assert the right to express opinions without fear of reprisal, and Robin Hood's Merry Men, an anti-McCarthy group that was established in 1954 to work on a campaign to recall the senator. In 1955, a broad range of campus leaders, including the president of the Wisconsin Student Association, signed and distributed a letter opposing the 1950 McCarran Act, also known as the Internal Security Act, which required communist organizations to register with the federal government and created a board to investigate potential subversion. Questioning the law's constitutionality and recalling some of former President Truman's own objections (Congress had overridden Truman's veto in order to pass the law), the students argued that the legislation threatened young people's right to freely associate and exchange ideas.[46]

Even within the state legislature, from which Senator Bubolz had threatened to investigate the university, there was a good deal of support for the university's traditional stance on student groups and outside speakers. Madison may have been one of the more liberal cities in the state, but there were many other parts of Wisconsin that had been deeply influenced by the early twentieth-century Progressive movement, not to mention the continuing strength of socialists in Milwaukee, the state's largest city. The Wisconsin Legislative Council that requested materials from the university in the wake of Berry's campus appearance showed little interest in campus radicals, and the group's report, issued in 1954, took a much more general approach, trumpeting the importance of higher education in the state and echoing the university's oft-stated concern about the need to educate mature citizens who can make their own evaluation of truth and falsehood. Led by Republican state senator and future governor Warren Knowles, the committee's report made little specific mention of speakers and student groups at the university, concluding simply that "the university should continue its present policy of placing no restrictions on freedom of speech or assembly beyond those established by state or federal laws."[47]

That Wisconsin's state government, dominated by Republicans and working at the height of McCarthy's national power, would take such a mild approach to the issue of radicalism at the university indicates McCarthy's complicated position in his home state. McCarthy was certainly popular, winning with 61 percent of the vote when he was first elected as a relative unknown in 1946 and with 54 percent of the vote in his 1952 reelection campaign, after he had gained national prominence for his tough anticommunism, but he actually underperformed other Republicans in the latter election. Among the six Wisconsin Republicans vying for statewide offices that year, his 9-point win represented the smallest margin of victory. Republican Walter Kohler Jr. won the governor's race that year by 25 points, while Dwight Eisenhower carried the state in the presidential election by a similar margin of 22 points.

This might help explain why McCarthy rarely attacked opponents in his home state. When he did, his attacks were not always well received, such as when he directed his fire at Lawrence University president Nathan Pusey, a McCarthy critic who found wide support even though Lawrence was located in McCarthy's hometown of Appleton (Pusey would later go on to be the president of Harvard University from 1953 until 1971). McCarthy miscalculated again in

1954 when he denounced Stoughton, Wisconsin, native General Ralph Zwicker, a hero of the Battle of the Bulge, during his investigation of the U.S. Army. The attack on Zwicker was one of several factors behind the "Joe Must Go" recall campaign the same year, a campaign that was ultimately unsuccessful but that gathered between three and four hundred thousand signatures over the course of several months. McCarthy also found it difficult to attack the University of Wisconsin; even though the university was located in the relatively liberal confines of Madison, Republican governors had appointed most of the members of the university's Board of Regents, and many of the regents were prominent Republicans who were well regarded throughout the state.[48]

By the end of 1953, then, after ten months of deliberation amid the tangle of university and state politics, the university finally released its verdict on the question of student groups and outside speakers. The issue had gone through at least two committees, including the Student Life and Interests Committee, which normally oversaw student groups, and an ad hoc committee formed by President Fred to advise him separately. The latter committee issued a majority report recommending that the university change its policy to deny the use of facilities for outside speakers known to be members of communist or communist front organizations, but Fred ultimately proceeded with the committee's minority opinion as well as the unanimous recommendations of SLIC. Despite the tumult caused by the appearance of two speakers associated with the newspaper of the Communist Party and the clear political risks near the height of the McCarthy era, the university simply reaffirmed its existing policy of free speech and student political expression. Based on that reaffirmation, it took no action against the Labor Youth League or any other student organizations.[49]

When the results of the policy review were announced, in November, they were couched in the same language of support for critical inquiry on which university officials had drawn for the last half century or more. As Dean of Men Theodore Zillman put it in the cover letter attached to the report, the university's current policy was educationally sound, consistent with state and federal laws, good for long-term public relations, and avoided the practical difficulty of deciding which groups to censor. At many other universities, of course, the actions of faculty and administrators indicate that they were not so sanguine about the educational or public relations benefits of a policy that allowed communist student groups and speakers onto campus, but the committee drew on the history of the university and the nation in its unqualified support for free inquiry. "Faith in freedom, not fear of freedom, is our heritage," the committee concluded. "The founders of this republic, though faced with uncertainty and danger, created a free society with full allowance for divergent views. The early leaders of this university, when freedom was challenged, made untrammeled inquiry the guiding spirit for a great university. We propose that the wisdom of this heritage be applied to the problems of today."[50]

Ultimately, Wisconsin provided an institutional space for dissent that did not exist on many university campuses in the two decades after the end of World War II, let alone places outside of higher education. Certainly, Fred and others disagreed with radical students on the merits of capitalism and American foreign policy, among other things, but they firmly believed that the best way to deal with potentially subversive elements (at least student elements—they were not so certain about communists among the university's staff) was to let them compete in the marketplace of ideas, a competition that they believed communists and other radicals would surely lose. In response to an Indiana woman who wrote him in 1953, urging him to crack down on campus radicals, Fred responded succinctly: "We agree that our country has much at stake. We differ on ways to combat the menace." President Harrington would take the same position when he took the university's reigns in 1962, declaring in a letter to an alumnus that year that "There are many good ways of fighting communism; but these do not include suppressing free speech." Controversies continued to erupt occasionally over student organizations and especially the radical speakers they sometimes invited to campus, but the 1953 review of university policies stood for the rest of this era. One event that did prompt some outrage from around the state, a Socialist Club–sponsored speech by U.S. Communist Party leader Gus Hall in 1962, shows how little interest there was among Wisconsin's administrators for another extended policy review. Dean Zillman, writing a memo to Dean of Students LeRoy Luberg, summarized the issue succinctly, suggesting that the administration should simply "let the rascal speak."[51]

❖

It was within this context at the University of Wisconsin that an increasingly energized student politics and the first indications of a new left emerged. American Youth for Democracy and the Labor Youth League were rooted in the Old Left, youth auxiliaries of the Communist Party, but one of the most important developments in Madison was the break from this political tradition that occurred during the 1950s. If the LYL represented an extension of the Old Left, even if the link was somewhat tenuous considering that Wisconsin students operated half a continent away from the Old Left's center of gravity in New York City, the Socialist Club and Student Peace Center represented both continuity and change. There were many students in the Socialist Club and

Peace Center who had been members of the LYL only a year or two earlier, but the continued withering of the Old Left amid McCarthy-era repression, disillusionment over the Soviet Union's 1956 invasion of Hungary, and the revelation of atrocities committed by Joseph Stalin created an opportunity to rethink basic assumptions for many leftists. The sixties still seemed distant in some ways, but the Socialist Club and Student Peace Center pointed to developments that would become increasingly familiar in the years ahead: students in Madison were less concerned with the internecine fighting that had consumed so much energy within the Old Left, and they incorporated a cultural element in their politics even as they began to utilize direct action.[52]

The Socialist Club especially symbolized a blending of New York and Madison, a mixing of the Old Left and a new political sensibility, in a way that the transplanted Labor Youth League did not. Particularly important, the Socialist Club was independent from any national organizations, declaring among its founding principles that it would represent "every shade of socialist thought." Ideological orthodoxy had been prized in the Old Left, but the Socialist Club acted as a kind of meeting place for leftists of various stripes in the late fifties and early sixties, including among its membership some former LYL members along with many others attracted to socialism. In 1963, the club's summer president, C. Clark Kissinger, declared with pride that "whenever you get ten socialists together, you have at least seventeen different factions"; this ideological diversity would be a hallmark of the New Left, part of the open-ended discussion and debate on how to tackle such deep-rooted issues as imperialism, racism, and income inequality.[53]

Even more than the Socialist Club, the Peace Center stood out from other leftist groups, significant for cutting something of a new direction in campus politics. This was certainly influenced by the group's Christian and pacifist origins, but it continued even after the Center's membership started to look more like that of the Socialist Club in the late fifties. "Everything was done by consensus," former Peace Center chair Nina Serrano recalls of the group's early years, anticipating the mood of the New Left as well as, perhaps, the women's movement. "Feelings counted, not just well-reasoned discourses, like the Marxist study groups. There were no bureaucratic trappings, like offices in New York making the major decisions." The Anti-Military Balls in particular were more closely related to the countercultural activism of the late 1960s than the more studied and serious programs of other left groups, a development that helped to bridge the divide between leftist students and the rest of the campus. Saul Landau, who had been involved in the Labor Youth League and then the Socialist Club and Student Peace Center (and was married to Serrano at the time), puts the difference between the league and these later groups in simple terms: without the need to adhere to a party line and freed of the discipline of the Communist Party, the campus left in the late 1950s was simply "more fun."[54]

The Peace Center also helped re-introduce direct action to the campus, though it did so tentatively. No doubt influenced by the national peace movement, which included direct action protests against civil defense programs and other symbols of the Cold War in the 1950s, the Peace Center included a committee on direct action, and in 1957 it reprised the 1950 anti-ROTC protest. In the early 1960s, the SPC became more active, especially on the issues of nuclear testing and civil defense, which were gaining national attention at the time. Holding a number of protests in 1961 and 1962, the group helped lead the way, along with the growing civil rights movement on campus, in developing a direct action politics that would become an important part of the New Left.[55]

These developments in the late 1950s, developments that built on the state's Progressive tradition and the university's commitment to civil liberties, point to a crucial moment in the emergence of a new left in Madison and in the United States. They coincided with the waning of McCarthyism from its peak in the early 1950s (though domestic anticommunism would remain a powerful force for many years), and they also suggest a degree of continuity between the 1950s and 1960s that is easily missed given the much more vocal left that emerged in later years. Universities were becoming increasingly important to the nation's Cold War struggle, but students in Madison and at some of the nation's other leading universities continued to nurture alternative perspectives on the Cold War. These students had little idea that a powerful new left would exist within a few short years, but their efforts laid an important foundation for the great changes in American culture and society that would take place during the sixties.

3

"A constant struggle with ideas"

Intellectual Community in the Sixties

As the 1960s dawned, Madison was one of a small number of places in the country where students were struggling toward a new left. Though its shape and future direction remained inchoate, young radicals were disillusioned with the status quo, skeptical of America's aggressive Cold War policies, and doubtful about liberals' commitment to civil liberties and civil rights. Direct action would come to dominate sixties politics, with young people emphasizing the need to put their bodies on the line in order to demonstrate their commitment, but in the emerging New Left of the early sixties, ideas provided the movement with a crucial underpinning. The New Left is rarely recognized for its intellectual depth and has often been condemned (or, from another perspective, celebrated) for its supposed anti-intellectualism, yet Madison highlights the importance of intellectual exchange. Young radicals in the late 1950s and early 1960s were groping for an understanding of the failures of the left, a framework for comprehending the problems of Cold War America, and a direction forward. Many of their ideas ran counter to America's Cold War orthodoxy, but the forces of McCarthyism could not stamp out debate and discussion of unorthodox ideas just as they could not close the door on radical student organizations.[1]

In Madison, the intellectual community that emerged in the late 1950s included student organizations like the Socialist Club and the Student Peace Center, but another key element was Wisconsin's generally excellent and sometimes irreverent faculty. University professors have played only a small role in histories of the sixties, but even as professors often faced more pressure from McCarthyism than did their students, with most of them veering toward the middle of the ideological and scholarly spectrum, there was always a small group of professors who belied these trends. In Madison, these faculty members were spread throughout the university, with an important concentration in the history department, and they created a rigorous academic environment where ideas, even radical ideas, were taken seriously. Few of them were radicals themselves, but they exposed students to political theory and intellectual history and challenged them to refine their ideas. A few set an important example with their own political activism, while diplomatic historian William Appleman Williams stands out most prominently for providing a model of radical scholarship that would take deep root in Madison and would spread throughout the nation.

The clearest expression of intellectual development in Madison was the publication of *Studies on the Left*, a scholarly journal established by a group of Wisconsin graduate students in 1959. *Studies* connected the many parts of the university's intellectual community, including Wisconsin and out-of-state students, Jews and non-Jews, and students and faculty. UW sociologist Hans Gerth contributed an article to the first issue, and Williams's penetrating view of diplomatic history underscored the journal's critique of American foreign relations and the American liberal tradition. Extending the work of groups like the Socialist Club and the Student Peace Center (many of the editors were also members of one or both of these organizations), *Studies* furthered the break with the Old Left. As young radicals across the country searched for a framework for understanding the nation's history and politics, the journal played a crucial role in providing a foundation for the New Left's wide-ranging and powerful critique of America.

❖

Just as McCarthyism provided a significant obstacle for student activism in the decades after the Second World War, university professors, a central component of intellectual communities in Madison and elsewhere, were also subject to the powerful forces of domestic anticommunism. While the University of Wisconsin stands out for its relative tolerance of controversial student groups, the issue of student organizations and speakers was only one part of the much broader collision between higher education and McCarthyism. As early as 1948, the possible presence of communist teachers on the nation's university and college campuses attracted the attention of domestic anticommunists, with a rapidly developing consensus among many officials in higher education that communists were unfit for membership in the academic community. At the University of Wisconsin, too, administrators disavowed communist professors, essentially drawing a distinction between communist students, misguided but not in a position of influence, and communist teachers, who violated the integrity of the university.

Historian Ellen Schrecker, whose work is the most comprehensive on the effect of McCarthyism in academia, concludes that domestic anticommunism altered both the intellectual and institutional structure of the nation's universities. "The academy did not fight McCarthyism," she argues, "it contributed to it." Investigating committees like the House Un-American Activities Committee (HUAC) set their sights on higher education, but universities often took up this effort as their own even as they maintained a rhetorical commitment to academic freedom and civil liberties. At least some in the university community redefined the concept of academic freedom altogether: instead of protecting individual scholars and their freedom to consider otherwise controversial ideas as it had in the past, the notion of academic freedom became a way to protect the institutions themselves from outside interference.[2]

One of the first investigations to draw significant attention to the issue of communist faculty members occurred at the University of Washington in 1948. That year, the state legislature's Fact-Finding Committee on Un-American Activities called several professors to testify, with three admitting prior participation in the Communist Party but refusing to name names and three others almost completely uncooperative. The university then began its own investigation (a common follow-up to the work of legislative committees, which did not have the power to fire or otherwise discipline faculty members), and while the investigation initially focused on the professors' truthfulness, the admission by two professors that they were still members of the Communist Party turned the issue to whether communists were, by definition, unfit to teach. There was no evidence that their politics had affected their scholarship or teaching, and the charges boiled down to the relatively simple question of whether or not their allegiance to the Communist Party meant that they lacked intellectual independence. After an extended process, the university fired both professors, English professor Joseph Butterworth and philosophy professor Herbert Phillips, as well as another professor, psychologist Ralph Gundlach, who had refused to cooperate with the university investigation. The result was an important precedent in how universities would deal with communists during the McCarthy era, a precedent made all the more effective since each of the three had been tenured and none of them were again able to find regular teaching positions.[3]

Over the next several years, little happened to challenge the consensus that communists were unfit for higher education, and at the same time, what was initially a somewhat haphazard attempt to examine radicalism in the nation's universities took a more organized turn. In 1953, the new chairman of HUAC, Illinois representative Harold Velde, announced that the committee would conduct an in-depth examination of higher education. The Senate Internal Security Subcommittee and Joseph McCarthy's Committee on Government Operations also turned their attention to communism in universities, and the three congressional committees between them called more than one hundred professors to testify in 1953 and several dozen more in 1954. The American Association of University Professors made some attempts to protect faculty from the excesses of domestic anticommunism, including their official position that professors should be judged by the quality of their scholarship and teaching rather than their past or current politics, but these limited efforts had even more limited success.[4]

Academics responded in many different ways to subpoenas from legislative investigators. Some invoked the first or fifth amendments, some took the "soft fifth," meaning that they were willing to discuss their own political activities but were not willing to answer questions about others, and some cooperated more fully. While it became clear from court decisions in the early 1950s that the fifth amendment offered those testifying the most protection from the law, it became just as clear that this defense offered little protection from university investigators. To university review boards and appeals committees, taking the fifth was often equated with admitting guilt or, at the very least, displaying a degree of deception that was deemed unacceptable for a scholar and a teacher; though there were exceptions, the general rule was that the more professors cooperated with investigating committees, the more likely they were to keep their jobs. While one historian counts sixty-nine faculty members who were fired for political reasons during the McCarthy era, this is a conservative figure, one that does not include professors who were denied tenure, were pressured into resignation, or were removed by some other means short of termination.[5]

Berkeley and Michigan were among the public universities that experienced some of the worst convulsions of the McCarthy era, but Wisconsin, as it did with student organizations, produced a more mixed record. Radical student groups were mostly tolerated by the administration, but the university generally fell into line when it came to the issue of communists among the faculty. Fred Harvey Harrington, who became university president in 1962 and had already worked in the administration for several years, recalls that both of his predecessors, E. B. Fred and Conrad Elvehjem, were opposed to communists on the faculty. In a January 1953 speech, near the height of the anticommunist hysteria, Fred made it public that he would not tolerate communist faculty members: "The university has an obligation to seek for its staff men of intellectual integrity and devoted citizenship," Fred declared. "I have no use for communists, or other individuals or groups, whose purposes are inimical to the welfare of our state or country. Speaking for myself personally, I will not knowingly recommend the appointment of a member of the Communist Party to the staff of the university, and I shall recommend the termination of the services of any staff members whose activities are proved to be subversive of our government." He expressed some reservations, but Fred also signed on to a statement from the Association of American Universities that same year, the statement declaring what was already widely acknowledged, that communism disqualified one from membership in the academic community. "Above all," the statement read, "a scholar must have integrity and independence. This renders impossible adherence to such a regime as that of Russia and its satellites. No person who accepts or advocates such principles has any place in a university."[6]

Despite these public statements, it is still notable that Wisconsin avoided the worst excesses of McCarthyism when it came to the treatment of its faculty. State universities were particularly susceptible to the era's political winds, but even though Wisconsin's legislature was ensconced less than a mile from the university campus, the state's political heritage provided at least some protection from domestic anticommunism. In 1949, for example, the Board of Regents, most of them appointed by Republican governors, restated the university's traditional policy on academic freedom, including the declaration that "an opportunity critically to study the proposals and claims of systems alien to our own is the intellectual right of every student. And freedom to explore and discuss the issues in the field of his special competence is the right of every teacher." President Fred was also instrumental in keeping Wisconsin from adopting a loyalty oath similar to those established in many places across the country, including the University of California, where thirty-one professors were fired for their principled refusal to sign the oath (some were reinstated after a lengthy court battle). While political calculations undoubtedly figured into hiring and promotion decisions at Wisconsin, Madison managed to avoid the kind of high-profile cases that broke out in many other parts of the nation.[7]

Whatever took place on individual university campuses, however, the investigations into professors' backgrounds and the attention to higher education produced an even broader impact on the academic world and was reflected in much of the research and scholarship produced in American universities. Some university scientists and engineers, of course, were deeply involved in military and other research related to the Cold War, and other fields, too, helped to create an ideological foundation for the struggle between East and West. In the humanities and social sciences, scholarship during the early Cold War was certainly not monolithic, but it was notable for its lack of fundamental criticism of mainstream American policies and values. As the United States engaged in an ideological war with the Soviet Union and radicalism was largely discredited, it was assumed by most scholars that the essential questions about American society had been answered. In this view, the theoretical underpinnings of American democracy and capitalism had triumphed, a point echoed in Daniel Bell's famous 1960 book, *The End of Ideology: On the Exhaustion of Political Ideas in the Fifties.*[8]

Historians, like scholars in many fields, were affected by the mood of the early Cold War decades, and criticism of American institutions and ideals were often tempered in the postwar years. Radical historians like Herbert Aptheker and Philip Foner (whose scholarship focused on, respectively, African American history and labor history) were marginalized, while so-called "consensus history" outlined a narrative of America's past that downplayed the importance of social and political conflict. Consensus historians pointed to Americans' shared values and their ongoing struggle for freedom, producing a history that, as historian John Higham puts it, revealed America as "a relatively homogenous society with a relatively conservative history." Though consensus historians never fit into a simple mold—leading scholar Daniel Boorstin, for example, celebrated American consensus while another, Louis Hartz, disparaged it—they offered a narrative that squared with the imperatives of the early Cold War, especially its emphasis on Americans' shared values and the sharp contrast between American democracy and communist totalitarianism.[9]

A key element in this project was the reevaluation of the work of Progressive historians, a group that had held sway especially in the years between the world wars. Charles Beard, the most well-known Progressive historian, came in for particular criticism, a task made easier by Beard's opposition to America's entrance into World War II. Progressive history's emphasis on conflict and division in America's past (a reflection of the debate over the successes and failures of American capitalism during the first decades of the twentieth century), no longer resonated, nor did moral relativism, a common tool of Progressive historians that came under especially withering attack. In the politically charged atmosphere of the Cold War, where democracy seemed to offer a sharp contrast with totalitarianism, freedom with oppression, religion with godless communism, and so on, moral truths seemed increasingly self-evident; moral relativism, according to its critics, meant no morals at all. As University of Pennsylvania professor Conyers Read argued in his 1949 presidential address to the American Historical Association, historians "must recognize certain fundamental values as beyond dispute." Calling on historians to defend these values and drawing a parallel with the role of science in America's national security, Read suggested that "the historian is no freer from this obligation than the physicist." Over the next decade or more, many historians, like their colleagues in other disciplines, followed Read's example.[10]

Despite the powerful shift in the scholarly winds, the University of Wisconsin remained an outpost against at least some of the prevailing attitudes of the postwar decades. Like other large institutions, Wisconsin was drawn deeply into Cold War service, but despite the federal government's investment in higher education and the efforts of domestic anticommunists to root out radical ideas from colleges and universities, Wisconsin maintained an atmosphere where ideas were generally respected, even ideas that challenged the Cold War consensus. Student organizations contributed to this environment, and despite the influence of McCarthyism, so did small numbers of professors in significant corners of the university.

Crucial to the atmosphere in Madison was the support for civil liberties from a number of respected and outspoken faculty members. Soils science professor Francis Hole, a Quaker and a conscientious objector during World War II, was one vocal supporter of both civil liberties and nonviolence after he started teaching in Madison in 1946. In addition to regular efforts opposing compulsory ROTC, Hole wrote a letter to President Fred protesting Fred's acceptance of the Association of American Universities' 1953 statement on academic freedom and declaring his own unwillingness to cooperate with legislative investigations. Meanwhile, biochemist Karl Paul Link, who discovered dicumarol, a widely used anticlotting agent that also turned out to be a highly effective rat poison, leveraged the immense financial gains that his research brought the university against his role as faculty adviser to radical student groups like the John Cookson Marxist Club and the Labor Youth League. Without a faculty adviser, these groups would have been unable to register on campus, a fate that befell radical groups at many other universities.[11]

Law professor William Rice was a particularly important supporter of civil liberties on the UW campus and throughout the country. After serving in World War I and clerking for Supreme Court Justice Louis Brandeis, Rice was a fixture on Madison's campus from 1922 until his retirement in the early 1960s.

He was active in local, state, and national Democratic Party politics, working in the New Deal and on the National War Labor Board, and he was chairman of the Wisconsin Civil Liberties Union for several years in the 1950s and 1960s. In Madison, he was involved in disputes over campus civil liberties as early as the 1920s, and he spoke at an American Youth for Democracy rally in 1947, publicly protesting the university's decision to ban suspected communist Gerhard Eisler from speaking on campus. Later, in 1961, and with many students in attendance, he testified before the Wisconsin state legislature, urging them to help put HUAC out of business. In his final years, he would also support the early civil rights and antiwar movements on campus.[12]

Some prominent professors demonstrated their opposition to domestic anticommunism by working against Senator McCarthy himself. Biochemist Henry Lardy, who would participate in a 1965 petition drive of professors opposed to the war in Vietnam, was active in Democratic campaigns against McCarthy and in the 1954 "Joe Must Go" recall movement. According to Lardy, there was virulent opposition from Wisconsin citizens who believed that opposition to McCarthy was a kind of communist plot, but there was not much outright support for McCarthy among the faculty, even if there was a certain amount of fear. Geneticist James Crow, known nationally for his research and teaching, was another professor involved in the recall movement; he had been active in the 1930s peace movement as a college student and, like Lardy and many others, would later oppose the Vietnam War. Henry Wortis, one of the few openly communist students on campus in the mid-1950s, remembers that Crow hired him to work in his lab and treated him in a "very straightforward way." Like many of his colleagues, Crow worked against some of the excesses of the Cold War and took radical ideas and those who professed them seriously, helping to cultivate a space in which Cold War dissent was possible.[13]

These professors and others helped create a context where unorthodox ideas could survive, but it was left to an even smaller group of faculty who helped shape the intellectual environment in which these ideas thrived. One of these was German émigré sociologist Hans Gerth, who suffered from a kind of academic exile in Madison. While many non-Jewish academics had left Germany in the early 1930s, Gerth stayed until 1937, his work for a major Berlin newspaper contributing to the perception that he was something of a last-minute antifascist. During World War II, Gerth was practically a prisoner in Madison, registered and fingerprinted as an enemy alien and subject to a number of restrictions on his travel and activities. Yet Gerth had been a minor figure in the Frankfurt School, the group of neo-Marxist political and social theorists that had emerged in Germany in the 1920s, and he imparted to his students in Madison a theoretical sophistication that could not be found in many other places in the university, introducing them to such thinkers as Karl Mannheim, Theodor Adorno, and Erich Fromm. Something of an "absent-minded professor" and not on the left himself, he became a key source of Wisconsin's radical milieu from the 1940s through the 1960s, mentoring a number of radical students, including future UW professor William Appleman Williams and New Left hero C. Wright Mills, both Wisconsin graduate students in the 1940s.[14]

Like Gerth, another Wisconsin professor known for his engagement with leftist students, even if he was not a political radical himself, was European historian George Mosse. Heir to a wealthy German publishing house that had been seized by the Nazis, Mosse arrived in Madison in 1955 and was a presence in the department and the university until his retirement more than thirty years later. Like Gerth, he was steeped in European political theory, and he introduced his students to the writings of Marx, Nietzsche, and Antonio Gramsci, among others. Though he remained a critic of Marxism, he took the Marxist tradition seriously, and he had a large following of graduate and undergraduate students who would gather with him informally, in the Union building or elsewhere on campus, to discuss European history and radical ideas. In a sign of students' appetite for ideas as well as the relevance of history to the sixties, Mosse's lectures on European history and politics were often jam-packed later in the era, attracting many students who were not even enrolled in his courses. Of course, it didn't hurt that Mosse, in his accented English, was a masterful lecturer: warm, engaging, charismatic. "When I signed up for History 3 [one of Mosse's courses]," remembers Paul Breines, then an undergraduate but who later returned to work with Mosse on his PhD, "basketball, rather than ideas, was my passion; yet ten minutes into the first lecture, I had found my calling: I wanted to be Professor Mosse, to do what he was doing in the ways in which he was doing it."[15]

A historian, Mosse was a member of one of the most distinguished and certainly the most unorthodox departments at the University of Wisconsin. Indeed, the history department provided something of a critical mass of Cold War dissent even as its influence reached throughout the university, with one quarter of the university's student body taking at least one history course in the fall of 1961 alone. As described by Tom McCormick and Lloyd Gardner, both history graduate students in the late 1950s who would go on to distinguished academic careers of their own, the Wisconsin history department in the 1950s "remained something of an anachronism, or, looked at the other way around, ahead of its time." Professors' individual politics leaned in many different directions, but the collective result was a space where ideas were valued and where the power of the Cold War consensus was blunted.[16]

That some professors continued to work in the tradition of controversial Progressive historian Charles Beard was a sign of the department's challenge to the prevailing political climate. Class conflict and a skeptical eye toward state power were highlighted in the work of historians like Merrill Jensen, whose scholarship included an economic analysis of the early republic, and Howard Beale, who edited a volume on Beard in 1954. Beale also drew inspiration from Beard's role as a public intellectual. A member of the state's Commission on Human Rights in the 1950s and a founder of the student-faculty Stick Your Neck Out Club in 1952, Beale was a vocal advocate for civil liberties and academic freedom as well as a critic of U.S. imperialism. Other important figures included the well-respected Civil War historian William B. Hesseltine and diplomatic historian and future UW president Fred Harvey Harrington, a tall and physically imposing professor known to "smoke" paperclips during his seminars. Like others at Wisconsin, Harrington followed Beard's interest in the historical importance of economics, and he took a much more critical view of the State Department than other diplomatic historians at the time. Later, as university president, he would support many of the early developments in the student movement but would have a difficult time navigating the more tumultuous late sixties.[17]

Perhaps the most prominent member among the history faculty was Merle Curti. The son of a Swiss-American pacifist, Curti had studied with acclaimed historian Frederick Jackson Turner at Harvard (Turner was born in Portage, Wisconsin, and taught at the University of Wisconsin from 1890 until 1910) and arrived in Madison in the early 1940s, enhancing his already established reputation with a 1944 Pulitzer Prize for *The Growth of American Thought*. Well known among historians for his criticism of American foreign policy and his support for civil liberties, Curti was targeted by some in the profession, like former American Historical Association (AHA) president Conyers Read, who believed that historians should lend strong support to the Cold War. In his own 1954 presidential address to the AHA, the most prominent organization of professional historians, Curti hit back, staking out a strong position against some of the currents in the historical profession and in American society more broadly. Suggesting the need for courage in difficult times, he accused political demagogues of revitalizing a tradition of anti-intellectualism with their attacks on "subversion" within higher education. Historians needed to "uphold the integrity of the truth-seeking process," he declared, and remain true to the essential functions of their craft: "criticism, experimentation, and the effort to bridge different cultures of the world through understanding."[18]

For George Rawick, a graduate student in Madison in the early and middle fifties who would later become a professional historian himself, Merle Curti had a particularly lasting influence. Unimpressed by some of the history faculty (though with a good deal of praise for Hans Gerth), Rawick was forever impressed by Curti's ideals. "His deep-seated commitment to American grass-roots democracy made an indelible impression on me," Rawick recalls. "His presidential address to the American Historical Association in which he directly challenged the themes of his predecessors in the AHA presidency, Conyers Read and Samuel Eliot Morison . . . was one of the most remarkable experiences of my life." As happened in this and many other cases, Rawick was more radical than his teacher, but this was of little consequence. For Curti, Jensen, Beale, and others, it was their commitment to American ideals and their independence from cultural and political orthodoxy that rubbed off on their students. "These professors didn't agree with us," writes another former student, Saul Landau, "but they welcomed a challenge they didn't get from most graduate and undergraduate students." According to Paul Breines, "Even when we disagreed with him [Mosse] most vehemently, he was the one who transmitted the key values, images, and secrets with which we tried to form ourselves as a certain kind of leftist intellectual."[19]

Finally, among the many significant faculty members in the history department, the professor who most came to represent the unorthodox tradition was William Appleman Williams. Unlike Curti, Jensen, Beale, and others who were critical of the abuses of domestic anticommunism and the excesses of Cold War foreign policy but who remained within the political mainstream, Williams, born and raised in Iowa, a Naval Academy graduate and a Wisconsin PhD (1950), was a radical, a socialist but with little sympathy for communism or other variants of the Old Left. Part of his appeal was that his radicalism was distinctly "American," a contrast with the transplanted ideologies that suffused much of the left. Some of the graduate students who worked with him described him as a humanist or perhaps a Christian socialist, and speaking of the world he wanted to create, Williams emphasized the importance of "an American community," one that "is neither aristocratic nor stratified, skewed or paradoxical. It is democratic and equitable, straightforward and loving. This kind of community involves . . . a different hierarchy of values. Love comes before power and participation before passivity. Equity and equality come before efficiency and ease." Williams would be the single most important professor on campus in producing a counternarrative to the dominant view of the Cold

War, a key figure in campus politics and the intellectual community until his departure for Oregon State University in 1968.[20]

Williams' scholarship was central to his outsized influence among Madison radicals, and even before he started teaching in Madison in 1957 he had already developed a reputation for challenging America's Cold War orthodoxy. Though still a minor figure in the profession, he made waves at the 1950 meeting of the AHA with a denunciation of America's aggressive foreign policy, and he continued to push the envelope of Cold War–era history in his first book, *American-Russian Relations, 1781–1947*, published in 1952. Drawing heavily on his dissertation on Raymond Robbins, a Midwestern Progressive and diplomat who worked tirelessly for improved relations between the Soviet Union and the United States in the early twentieth century, the exhaustive monograph included a heavy emphasis on economic and business interests in the making of American foreign policy toward Russia. Williams argued that the Bolsheviks were willing to deal in good faith with Washington in the years after World War I, but President Woodrow Wilson and other American policymakers chose repeatedly to undermine the new government, using a variety of means, including military force.[21]

Even more explosive than this view of America's interwar foreign policy as overly aggressive and short-sighted—Williams blamed Wilson for the failures of the Versailles Treaty that helped lead to World War II—was the book's twenty-five page coda. Written at the height of the Cold War, the coda laid the blame for the post–World War II hostility between the United States and the Soviet Union directly at the feet of American policymakers. While Williams offered little support for the Soviet system, he believed that they were an essentially benign power and that it was the United States that had refused to deal honestly, both during and after the war. Moreover, Williams trained his sights directly on George Foster Kennan, the American diplomat who was an influential voice in the Truman administration's foreign policy and a key architect of the postwar policy of containment. Disputing Kennan's findings on a number of fronts and accusing him of overlooking America's long-held antagonism toward the Soviet Union and overstating the threat that the Soviets posed to the United States after World War II (it was the Americans, after all, who possessed the bomb in the late 1940s, Williams reminded readers), Williams called for "mutual accommodation" and "negotiated settlements," concluding that "freedom is not nurtured by states preparing for war."[22]

American-Russian Relations laid out many of the themes that Williams would return to in his later works, but it was not until *The Tragedy of American Diplomacy*, published in 1959, that he set himself apart as a groundbreaking and controversial historian and constructed the historical framework that would influence the New Left's understanding of Vietnam and the Cold War. Making the case for a thorough re-examination of the history of American foreign relations from the 1890s through the post–World War II years, Williams departed from the common view that America's dominant role in the world had been more or less accidental, an essentially unintentional response to events like the Spanish-American and First World wars. Instead, Williams argued that the creation of an American "empire" was a deliberate policy based on the need to find outlets for American goods and to stabilize an economy that experienced wild swings in the decades after the Civil War. First articulated in the 1890s was Americans' insistence on an "open door" throughout the world, a means for spreading American ideas as well as commerce. U.S. policymakers often presented the open door in terms of the benefits that American assistance brought to peoples around the world, but Williams made clear that the policy's ultimate goal was to support American expansion and supremacy, a goal that distorted American ideals even as it was resented by the very peoples it was supposed to help.[23]

Tragedy was also important for laying out Williams's own politics, his alternative to the open door. "The problem," Williams wrote in the book's introduction, "is to come to terms with the hard fact . . . that the Soviet Union has broken the monopoly of Anglo-Saxon leadership; and then to admit that Russia is an equal even though it is a rival and proceed to work out a program for living with it in a world that America no longer dominates as it did in the past." Though not an apologist for Joseph Stalin or the Soviets, Williams believed that the United States had fundamentally overestimated the threat from the Soviet Union; this miscalculation, moreover, had distorted American policies. America could accommodate the Soviets and other international rivals and, on the flip side, could use the resources that it was expending on the Cold War to solve its own domestic problems. The first step was a basic reassessment of "the accepted thesis that America's freedom and prosperity depend upon the continued expansion of its economic and ideological system through the policy of the open door. . . . *Instead, it appears that America's political and economic well-being depend upon the rational and equitable use of its own human and material resources at home and in interdependent cooperation with all other peoples of the world"* (italics in original).[24]

This view would become almost standard among 1960s activists (and many future historians), but in the 1950s these were daring words. Scholarly reviews were generally negative, and the book captured the attention of domestic anticommunists, with Williams receiving a summons from HUAC in 1960 and the committee demanding to see a copy of the manuscript for his next book, *The*

Contours of American History. Nor was this Williams's first brush with domestic anticommunism. The initial publisher of *Tragedy* had backed out of the deal for political reasons, while Williams was unable to get his work published in some of the best historical journals for several years. Williams's summons was ultimately cancelled before he was scheduled to testify in front of the House committee (he still met privately with committee members), but the FBI's assessment was that he remained a risk to national security. The FBI accurately determined that Williams was a socialist and not a communist, but it concluded that he needed to be monitored. "In view of Williams' profession," a late 1950s memo in his FBI file reads, "in time of national emergency, he would be in a position to influence others against the national interest."[25]

Despite this pressure from domestic anticommunists, Williams remained a pivotal figure within Madison's leftist community. Known for smoking cigars and for his broad intellectual interests—he made regular trips to the graduate library to read through new academic journals, not just in history—he was larger-than-life, and *Tragedy* was a kind of "sacred text" for those searching for a framework for understanding American imperialism and the failures of the Cold War. Tom McCormick recalls that when he arrived in Madison, Williams's influence on him was "immediate and electrifying." Even among those who were inclined to reject his radicalism, his charisma forced his students to grapple seriously with his ideas. "You have to have somebody who challenges you enough," McCormick recalls, "that you're nonetheless willing to let your ideas rub against his and do battle with his. . . . Not many people can persuade you to do that." Moreover, while the influence of most Wisconsin professors was limited to their students in Madison, Williams's scholarship was read widely throughout the New Left, and his criticism of American liberalism and the open door runs through much of the New Left's ideology as it developed during the sixties.[26]

Finally, though few Wisconsin faculty could easily be termed "activists," Williams was one of several who made an impact as a public figure. Like Howard Beale, William Rice, and a handful of others, Williams met regularly with liberal and leftist student organizations, and he and Rice testified publicly before the state legislature in 1961, urging the legislators to help shut down HUAC. With demonstrators and counterdemonstrators outside the state capitol building, Williams refused to back down against the hostile legislators. Faced with questions about his teaching, questions straight out of the anticommunist playbook, his answer—"I teach people to think"—brought a thunderous applause from his supporters in the galleries. Williams was also one of more than two dozen professors who participated in Madison's first teach-in, in the spring of

1965; later that year he participated in a national teach-in, evidence of his national profile as well as his skill as a public speaker.[27]

Williams and others were certainly popular on campus, but the process by which Wisconsin's unorthodox professors influenced students in Madison was a complicated one. In the broadest sense, faculty created a genuinely exciting intellectual atmosphere in which students with radical interests and deep intellectual curiosity thrived. Centered in the history department, but with outlets throughout the university, this atmosphere led to a vital mix of professors, graduate students, and undergrads: midwestern and eastern, Jewish and non-Jewish, radical, liberal, and even conservative. Not every student in law professor William Rice's classroom emerged a champion of civil liberties, nor did every student in William Appleman Williams's courses accept his criticism of the Cold War as his or her own, but there was a significant minority who did. In some cases, students were predisposed to accept these messages, with many of the students in groups like the Socialist Club and Student Peace Center coming to Madison with a family history of leftist politics. Brought up with a suspicion of American foreign policy and with family or friends who had been targeted by domestic anticommunists, they were drawn to professors who shared their views. Others, however, came to Wisconsin with much more conventional views. Williams's student and future historian Tom McCormick would leave graduate school in Wisconsin in 1960 a socialist, but there was no hint of this future in his small-town upbringing in Ohio. Indeed, following in the footsteps of his grandfather, who had been deeply involved in local Republican politics, McCormick had been the head of the Young Republicans as an undergraduate at the University of Cincinnati.[28]

This intellectual environment exerted a powerful force and helped create the foundation for students charting a new left. As Milwaukee native Bertell Ollman—president of the Madison chapter of the liberal-left Student League for Industrial Democracy in the mid-fifties and later a Marxist—put it, the keys to his development "were the great variety of viewpoints and the encouragement to think for oneself that were the hallmarks of university life in Madison." This encouragement and variety of perspectives, combined with the growing student body, especially the growth in the graduate school, meant a peer network that was influenced by professors but that increasingly operated outside the more formal interactions with faculty. The Wisconsin Historical Society reading room, campus hallways, the Union's Rathskeller, off-campus apartments— these were the spaces where a growing number of students argued and debated, probed and prodded. Paul Breines, then an undergraduate, remembers that the history graduate students living in his building played a key mentoring role, and many former Wisconsin students have fond memories of the community that developed in the late 1950s and early 1960s. "This was the most ideal intellectual community I could have imagined," recalls Saul Landau of the peer exchange that occurred in Madison. "It was a constant struggle with ideas."[29]

❖

The most concrete product of the political and intellectual environment that existed in Madison in the 1950s and early 1960s was the journal *Studies on the Left*, which began publishing in 1959 and joined a small number of similar journals started by students at other American universities. Established by a group of UW graduate students, many of them in the history department, the journal was an attempt to develop a new direction for the left and was a testament to the world of ideas that existed in Madison. Influenced by the tradition of radical student organizations that had persisted throughout the 1950s, especially the Socialist Club, to which many of the journal's editors belonged, the journal took many of its cues from thinkers like sociologist C. Wright Mills, a persistent critic of Cold War America, as well as from influential Wisconsin professors, including Hans Gerth, who contributed an essay for the journal's first issue, and, of course, William Appleman Williams.

Sixties activists have often been accused of being "anti-intellectual," but *Studies* highlights a more complicated picture. Although there was always a tension between activism and intellectual work in Madison and even among the journal's editors, with some of them primarily interested in developing a scholarly basis for a new socialist politics and some more interested in tying the journal to the activism then emerging in the civil rights and antiwar movements, the journal points to the importance of ideas to many involved in the New Left. As *Studies* editor James Weinstein puts it, the journal was an attempt to "understand our roots and transcend them, which only a new understanding of our history—and that of the nation—could make possible." As young people struggled to make sense of the world around them and to develop a framework for challenging the Cold War, this was an important project, and one that paid significant dividends throughout the rest of the era.[30]

From the journal's very beginnings, *Studies* editors were highly critical of the American left as it existed in the late 1950s, made up as it was of a number of small groupings—Stalinists, Trotskyites, democratic socialists, and others— that were consumed primarily with fighting for their survival against the forces of domestic anticommunism and, when they had time, infighting among each other. *Studies'* founders shared an "awareness of the severe failure of the Old

Left," former editors David Eakins and James Weinstein wrote after the journal's demise in 1967, "and a commitment to participate in the development of a body of theory to stimulate the creation of a new revolutionary movement in the United States." More specifically, the editors concluded in 1962 that "where thoughtful discussion and rigorous analysis have been called for, the various groups in what remains of the organized left have responded with concerted attempts to force history and ideas into a preconceived mold. All of these organizations have become frozen into or imprisoned by attitudes and experiences of the twenty years from 1919 to 1939." Though lacking a clear direction, these young radicals were nonetheless committed to a new beginning.[31]

The group associated with *Studies*, then, continued the break with the Old Left, a break that had started in Madison with the establishment of the Student Peace Center and the Socialist Club earlier in the 1950s and that would gain speed in the early 1960s. Early editors included some, like Marty Sklar and Saul Landau, who had grown up in the Old Left and had been members of the Labor Youth League, but the editors also included David Eakins, who had been blacklisted for his work with a Denver meat-packing union, and Lloyd Gardner, who was from a Protestant, midwestern, and politically centrist family. Lee Baxandall, from a Republican family in Oshkosh, Wisconsin, was one of a number of English students associated with *Studies*, and another was Eleanor Hakim, the most prominent among the several women who worked on the journal. (From New York but without a radical family background, Hakim was something of a mysterious figure; with long black hair and thick glasses, she regularly told people that she was going to die young, which she did, in 1983.) Far from the centers of the Old Left on the East and West Coasts, and with a mix of distinctive perspectives, Madison provided a space for the exploration of new ideas and directions.[32]

The freshness of *Studies* was evident in the first issue's editorial statement, "The Radicalism of Disclosure." Embracing the mantle of "radical" historians, the editors proclaimed that history was about the problems of "man and society," offering at the same time a scathing indictment of their own profession as stagnant and cloaked in false claims of "dispassion" and "objectivity." Objectivity, Sklar and company argued, was little more than a stand-in for prevailing opinion, a method for de-legitimizing alternative viewpoints as biased and distancing scholars from pressing contemporary issues that could benefit from their knowledge and understanding. Rather, the editors suggested, dispassion did not necessarily correlate with less bias; the radical scholar was more impassioned, but not necessarily more biased. Historians, the editors concluded, needed to break down the wall that separated them from their work. Bringing their own sensibilities to scholarly inquiry would lead to a better and more usable history.[33]

Early issues of the journal (it was planned as a quarterly but issues went out irregularly) explored a variety of disciplines and included articles from young authors as well as more established scholars. One typical article, "New Deal to New Frontiers: 1937–1941" by *Studies* editor and UW graduate student Lloyd Gardner, appeared in the first issue and closely followed Williams's scholarship. Emphasizing Franklin Roosevelt's commitment to the open door, Gardner argued that the efforts to expand markets overseas brought the United States into increasing conflict with Germany's and Japan's own expansionist foreign policies, thus setting the stage for America's entrance into the war on the side of the Allies. Other history articles included "William E. Borah: Critic of American Foreign Policy" by Orde S. Pinckney, "The Rise of the American Mediterranean" by Gordon K. Lewis, "The Socialist Party: Its Roots and Strength, 1912–1919," by *Studies* editor James Weinstein, and "Samuel Adams: Calvinist, Mercantilist, Revolutionary" by William Appleman Williams himself. Articles in other disciplines included "Dialectics: A Philosophical Analysis" by Gerald Dworkin, "Modern Marxism and Modern Science: Any Common Ground?" by Hans Freistadt, "The Support of the Mysteries: A Look at the Literary Prophets of the Beat Middle Class" by Paul Breslow, and a translation of Walter Benjamin's "The Work of Art in the Epoch of Mechanical Reproduction."[34]

One event that received particular attention in the journal's pages and that was crucial to the editors' understanding of American history was the Cuban Revolution in 1959, the same year that *Studies* was founded. The revolution was immediately a signal event throughout the nascent New Left, an example of the kind of movement that might be replicated in other parts of the world, perhaps even the United States. Moreover, for many young radicals, Fidel Castro himself was especially important; historian Van Gosse emphasizes the appeal of his spontaneity, nonconformity, and "hipness," especially for young men. Likewise, for Saul Landau, who visited Cuba soon after the revolution and became a key member in the national Fair Play for Cuba Committee, a group that worked for better Cuban-American relations, it was the revolution's youthfulness that was particularly significant. Most of the people who had made the revolution were young in years, including Castro himself, who was then in his early thirties and was among the older of the revolutionaries, and the revolution as a whole, as Landau puts it, was "refreshingly new. . . . It was open and it was fun-loving, and it was bold and daring to stick its finger straight in Uncle Sam's eye."[35]

The excitement about Cuba in Madison and throughout the American left was reflected in *Studies'* decision to devote its entire third issue to the revolution and to print twelve thousand copies, more than three times the number for the first and second issues but still not enough to satisfy demand. Brushing aside concerns about the nationalization of American property and the threat of communism, concerns that had led American policymakers to quickly turn against Castro, the editors highlighted their enthusiasm for the revolution, portraying it as a movement for freedom and an attempt to create a "humane society." "These revolutions," the editors wrote of the revolutionary movements in the third world, including Cuba, "were not created by devils; they arose in fulfillment of the long-held aspirations of the hungry people of the world." In other words, the Cuban Revolution and other third world revolutions, despite official American opposition, were essentially just. Following Williams's lead again, the editors rejected a central foundation of American foreign policy, that American power was ultimately beneficial to the rest of the world. Their criticism of American power, or what Williams called "empire," meant an alternative perspective on revolution in Cuba and elsewhere in the world.[36]

The editors indicted American Cold War ideology for its inability to view the Cuban Revolution outside of an oversimplified dualism of "us" versus "them." The dichotomy between freedom and communism and the reduction of the world into two camps, the editors argued, was a "sham." Accommodation was a genuine possibility if not for the inflexibility of the Cold War, which, in Cuba, left only two possibilities: an intensification of the Cold War or, as some favored, outright invasion. Ultimately, this was the result of American foreign policymakers' inability to recognize and deal with the complex reality of Third World revolution; all revolutions that posed even a potential threat to American interests were labeled as communist no matter the real underlying conditions. This framework for understanding Cuba, much of which would later be applied to Vietnam, was not original to *Studies*, but the journal provided a space for young radicals in Madison and throughout the country to discuss the Cold War and explore alternatives to conventional American foreign policy. "Cuba presents us with an urgent task," the editors concluded, "and, at the same time, with the best opportunity to expose and destroy Cold War ideology."[37]

More original to the pages of *Studies*, and just as important to the development of the New Left, was the editors' hard-hitting attack on liberalism. From its beginnings, *Studies* had little sympathy for liberalism or for liberal icons like Franklin Roosevelt, Woodrow Wilson, or, after his election, John Kennedy.

This distrust of liberalism was certainly influenced by the Old Left background of several *Studies* editors—they had seen liberals abandon and then attack the left in the post–World War II years—and it was also influenced by liberalism's turn away from a critique of modern capitalism. The economic program of Americans for Democratic Action, the premier liberal organization whose membership included Eleanor Roosevelt as well as historian and Kennedy adviser Arthur Schlesinger Jr., accepted the main contours of a capitalist economy, suggesting that economic growth would provide the resources to solve poverty and other problems. Liberals no longer needed to worry about capitalism, argued Harvard economist John Kenneth Galbraith in the 1950s, nor were large corporations the enemy.[38]

Studies' disdain for liberals was also influenced by William Appleman Williams, who disparaged both liberals and conservatives for their support of the open door. In *American-Russian Relations*, Williams had criticized Woodrow Wilson for his commitment to open door foreign policy and for his unwillingness to deal openly with the Bolsheviks, and following up in his massive 1961 work, *The Contours of American History*, Williams made little distinction between liberals and conservatives in their support of an expansive American foreign policy. The period dating back to the late nineteenth century had been marked by "corporate capitalism," he argued, and though liberals, or "reformers," had made a variety of efforts to make capitalism work more smoothly and equitably, their commitment to private property rendered them unable to truly grapple with the problems in American society. Williams lionized Eugene Debs's brand of socialism, but he had little positive to say about Franklin Roosevelt, the great liberal hero. "The New Deal saved the [capitalist] system," Williams wrote in *Contours*. "It did not end it."[39]

Studies extended the work of Williams and made its own contribution to the critique of liberalism when editor Marty Sklar coined the term "corporate liberalism" to describe the historical blending of corporate capitalism with the American liberal tradition. Sklar's 1960 essay on Woodrow Wilson, published in *Studies*, rejected what he saw as the oft-accepted distinction between Wilson the "moralist" and Wilson the "commercialist," contending that Wilson's deep belief in capitalism was actually an essential part of his morality. Wilson's expansionist foreign policy, then, rather than being an aberration, was an extension of his view of American liberalism. More broadly, *Studies* editors believed that the Progressive Era in the late nineteenth and early twentieth centuries was a formative moment; it was during this period when liberals and corporate leaders came to agree on the necessity of a regulated market (notwithstanding disagreement over the extent of regulation) and liberal "reform" efforts helped solidify corporate control over the American economy.[40]

Studies also extended a contemporary, not just historical, critique of liberalism, using a 1962 editorial to set its sights on what it termed "corporate, Cold War liberalism." What was so striking about this statement was the argument that the real threat to the left was not from the political right (the "ultra-right" or "ultras," as the editors called them), but it was liberalism that served as the real roadblock to fundamental change in America. "The ultras may feel that more stringent measures are needed to defeat the devil," the editorial read, "but they did not concoct the cold war; nor did they originate the concept that the forces of justice must triumph against communism or perish—that idea goes back to Woodrow Wilson. Their attitude in this respect is not essentially incompatible with that of such liberals as Rockefeller, Kennedy, Rusk, Stevenson, Rostow, Berle, and their corporate allies." Rather than a force lined up against liberalism, the right was a *product* of liberalism: "As architects and custodians of the warfare state," it was liberals who were responsible for America's antidemocratic trends. The left's mistake was in "defining the right wing as a menace to an extant liberal society, rather than as a concomitant of the increasingly authoritarian liberal mechanism for responsibly waging the cold war."[41]

For the New Left, this was a groundbreaking declaration. In contrast, the "Port Huron Statement," which was published by Students for a Democratic Society (SDS) in 1962 and is considered perhaps the most significant document ever produced by the New Left, took a much more mixed position on liberalism. The lengthy document made a powerful case for a new movement of young people alienated by the contours of the postwar world, yet it tread softly when it came to President Kennedy and held out hope that liberalism, though in decline, could be redeemed. SDS would soon move away from this position, with President Johnson's escalation of the war in Vietnam and the Democratic Party's poor record on civil rights extinguishing any hope of working with liberals, while *Studies'* view of liberalism would become a mainstay of New Left ideology. In a 1965 speech at an antiwar rally in Washington, D.C., SDS president Carl Oglesby announced to the crowd that they had to do more than protest one example of the nation's foreign policy: they had to "name the system" that was at the root of America's problems. Channeling the analysis that *Studies* editors had been developing for several years, he criticized liberals for America's Cold War foreign policy, including the corporate interests that benefited from many of those policies. The system that was at the root of America's problems, he declared, was "corporate liberalism."[42]

Studies remained too scholarly for some activists—"very professional and very dull," Saul Landau wrote to his fellow editors about the journal in 1961— but it was an important forum in the early years of the New Left, joining journals like *Root and Branch* out of Berkeley and *New University Thought* out of the University of Chicago in exploring ideas that would be tested as the 1960s wore on. *Studies* sold out the first issue's print run of three thousand copies, and circulation rose slowly after that. The journal also made increasing contacts outside of Madison. All but one of the original editors was based in Madison, but there quickly developed a much broader network of editors, associate editors, and representatives nationally and even internationally. By the third issue, there were associate editors based at the University of Minnesota, the University of Chicago, Iowa State University, and Michigan State University. By the following issue, these had been joined by associate editors at Berkeley and Columbia as well as "representatives" in London and Paris. Some of these were fellow graduate students, some were established scholars, and some were the journal's original editors as they moved out of Madison and into other institutions across the country. Eventually the journal itself moved (though maintaining an office in Madison), relocating to New York City in 1963 after several of the editors had already moved there.[43]

And while *Studies* never fit comfortably in the activism-fueled middle and late sixties—it was split between those who wanted a journal closely associated with the movement and those who wanted to focus on building a theoretical framework for a new politics, a split that ultimately led the journal to dissolve in 1967—it made important contacts with activists, including Students for a Democratic Society. The editors were impressed by the burgeoning civil rights activism on college campuses, activism that they wrote was "sweeping away a fog of apathy," and they tried to provide analysis of the growing campus movement over the years. C. Clark Kissinger, a math graduate student and associate editor who established Madison's SDS chapter in 1963 and became SDS's national secretary the next year, helped to build an informal relationship between the two groups and peddled copies of the journal at conferences and other meetings. Tom Hayden, the primary author of the "Port Huron Statement" and a key figure in SDS and throughout the New Left, joined the journal's editorial board in the fall of 1963, though he would leave in 1966 amid differences with many of the other editors.[44]

Studies on the Left, then, highlights the vitality of the intellectual community in Madison in the 1950s and 1960s as well as the importance of intellectual exchange in the history of the New Left. Universities like Wisconsin became Cold War institutions in the postwar decades, yet with their growing prominence and the expansion of the student body, they also provided the foundation for a dynamic movement to change America. Though Madison remained a mostly conservative place during these years—not so different from other college towns throughout the nation—student leftists persevered even during the worst of the McCarthy years, and there were professors in significant corners of the university who challenged the Cold War consensus and took ideas, even radical ideas, seriously. In this context, the students who worked on *Studies*, as well as those who several years later started another journal in Madison, *Radical America*, began to reckon with the world they had inherited and move toward the powerful youth movement that would define the era.

State Street at night, 1965. The approximately mile-long avenue connects the university and the state capitol. (courtesy of the UW–Madison Archives)

Der Rathskeller, University of Wisconsin Memorial Union, 1950s. The Rathskeller served as a meeting place for many students, including political radicals. (courtesy of the UW–Madison Archives)

Chemistry Building, 1960s. The two parts of the Chemistry Building were built in the 1950s and early 1960s with state and federal funding. The taller building in the complex was named after UW chemist Farrington Daniels, who worked in the Manhattan Project during World War II. (courtesy of the UW–Madison Archives)

University of Wisconsin–Madison graduation in 1961, a year that saw 4,367 students receive degrees. The number of graduates increased every year between 1955 and 1971. (courtesy of the UW–Madison Archives)

Nuclear Attack Survival Kit, 1962. The kit was prepared as a part of the university's civil defense efforts during the Cold War. (courtesy of the UW–Madison Archives)

President E. B. Fred (*right*) with "sifting and winnowing" plaque, 1950
dedicated in 1910 and recalled the university's commitment to acader
of the UW–Madison Archives)

Protest at ROTC Review, 1950. (courtesy of the UW–Madison Archiv

Students departing for the March on Washington, 1963. (courtesy of the UW–Madison Archives)

Top left: ROTC protest, 1950. (courtesy of the UW–Madison Archives)

Bottom left: Fred Harvey Harrington (*left*) and William Appleman Williams (*right*). The figure in the center is Charles Vevier, vice-chancellor of the University of Wisconsin–Milwaukee. (courtesy of the UW–Madison Archives)

Early demonstration against U.S. involvement in Vietnam, ca. 1965. (courtesy of the UW–Madison Archives)

Antiwar demonstration on the steps of the State Historical Society of Wisconsin, ca. 1965. (courtesy of the UW–Madison Archives)

Draft sit-in, 1966. Students peacefully occupied the campus Administration Building for more than three days and nights. (courtesy of the UW–Madison Archives)

Draft sit-in, 1966. (courtesy of the UW–Madison Archives)

Dow Chemical Co. protest, 1967. The glass in Commerce Hall had broken when police removed students from the building. (courtesy of the UW–Madison Archives)

Dow Chemical Co. protest, 1967. (courtesy of the UW–Madison Archives)

Bascom Hill, near the center of campus, 1968. A statue of Abraham Lincoln is in the foreground. (courtesy of the UW–Madison Archives)

Police guarding Bascom Hall, ca. 1969. (courtesy of the UW–Madison Archives)

Demonstration during the Black Strike, 1969. (courtesy of the UW–Madison Archives)

National Guard on campus during the Black Strike, 1969. (courtesy of the UW–Madison Archives)

Teaching Assistants Association strike, 1970. (courtesy of the UW–Madison Archives)

Bombing of Sterling Hall, 1970. (courtesy of the UW–Madison Archives)

Top left: Antiwar demonstration, 1970. This demonstration was to protest the American invasion of Cambodia and the shooting of students at Kent State University several days earlier. (courtesy of the UW–Madison Archives)

Bottom left: Bombing of Sterling Hall, 1970. (courtesy of the UW–Madison Archives)

4

"I can't be calm, cool, and detached any longer"

The Beginnings of a Mass Movement

At the end of the 1950s, Madison possessed a number of factors that would be crucial to the development of a powerful protest movement in the next decade: a tradition of student radicalism; a relatively tolerant administration; a number of charismatic and unorthodox professors; a critique of American politics and foreign policy; and a network of critical student organizations. Still, as the 1960s dawned, there was little indication that "the sixties," including all that era has come to be known for, had started or was just around the corner. Civil rights were a regular but minor political issue, hints of what would become known as the counterculture were rare, and American involvement in Vietnam, which would focus so much of sixties energy, was relatively minor. Surveying the campus, keen observers might have discerned a slight increase in the vitality of student politics—the recent establishment of *Studies on the Left*, for example—as well as the new directions pioneered by groups like the Socialist Club and the Student Peace Center, but even for those who might have been looking, a powerful "new left" still seemed far off.

Just six years later, however, the situation had changed drastically. By 1966, as students occupied the campus administration building to protest the university's cooperation with the Selective Service System, demonstrations were a regular part of campus and city life, and the subdued politics of the 1950s were little more than a rumor to the vast majority of students who had started college several years later. The left had been a fringe element of campus politics for most of the postwar years; now it occupied a larger and more vital place than ever before. The civil rights movement, in particular, sparked the era of campus protests, beginning with the southern sit-in movement in the spring of 1960 and especially the model of courage and defiance displayed by black youths. For those who participated in the movement in Madison and especially for the several dozen Wisconsin students who experienced the southern movement directly, civil rights provided a powerful example and a compelling moral idealism that would come to rest near the core of the sixties.

By the time of the draft sit-in, the New Left had become a mass movement in Madison and throughout the nation. With Vietnam supplanting civil rights as the key issue on campus, mirroring President Johnson's escalation of the war in early 1965, hundreds and sometimes even thousands of Wisconsin students participated in rallies, marches, teach-ins, and other types of action. Some were drawn into the movement by family or friends, some by the power of ideas found in the classroom or in the pages of books and journals like *Studies on the Left*, and some by their fierce reaction to American policy on civil rights or Vietnam, but all of them were searching for ways to reshape American policies at home and abroad. The draft sit-in was the culmination of this period, a mark of how much the campus had changed as well as a sign of things to come. Though it ended peacefully, it highlighted the emergence of direct action as a crucial tool of the movement, and it was the first major campus protest directed at the university itself, an outgrowth of the contradictions of Cold War–era higher education that had been growing steadily since the end of World War II. As involvement in Vietnam laid bare the relationship between universities and America's national security, the sit-in foreshadowed the kinds of confrontations that would become a central part of the era's fabric.

❖

Civil rights would provide a political proving ground for many sixties activists and would shape the texture as well as the politics of the New Left, but just as the national civil rights movement had a long history that extended before the 1960 sit-ins and even before the Montgomery bus boycott and the Supreme Court's decision in *Brown v. Board of Education*, the University of Wisconsin also had a much longer resume on civil rights. In the immediate postwar years, many students advocated for what they usually called "human rights" and pushed others in the university—fellow students, faculty, and the administration—to combat discrimination based on race and religion. Housing was a particularly controversial issue, and there were regular efforts to end discrimination in university housing as well as in university-approved private housing. Though halting and ultimately incomplete, these efforts provided a foundation for the much larger movement to come.

In the years immediately after World War II, returning veterans provided one of the key constituencies in the fight for human rights. In 1947, when Madison's Three Bells Tavern refused to serve African American law student Theodore Coggs, the campus chapter of the liberal-leaning American Veterans Committee organized a boycott of the tavern, calling on Madisonians "not to subsidize plain injustice. . . . Let's practice a little real Americanism." Veterans also used their dominance of student government to press the issue of civil rights, and they formed a Committee on Discrimination that documented several examples of discrimination against students, some of them by the university. The committee's primary complaint was that the administration was tolerating discrimination by university-approved off-campus housing providers, landlords over which the administration had a good deal of leverage. The group called on the university to act, and one of its specific recommendations was the formation of a student-faculty committee to investigate instances of discrimination.[1]

At least some university faculty were sufficiently impressed by the need to respond. The faculty-run Student Life and Interests Committee cited the work of the Committee on Discrimination in its 1949 recommendations for changes to campus policy, and another faculty report, by the powerful University Committee, went even further in acknowledging the existence of discrimination. Approved as Faculty Document 933 in 1950, the report called for a "positive, vigorous, and continuing program against prejudice, discrimination and segregation at the university and by the university." It recommended the establishment of a student-faculty human rights committee, a color-blind policy in residence hall room assignments, more action on discrimination in university-approved housing, and, aimed primarily at Greek fraternal organizations, the end of discriminatory charters in student groups. It would take some time before the Board of Regents would approve Document 933—some members were initially concerned with the document's apparent acknowledgment of past discrimination—but the university ultimately made an effort to implement each of these recommendations in the following years.[2]

Students worked to secure human rights on campus throughout the late 1940s and 1950s, but it was the Greensboro, North Carolina, sit-in on February 1, 1960, that provided the crucial spark. Though not the first sit-in of its kind, the simple act of courage and defiance, as black youths sat down at a segregated lunch counter and asked to be served, ignited the passion of many African Americans and spread quickly through the South. The sit-in movement led to the creation of the Student Non-Violent Coordinating Committee (SNCC), one of the most important civil rights organizations of the era, and it also changed the nature of the fight for civil rights among the primarily white students on northern campuses. Making its way into the consciousness of students in Madison over the course of the next several weeks and months—discussed in students' informal networks and covered in leftist newspapers and magazines as well as the *Daily Cardinal*—it was a critical turning point for the New Left, injecting direct action into students' lexicon and changing the tone of campus activism for the rest of the sixties.

By the end of February, small numbers of Wisconsin students were already taking action. Some of the first meetings were held in the living room of Franklynn Peterson, a senior from Port Edwards, Wisconsin, and the chair of the Socialist Club, and a group of about fifty students and a few community members set up the first picket outside of the downtown Madison Woolworth's— the same store that black youth in the South had initially targeted. Enduring the subfreezing temperatures were several students from the Socialist Club, including Peterson, Fred Underhill, and Paul Breines, while some came from the campus NAACP or, like Judy Cowan, who would attend SDS's Port Huron conference two years later, from the Wisconsin Student Association's Human Relations Committee; indeed, some of them belonged to more than one of these organizations. In the following weeks, the group picketed several more times, growing in number and widening their protest to include other national chain stores in downtown Madison.[3]

While thousands of students from around the country joined in this nation-wide current, at such universities as Berkeley, Michigan, Vassar, and Cornell, students in Madison also held two civil rights rallies that spring of 1960, the first events of their kind in recent memory and a clear indication of the rapid change in the campus mood. On March 3, many of the same students who had picketed outside of Woolworth's, including Gary Weissman, a former president of the Wisconsin Student Association who, like Judy Cowan, would also go on to attend SDS's famous Port Huron conference, organized a campus rally in support of civil rights, with more than five hundred students gathering on the steps of the Wisconsin Historical Society at the east end of campus. Two months later, at a May 17 demonstration marking the anniversary of the Supreme Court's *Brown v. Board of Education* decision, six hundred students marched single file and in silence the several blocks from the campus Memorial Union building to the state capitol.[4]

In Madison, the events of spring and summer 1960 heralded a shift in student activism, as several hundred students participated in nonviolent rallies, marches, and pickets. One of the interesting developments was that the growing movement attracted a broad mix of students, some of them from the same left and liberal-left backgrounds that led students into the Socialist Club and Student Peace Center, but many of the participating students had not been active in campus politics before and had no family or community tradition of political action. The rallies also gained considerable support across the campus, as the Student Senate voted 21–3 to support the March rally, and the *Daily Cardinal* concluded afterward that the rally had been "well done." Wisconsin governor and future U.S. senator Gaylord Nelson offered his encouragement as well. "Many attacks have been written to the effect that today's college students are nothing but materialists, interested only in learning how to make money," the governor said in a written message to the demonstrators. "This assembly shows that this is not true—that there are some of you at least who are still idealists, who believe in moral principles and believe strongly enough to do something about your beliefs. I wish you success." The May demonstration, too, gained wide support, including backing from such community groups as the Madison Federation of Labor, the American Civil Liberties Union, and the Women's International League for Peace and Freedom. At the rally that followed the march to the capitol, speakers included Governor Nelson, Lieutenant Governor Philleo Nash, and UW President Conrad Elvehjem. Afterward, Dean of Students LeRoy Luberg commented that the protest had been "dignified, spirited, and useful."[5]

Despite wide support, however, some students expressed concern over the newfound activism, the beginning of a discussion about the nature of student politics that would continue throughout the sixties. In the debate over whether the student government should officially support the March rally, for example, it became clear that some students wanted to move faster than others. Although the Student Senate overwhelmingly supported the rally, they did so only after voting down, 19–10, a proposed silent march to the capitol. Student activism of this kind was practically unknown at the time, with some student senators raising doubts about the effectiveness of a march, as opposed to a rally, and others expressing concern over the potential for student opposition and perhaps even violence.

In the campus paper, too, several students questioned the demonstrations, focusing especially on a criticism of rallies as ineffective and potentially danger-ous and often drawing a sharp distinction between a "rational" approach to solving problems and the "emotional" approach signified by public protests. Graduate Club president Charles Gruneisen told a *Cardinal* reporter that the March rally was a "futile, emotional gesture," while another student called for some form of peaceful arbitration to solve the problem of civil rights. To the *Cardinal*'s editorial staff, which had praised the rally, the latter student directed some sharp invective: "Why don't you and your rabble rousing friends use your heads and brains instead of depending on emotion and a mob of easily led followers to accomplish what you seek?" A third student compared the May protest to commemorate the anniversary of *Brown* to the mass actions of Nazi Germany or Soviet Russia: "In America," he declared, "we have legislation, ballots, and courts to settle our differences."[6]

Others in the community were also equivocal about the newfound spirit of activism. In the aftermath of the March rally, UW president Conrad Elvehjem specified his support for what he termed "the intellectual rather than the emotional approach to protesting," and the Madison chapter of the NAACP (distinct from the campus chapter, which folded sometime in the spring of 1960 as new organizations emerged to take its place) also expressed ambivalence about the recent direction of civil rights protests in the city. Madison NAACP leader Odell Taliaferro apologized publicly to the community for his inability to avert the chain store picketing in February, telling a Madison newspaper reporter that while "it is indeed heartening to discover that so many of our young people feel so strongly about human rights," he would have liked to discuss with students the "advisability of the contemplated action." Taliaferro would later backtrack on his critical approach to student protesters, but the point was clear: not everyone was encouraged by the newfound spirit of activism.[7]

Following the busy spring and summer of 1960, civil rights remained a regular campus concern. Though the level of activism rose and fell over the next several years, often coinciding with the rhythms of the academic calendar and with the course of national events, a new style of activism was plainly evident, one that was distinct from the more tentative efforts on behalf of human rights and other issues in the 1940s and 1950s. Issues other than civil rights occasionally occupied students' attention—nuclear testing, civil defense, the House Un-American Activities Committee, and the stirrings of war in Southeast Asia, for example—but at least until the beginning of 1965, civil rights remained the most pressing. During these years, what had been something of a latent activism became fully energized. It would be the Vietnam War that would tear most forcefully at many campuses in the late 1960s, but the first half of the decade, centered on the movement for civil rights and especially the example of black youths in the southern movement, was crucial in shaping later events.

There were many ways that the civil rights movement manifested itself on campuses like Wisconsin in the early 1960s. One was the procession of national figures who traveled to northern universities, which, in Madison, included

Martin Luther King Jr., SNCC leader Stokely Carmichael, former baseball star Jackie Robinson, and black nationalist leader Malcolm X, just to name the most prominent. News of events in the South was also important. The 1961 Freedom Rides, the violent opposition to James Meredith's entrance into the University of Mississippi in 1962, the 1963 March on Washington—all of these and other milestones of the civil rights movement were the focus of local events. In Madison in June 1961, one hundred and fifty students marched to the capitol to petition Governor Nelson to intercede on behalf of former UW student James Wahlstrom, who was then in jail for his participation in the Freedom Rides. In November 1962, about four hundred students gathered in front of the statue of Abraham Lincoln at the top of Bascom Hill in support of James Meredith, while starting in 1963, as the southern civil rights movement gained steam from massive demonstrations in Birmingham and the famous March on Washington, so did the movement in Madison. In September of that year, over seven hundred students and community members marched around the capitol square to demonstrate against the death of four children in a Birmingham church bombing. In June 1964, with Freedom Summer volunteers, including more than a dozen UW students, in Mississippi to work on a massive voter registration effort, a hundred activists endured the ninety-four-degree tempera-ture to gather and push for action on three missing civil rights workers whose disappearance had attracted national attention. One of the civil rights workers, Andrew Goodman, had been a UW student for part of his freshman year; all three of them were later found dead, murdered by the local KKK and with the help of several police officers.[8]

Finally, in March 1965, even as the Vietnam War was beginning to take center stage on campus, events in Selma, Alabama, provoked a massive response. With the voting rights campaign there confronted with police violence—the crackdown by state troopers as protesters attempted to march from Selma to Montgomery came to be known as Bloody Sunday—students picketed the Madison federal building on March 10 to protest the lack of federal protection. In the days that followed, UW and Beloit College students rallied at the capitol, including Nancy Fleming, a Beloit College student and the daughter of UW chancellor Robben Fleming, while more than one thousand students and residents gathered for a separate prayer vigil. Three busloads of students left Madison to join thousands of other protesters in Washington, D.C., while a smaller group, including twenty-three Madison students, journalists, ministers, and lawyers, traveled to Selma by chartered plane. The flurry of activity marked a high point for civil rights in Madison even though it would be several more years before the issue would again dominate student politics.[9]

One interesting result of the campus activism around events in the southern movement was that local issues often received little attention from Madison students. In the 1950s, when the national civil rights movement was much less visible, most civil rights activism in Madison had focused on the campus; by the 1960s, that had changed. The incredible drama of events in places like Greensboro, Birmingham, Jackson, and Selma was important, but the trend also reflected the belief by many white northerners that racism was primarily a southern problem. The lack of black students and faculty at the university— there were fewer than one hundred black students in 1964, and only nine black professors—might have highlighted the existence of discrimination in the university's admissions and hiring or at least raised the question of why so few blacks wanted to come to Madison, but white students, even those most active in campus civil rights groups, largely ignored the reality that was right in front of them. In 1963, it was Lloyd Barbee, a former UW law student from Memphis, Tennessee, and then director of the Wisconsin state NAACP, who publicly criticized the lack of black tenured faculty: "If this university wanted qualified Negroes on the faculty, they could find them. Now there's just a lot of pious talk—no action." Barbee went on to call on students to take direct action against the university, a call that went generally unheeded, at least until much later in the decade.[10]

Another facet of Madison activists' lack of engagement with local issues was their generally distant relationship with community-based civil rights groups. This distance was already evident in 1960, when the leader of the Madison NAACP reacted guardedly to the student picketing of Woolworth's; over the next several years, little changed. Faced with an overwhelming white majority (blacks made up about 2 percent of Madison's population in 1960), Madison's middle-class civil rights leaders usually preferred more conventional tactics over the kind of direct action politics that was increasingly popular among students. When the Madison chapter of the Congress of Racial Equality (CORE), made up largely of students, did turn its attention to local issues to protest alleged employment discrimination at the Madison Sears store in 1964, the NAACP declined an invitation to participate. Marshall Colston, an African American social worker who had taken over leadership of the Madison NAACP, had been dropping not-so-subtle hints less than a year earlier about the possible need for demonstrations in Madison, but now he took the opposite tack. "It is . . . our belief," Colston said, "that any evidence of discrimination in the fields of employment, housing, or public accommodation should be referred to the [Madison] Equal Opportunities Commission for full investigation and whatever disposition seems necessary as a result of that investigation." Students might have agreed with Colston's suggestion a few years earlier, but events had significantly changed their view of political tactics.[11]

On the rare occasion that the Madison NAACP did utilize direct action, cooperation with students still remained limited. In 1961, the state NAACP, led by the Madison chapter, sponsored a thirteen-day around-the-clock sit-in at the capitol building to press legislators to pass a number of civil rights bills that were being held up in committee; it was an orderly event, with sixteen participants at a time, including Anna Miller, who, at eighty-six, was the oldest protester, and Janet Nelson Lee, the governor's sister. But even as it received praise from many parts of the city, James McWilliams, one of a small number of black civil rights activists on campus and chairman of the campus Student Council for Civil Rights (SCCR), was not so sanguine. In a letter to the leaders of the sit-in, he commended the effort and declared his support for "direct action as a method by which citizens may present their grievances directly to the public at large or to their representatives," but he also claimed that some university students who wanted to participate were denied the opportunity, including one who was supposedly asked to leave because of her political beliefs. The response of Madison NAACP head Odell Taliaferro was just as revealing. Highlighting the embattled feeling within Madison's small black community as well as widespread suspicion of campus activists as radicals who had a much broader agenda than civil rights, he pointed out that the SCCR had "acquired additional enemies who we can not afford."[12]

Yet even as students in Madison and on some other northern campuses often missed the opportunity to link forcefully the glaring racism of the South with the more subtle, but still very real, racism in the North, the southern civil rights movement played a pivotal role in propelling sixties activism. The courageous and harrowing work of civil rights activists—at the lunch counter sit-ins, on the defiant march across Selma's Edmund Pettis Bridge, in the face of Birmingham police chief Bull Connor's fire hoses—this was the stuff of legend in the New Left, and young black activists in particular took on an almost iconic status for many white youth. For those Wisconsin students who participated in the movement from something of a distance, lending whatever support they could to activities in the South, it was an opportunity to participate in a national movement, one with compelling and clearly delineated principles. For the small number who participated directly in southern activism, the opportunity was even more significant. These students, perhaps four or five dozen from Madison in the first half of the 1960s, gained a firsthand look at the hardships of southern blacks and the commitment of activists in the movement, especially black youth in SNCC; ultimately, they provided a strong bridge between the southern civil rights movement and the Madison New Left.

Among the many Wisconsin students who participated directly in the southern movement, one of the first was Paul Breines, who gave up part of his 1961 summer break to participate in the Freedom Rides. Other UW students to participate that summer included Elizabeth Adler, Catherine Jo Prensky, and James Wahlstrom, while Beloit College student Jim Zwerg, who rode with SNCC leader and future congressman John Lewis, was severely beaten by a Montgomery, Alabama mob. The Freedom Rides were a series of racially integrated bus trips that challenged authorities to uphold a Supreme Court decision that segregation on interstate travel was unconstitutional, but the trips ended for many participants, including Breines, in Mississippi's infamous Parchman Penitentiary. Breines, whose best claim to fame might actually be the few weeks that aspiring musician Bob Dylan stayed in Madison with him and roommate Danny Kalb in 1960, had come from New York to Wisconsin with what he calls a "latent political consciousness"—his parents had been active in the left in the 1930s, though his main interest in high school was basketball, not politics—but the experience of the Freedom Rides was transformative. Of the three weeks he spent in Parchman, he recalls that "the inner details of being in jail, of being arrested, of being pushed around and knocked down and being in a collective struggle . . . was incredible." The black youths with whom he worked, activists who would continue the struggle even after he returned to Madison, made a particularly deep impression, while the experience of direct action, as many sixties activists would find, was exhilarating.[13]

Like Breines, participation in the Southern movement was crucial for fellow student Stuart Ewen. One of approximately fifteen Wisconsin students who participated in Freedom Summer, the 1964 effort to register black voters in heavily segregated Mississippi, Ewen worked in both Columbus and Tupelo during the summer and ended up staying on for several more months as a member of SNCC's staff. Ewen's experience in the southern movement did not turn him into a political radical, as his politics were certainly an important part of his decision to join Freedom Summer in the first place, but when he finally returned to Madison, in the spring of 1965, he had undergone a significant change. "It was a political education that changed who I was," he later wrote of the experience. "It taught me how to be an organizer, walking door to door and talking with folks who gave me more than I could give back. It was also a life of relative danger, not part of my suburban upbringing. I was in a war zone, a world of guns and shootings, being tailed and threatened. Our Freedom House was burned down one night. There was time spent in Mississippi jails."[14]

It should be no surprise that, for students across the country, experience in the southern civil rights movement translated into heightened activism at home, including the first major upheaval on a university campus, the 1964–65 Berkeley Free Speech Movement. Freedom Summer had brought several hundred full-time volunteers, mostly white college students, into Mississippi, and while they worked primarily in voter registration or taught in Freedom Schools, even these seemingly innocuous activities meant confronting directly America's legacy of racism and, in 1960s Mississippi, living in an atmosphere of considerable violence. Like the African Americans with whom they worked, students became acutely aware of the failure of the federal government to guarantee even basic rights and protections for some of its citizens. At Berkeley, many of the more than thirty students who had participated in Freedom Summer, including Mario Savio, became leaders of the campus movement, bringing to their efforts the moral energy of the civil rights movement as well as their newly acquired political skills. As one Berkeley student and Freedom Summer veteran commented on the standoff between Berkeley students and the university's administration, "A student who has been chased by the KKK in Mississippi is not easily scared by academic bureaucrats." Berkeley students remained relatively organized and disciplined during the Free Speech Movement, while the administration was caught off guard and remained on the defensive during much of the months-long standoff.[15]

Many Wisconsin students who participated directly in the southern movement also became campus leaders in civil rights and in other areas of campus politics. As Stuart Ewen explains the importance of civil rights work, "I returned to Madison in the spring of 1965 as someone for whom politics and action had become central. . . . I felt I had made some heavy life commitments, and I had brought back some practical lessons that were transported to student politics." While Paul Breines remained active in the Socialist Club and worked on the two journals that came out of Madison in the sixties, *Studies on the Left* and, later, *Radical America*, Ewen was involved especially in Madison's Committee to End the War in Vietnam (CEWV) and the Wisconsin Draft Resistance Union. He also teamed with another civil rights veteran, Robert Gabriner, who had worked with his wife Vicki on voter registration projects in Tennessee, to establish *Connections*, a countercultural newspaper that began publishing in Madison in 1966. Other students who made similar jumps included Harriet Tanzman, who worked at the SNCC national office during parts of 1963 and 1964 before co-organizing one of Madison's first anti-Vietnam protests; Christopher Hexter, another Freedom Summer veteran who was active in CEWV and the 1966 draft sit-in; and Dion Diamond, a black student who transferred to Madison in 1963 after working as a field representative for SNCC. Diamond had been arrested twenty-three times before he came to Madison, and he became chair of the campus chapter of the Friends of SNCC as well as a regular speaker at campus civil rights demonstrations.[16]

Ultimately, the civil rights movement, through individuals like Breines and Ewen as well as the thousands of students who participated in the Madison-based movement, brought organizing skills and a new and compelling energy to campus activism. Whereas demonstrations had been almost unheard of before 1960, they were so much a regular part of the campus fabric within a few years that a relatively quiet spring in 1963 led the *Daily Cardinal* to ask, "Is the silent generation returning to campus?" In absolute numbers, the campus left remained small in comparison to the later sixties, but this was a period of significant growth. Several civil rights groups emerged, older organizations, like the Socialist Club and the Student Peace Center, were re-invigorated, and a variety of new groups formed, including Students for a Democratic Society, established by math graduate student and future SDS national secretary C. Clark Kissinger in the fall of 1963.[17]

The mood of the campus had also shifted considerably. Elizabeth Ewen, who arrived in Madison in the fall of 1961, recalls that this was a time of changing student generations and a move from a more intellectual politics to one that was oriented toward action, exposing a tension that would continue through-out much of the sixties. "Being an intellectual earlier meant something like being a Talmudic scholar," Ewen remembers. "The civil rights movement did more than anything to change that; it caused people to join activist organizations, to *do something*. Being active now meant as much as the printed word." Observers, too, recognized the role of civil rights in the incredible changes at Wisconsin and other campuses. At a 1966 conference at the University of North Carolina, UW dean of students Joe Kauffman told his fellow deans that the effectiveness of the civil rights movement had given students an appreciation of tactics and commitment: "[Students] have seen laws changed, rules altered, practices discarded, and myths crumbled by resistance and defiance." Civil rights would fade from the forefront of campus politics in 1965, replaced by the Vietnam War, but the movement had imparted an energy and moral idealism, as well as practical experience, to Madison's activist leaders. Combined with the campus's longer tradition of radicalism, civil rights would play a significant role in bringing the sixties to life.[18]

❖

Although civil rights dominated activism in the early 1960s, the Cold War was still a prominent part of campus life, from the ever-increasing expansion of the university to the continuing activism on issues like nuclear testing, ROTC, and civil liberties. There were also strong connections between civil rights and Cold War activism, a point that was clear in the heavy overlap of students who worked on both issues. Indeed, as the 1960s dawned in Madison, the challenges facing the United States after more than a decade of Cold War struggle with the Soviet Union were on display at a university-organized symposium titled "The Sixties: Challenge to our Generation." That February, former British prime minister Clement Atlee, perennial Socialist Party presidential candidate Norman Thomas, and conservative writer William F. Buckley were just a few of the speakers who expounded on the challenges and opportunities for a generation of young Americans. Their perspectives differed considerably, but each agreed on the importance of finding a way forward in an increasingly dangerous world. "The main challenge facing us in the sixties," explained Norman Cousins, editor of the *Saturday Review* and another participant in the symposium, "is to stay alive and be free. The spiraling atomic arms race in a situation of mounting tensions—a nuclear arms race, moreover, that soon will involve perhaps a dozen nations—represents not just a challenge but a specific danger."[19]

Cousins, a founding member of the Committee for a Sane Nuclear Policy (SANE), was one of many voices that had joined the fight against America's Cold War policies in the late 1950s and early 1960s. Though they made little headway during these years, with both major political parties committed to an aggressive Cold War posture, a staunch group of liberals and radicals— journalists, intellectuals, clergy, scientists, politicians, and women's groups— began to lay the groundwork for the era's peace movement. The dangers of atmospheric testing and fallout, the quickening arms race, and the futility of civil defense drills were some of the key issues they raised, and they began to experiment as well with direct action. Twenty-eight pacifists were arrested for refusing to participate in a 1955 civil defense drill in New York City, while more than twenty-five thousand people across the country participated in a walk for peace in the spring of 1961.[20]

Students also played a role in the growing movement, both in Madison and in the rest of the country. Students at the University of Chicago founded a national group, the Student Peace Union, while SANE included a student auxiliary with numerous chapters, including one at the UW. In Madison,

Student Peace Center (SPC) members picketed a meeting of national civil defense leaders in March 1961, and SPC and the UW student chapter of SANE gathered about one hundred students to protest nuclear testing later that year. Students for Peace and Disarmament (SPAD, an independent peace group at the UW formed when SANE dissolved its student chapters) held another anti-testing protest in March 1962, and in October it worked with community groups Women for Peace and Women's International League for Peace and Freedom in organizing a picket against America's blockade of Cuba as the Cuban Missile Crisis brought the nation to the precipice of nuclear war.[21]

Like civil rights, peace activism in Madison helped develop a core of campus leaders who would be active in the more confrontational politics of the late sixties. Among these was James Hawley, who came to Madison in the fall of 1962 after attending Students for a Democratic Society's Port Huron convention that summer (as a visitor rather than a participant) and was active in a number of leftist groups. A member of SPAD, he was involved in organizing the first Madison rally against American involvement in Vietnam—in October 1963—and became a leader of the Madison Committee to End the War in Vietnam when it began in early 1965. Don Bluestone, a graduate student in history, was well known for his work in campus peace organizations before he became involved in the antiwar movement, while John Coatsworth, another graduate student in history, was likewise drawn into the left primarily by his opposition to American foreign policy. Coatsworth originally came to Madison to work with historian William Appleman Williams, and the many highlights of his years at Wisconsin included a well-attended campus talk on his 1963 summer trip to Cuba (in defiance of the State Department travel ban), his role in organizing a May 2, 1964, rally against U.S. involvement in Vietnam, and his leadership of the ad hoc committee that pulled together the initial student opposition to the U.S. escalation of the war in February 1965.[22]

While the national peace movement gained some momentum in the early 1960s, scoring a victory with the signing of a U.S.–Soviet Test Ban Treaty in 1963, it was the emergence of Vietnam as a major issue that brought the movement out from the margins of American politics. Actually, the United States had been involved in Vietnam for almost two decades by the time most peace activists focused their attention on Southeast Asia in the early 1960s. American policymakers had supported the French effort to reestablish colonial control over Vietnam after World War II (the Japanese had interrupted French control during the war) and had taken a more direct role when the French were defeated in 1954 by Vietnamese nationalist forces. Though overshadowed by Cold War events elsewhere around the world, Presidents Eisenhower and Kennedy committed American dollars over the next decade in an effort to maintain a friendly government in South Vietnam and prevent the expansion of the communist government that had taken hold in the North under the leadership of Ho Chi Minh. An American troop presence also grew over these years, especially in the early 1960s as the threat increased from the recently established National Liberation Front, or Viet Cong; by the end of 1962 there were more than eleven thousand American troops in Vietnam.[23]

This increase in troop strength, along with heightened concerns about corruption in the South Vietnamese government, helped bring the issue to the attention of activists in Madison and elsewhere. Demonstrations at the UW in the fall of 1963 and the spring of 1964 were part of coordinated efforts across the country, and the issue gained even more prominence after Congress passed the Gulf of Tonkin Resolution in August 1964, providing President Lyndon Johnson with the authority to escalate military action in Southeast Asia. Johnson ran for election that fall promising restraint in Vietnam, at least in comparison to Republican candidate Barry Goldwater, but his administration was already moving toward an increasing American commitment. An early February 1965 attack on American troops at Pleiku Air Base, in South Vietnam, gave Johnson an opening to act, and two battalions of Marines buttressed American forces already in the region, part of the increase in American troop strength from 23,000 at the beginning of 1965 to 184,000 by the end of the year. Operation Rolling Thunder began in February as well, a massive bombing campaign that targeted military and industrial targets in North Vietnam; originally supposed to last eight weeks, the operation continued for most of three years even as it failed to significantly impact the North's fighting ability.[24]

Antiwar activists in Madison responded quickly to these developments. While events in Washington, D.C., included a February "Mother's Lobby" and an April antiwar rally that was organized by Students for a Democratic Society and attracted twenty thousand protesters, Madison experienced its own rush of activity. John Coatsworth, who had co-organized an antiwar rally the previous spring, helped lead the ad hoc committee that brought out two hundred students for a February 9 march from the campus to the state capitol, including speeches by law professor William Rice, soils science professor Francis Hole, and sociology professor Maurice Zeitlin. A few days later, about three hundred students and community members joined an overnight vigil at the capitol, and other rallies and marches were part of a flurry of events that continued until the end of the spring semester. Meanwhile, the ad hoc committee that had initiated the protests became a permanent group, the Committee to End the War in Vietnam; starting with about one hundred and fifty members, the group would be the leading campus antiwar organization for most of the next two years.[25]

Among the many antiwar events in the spring of 1965, one that stands out is a week-long education and protest campaign organized by a coalition of CEWV and a group of about eighty-five professors. Calling itself the Faculty-Student Committee to End the War in Vietnam, the group organized an antiwar rally and a day-long teach-in, while the professors on the committee also distributed an open letter to President Johnson calling on him to move toward withdrawal from Vietnam. The involvement of professors reflected a history of cooperation between students and faculty in Madison as well as the emergence of university professors across the country as a significant constituency in the early antiwar movement. Faculty members played a key role in organizing the nation's first teach-in, at the University of Michigan, and the energy that emerged from this and similar events on other campuses led to the formation of the Inter-University Committee for a Public Hearing on Vietnam, with the group holding a national teach-in on May 15. Broadcast to campuses across the country and including more than fifteen hours of debate on the war, just a few of the most prominent scholars involved included historian Arthur M. Schlesinger Jr. (representing the administration's view), international relations expert Bernard Fall, and University of Chicago professor Hans Morgenthau.[26]

One of the most interesting developments of the week in Madison was the circulation of the faculty petition, which garnered the support of 132 professors across the campus. Dated April 3, 1965, the petition was in the form of an open letter to President Johnson and called for the de-escalation of the conflict and the ultimate withdrawal of American forces. It asserted that intellectuals had a critical role to play in the shaping of American opinion and policy. "In a democratic society," the faculty members declared, "the members of a university must be active and critical. Too often the intellectual community has remained silent when it was necessary for enlightened criticism to be heard." The signers included many who played an important role in campus politics in the 1950s and 1960s, including biochemist Henry Lardy, soils professor Francis Hole, law professor William Rice, physicist James Crow, and historians George Mosse, William Appleman Williams, and Harvey Goldberg. And while historians were the best represented in the university, with 21 of them signing the petition, support was spread across the campus. Among those who affixed their name were 12 sociologists, 10 English professors, 10 zoology professors, 7 anthropologists, and 5 physicists. Seven math professors also signed, including three who identified themselves as affiliated with the Army Mathematics Research Center.[27]

Indeed, this was only one of several petitions on the issue of Vietnam that circulated among the faculty in the 1960s. Just a few months before, sociologist

Maurice Zeitlin, a young faculty member who had received his PhD from Berkeley and was an early and vocal critic of American policy in Cuba, organized another petition drive among faculty. Calling on President Johnson to avoid escalation and seek peace through negotiation and a phased withdrawal of American troops, 117 professors signed this petition, including sociologist William Sewell, who would speak at an antiwar rally in April 1965 and would become chancellor of the Madison campus in the fall of 1967, a tragic figure caught between his own feelings about the war in Vietnam and his duty to uphold the university's policies. Though faculty signers were sometimes inconsistent—some might not have signed because they were out of town, on sabbatical, or simply unavailable—there was clearly a broad feeling among many professors that the United States needed to dramatically change course in Vietnam, with another petition in early 1967 garnering 279 signatures. Some professors signed more than one of these petitions, but there were nearly 400 different faculty members (out of a total faculty that numbered more than one thousand in the sixties) who were willing to publicly voice their dissent from American policy.[28]

The climax of the week organized by the Faculty-Student Committee to End the War in Vietnam was the teach-in on April 1, following by several days the era's first teach-in at the University of Michigan and part of a wave of similar events on campuses across the country that spring. In Madison, an estimated five thousand students jammed the Social Science building over the course of the day-long event, with some lectures and discussions so crowded that audio had to be piped into overflow rooms. The twenty-six professors who participated approached the issue of Vietnam from a variety of perspectives: Merle Curti spoke on "The Peace Movement: Historical Perspectives for the Present"; Francis Hole's talk was titled "Non-Violence versus Modern Warfare"; historian Laurence Veysey discussed "The American University and Dissent"; and Germaine Bree, a popular professor of French literature, lectured on "Sartre and Camus: Two Concepts of Commitment."[29]

After a long day, and as the hour approached midnight, William Appleman Williams rose to speak in what turned out to be a high point of the entire teach-in. Just as Williams had been so influential among the writers around *Studies on the Left*, he provided a framework for this generation of students coming to question America's role in the world. The reason that students, faculty, and community members had come together, Williams asserted, was because of the foreign policy failures of Presidents Kennedy and Johnson and the breakdown of representative government. America had become involved in Vietnam so it could continue to exert its economic, political, and cultural influence throughout the world, yet even America's immense power could not alter the reality that many formerly underdeveloped parts of the world had achieved a significant degree of independence over the past half century. "A few more men and planes [in Vietnam]," Williams argued, "are not enough to turn back the clock. . . . It is time to realize that we are trying to do the impossible, as well as doing the immoral." The United States, he suggested, needed to return to the principled idea of self-determination.[30]

The teach-in and the petition suggested the potential for an interesting coalition of activist students and professors. Wisconsin students and faculty had worked together before during the postwar years, starting with the Stick Your Neck Out Club, a group organized in 1952 to push back against the narrowing of accepted political opinions during the McCarthy years, and professors had played an important role in the development of a leftist intellectual community in Madison, including the beginning of *Studies on the Left*. The language of the faculty's open letter to President Johnson highlighted professors' interest in taking an active part in the national debate over Vietnam, while in 1965, around the same time as the teach-in, faculty and students also joined together in sometimes short-lived groups like Faculty and Students for Equality and the Student-Faculty Council on Civil Rights. Still, many students (and doubtless many faculty too) remained guarded about the potential for close cooperation. A document produced by CEWV later in the year noted the cooperation with faculty around the teach-in, yet it also remarked on the potential for conflict over how radical a faculty-student group could and should be. In the following years, this question would emerge with even more force, while the relationship between professors and students would be regularly tested.[31]

Even as the question of faculty-student cooperation remained, and despite the excitement within the ranks of the antiwar movement and the momentum of events that spring, not all students were quick to jump on the antiwar bandwagon. Just as the campus civil rights movement had been especially contentious when it began in earnest in the spring of 1960, so the antiwar movement elicited a variety of responses from students and community members. A *Newsweek* poll in March 1965 found that only about one-quarter of college students believed that American action in Vietnam was too strong, and in Madison at least some students organized to support the war effort. Claiming to represent the "frustrated majority" of students, a group calling itself the Committee to Support the People of South Vietnam provided an ideological as well as a stylistic contrast with CEWV. Pledging to carry out its program without the "buttons, placards, and emotional slogans which usually characterize mass movements," the group circulated a petition supporting U.S. policy and, remarkably, took only a matter of days to collect six thousand signatures from students and professors. Taking another swipe at the antiwar movement, one of the group's early leaders, Robert Gordon, asserted that CEWV was made up primarily of socialists, communists, and foreign students. Antiwar activists, Gordon suggested, were essentially maladjusted: "Their lack of personal hygiene and personality disorder reveals them to be the same students who were 'loners' in high school and who will make an equally poor adjustment after graduation."[32]

Indeed, despite the image of college campuses in the sixties as hotbeds of radicalism, Madison had a strong contingent of right-leaning students and conservative campus organizations. In the 1950s especially, conservative groups vied with liberals and radicals for influence. While mock campus elections showed Republican Dwight Eisenhower defeating Adlai Stevenson two to one in 1956 and Richard Nixon defeating John Kennedy in 1960 (Nixon actually swept all of the Big Ten universities that held mock elections that fall), conservative students also held prominent positions in student government and at the *Daily Cardinal.* The Young Republicans were active during these years, especially during election seasons, but a group calling itself the Conservative Club was home to many of the campus's most committed conservatives. Established in the mid-1950s, the group's principles included halting government centralization, emphasizing individual liberty, and publicizing the dangers of communism. In addition to distributing literature and inviting to campus prominent conservatives like William F. Buckley Jr. and M. Stanton Evans, many of the group's members were also involved in the publication of *Insight and Outlook*, a conservative magazine that began in Madison in 1959, the same year as *Studies on the Left. Insight and Outlook* claimed to be the first conservative student journal and had a print run in the thousands, continuing publication into the mid-sixties and establishing connections with conservatives on other college campuses, especially in the Midwest.[33]

The Conservative Club would continue to operate for several years, but it was another group, Young Americans for Freedom (YAF), that would become the most important conservative youth organization in Madison and across the country. Established at the Sharon, Connecticut, home of William F. Buckley Jr. in 1960, the group played a key role in Barry Goldwater's 1964 presidential nomination, provided a counter to young 1960s leftists, and, unlike most sixties groups, continued to play an important role in American politics long after the era ended. One UW student, Gale Pfund, attended the Sharon Conference in 1960, but it would be a few more years before another student, undergraduate David Keene from Fort Atkinson, Wisconsin, established a YAF chapter in Madison. Keene would go on to chair YAF's national organization in 1969 and would become a prominent conservative, leading the influential American Conservative Union from 1984 to 2011 and then taking over leadership of the National Rifle Association.[34]

Though the campus right was never able to match the left in terms of energy and noise in the sixties, it offered a credible opposition at times. Conservative students were more likely to be from Wisconsin than leftist students, and several campus groups supported the war, though some of them, like the Committee to Support the People of South Vietnam, were short-lived. Young Americans for Freedom even used direct action at times to champion the conservative cause, including a small 1965 protest at the state capitol in support of a section of the Taft-Hartley Act that limited the power of unions and was then under discussion by the state legislature. Conservatives also used the *Daily Cardinal* to publicize their views (though the paper was generally maligned by conservatives for its liberal and, later, radical bent). David Keene used the *Cardinal*'s pages to remind students in 1965 that "kindly uncle Ho Chi Minh is, after all, a communist," while James O'Connell, a conservative columnist off and on in the early and middle 1960s, offered a number of defenses of American action in Vietnam. In 1965, he argued that American credibility, rather than democracy or freedom, was as stake; America, he claimed, did not want a return to 1930s-style appeasement.[35]

Whatever opposition came from the right, however, did not stop the antiwar movement from pressing forward on a number of fronts in 1965. Demonstrations proceeded throughout the summer and fall, including a July rally on the Union steps to oppose escalation in Vietnam, a march in August to mark the twentieth anniversary of the bombing of Hiroshima, and an antiwar rally in October to kick off the first International Days of Protest. Indeed, the International Days of Protest were at least nominally coordinated in Madison, at the office of the National Coordinating Committee to End the War in Vietnam, a group that had been established at a conference of antiwar groups in Washington, D.C., that summer; with the office run by UW student Frank Emspak, it was something of a clearinghouse for the antiwar movement. Nearly a hundred thousand people around the United States and in a few other countries participated in the Days of Protest, and in Madison events included lectures, workshops, and rallies as well as a protest at the Milwaukee appearance of General Maxwell Taylor, a former army chief of staff and an early advocate of sending American ground forces into Vietnam.[36]

Behind most of this early activity in Madison was the Committee to End the War in Vietnam. While Students for a Democratic Society often sits at the center of accounts of the New Left, beginning with Kirkpatrick Sale's voluminous history of the group published in the early 1970s and continuing with many other well-regarded histories of the era, it was only one of several groups active in the Madison antiwar movement. SDS would become the most important New Left organization on many university campuses, especially campuses that did not have an extensive history of student activism and radical politics, but like Berkeley, where the 1964–65 Free Speech Movement emerged out of a tradition of student activism unrelated to SDS, Madison had a diversity of groups that took up the antiwar and other 1960s-era movements. SDS's widely read 1962 manifesto, "The Port Huron Statement," certainly influenced young activists throughout the country, but it was CEWV that was perhaps the largest political group in Madison in 1965 and 1966 and set the template that much of the campus New Left would follow in later years.[37]

As CEWV described itself, it was an educational as well as a protest organization. James Hawley remembers that there were sometimes a hundred or more students standing around the group's booth in the Memorial Union, a booth that the group maintained on an everyday basis to distribute literature about Vietnam and publicize its activities. It also sent representatives to speak to other student groups on campus and held workshops on American foreign policy; John Coatsworth remembers that the group made some attempts at community organizing, something that campus activists would try again and again over the next several years, not always successfully. CEWV would lose influence over the next two years and would be only one player among many by the time of the dramatic protests against Dow Chemical Company in 1967, but in 1965 and 1966 it would incorporate such defining elements of the New Left as participatory democracy, direct action, opposition to American racism and imperialism, and a strident critique of universities as authoritarian and in need of radical restructuring.[38]

The desire to take part in the decisions affecting one's life—popularized especially by SDS as "participatory democracy"—was vigorously promoted by CEWV in Madison. In a pamphlet written in late 1965 or early 1966 and intended as a kind of blueprint for other groups organizing to oppose the war, the Madison chapter made clear that its work was based on the belief that all citizens could participate in local and national decision making, even foreign policy decisions. "It is untrue," the group declared, "that foreign policy is somehow beyond the understanding of the average citizen and should be left to the 'experts.' . . . Any intelligent American can formulate a coherent understanding of American foreign policy and the Vietnam crisis [and] he has a right and an obligation to participate in the decision making process." Moreover, the group blamed what it saw as the misguided war in Vietnam on the very lack of citizen participation: if Americans had been informed about foreign policy and involved in national decision making, the thinking went, they would not have found themselves in the crisis in Vietnam.[39]

One result of the emphasis on participatory democracy was that CEWV, like many New Left groups, attempted to decentralize its organization. Even with a relatively complex structure, including an executive committee and numerous subcommittees, the group repeatedly stressed the need to keep the general membership well connected to the leadership. Frequent meetings were meant to keep members involved in the group's decisions, and the committee system was explicitly designed to diffuse power throughout the organization. Of course, this could backfire as well, and New Left lore is filled with stories of all-night meetings in search of consensus. In Madison, an observer noted in September 1965 that the committee was often bogged down in meetings rather than spending energy on action, and another account claimed that CEWV meetings tended to be "long, arduous, and abundant in polemic." Still, group members remained committed to decentralization. They observed that some of the Madison group's most important members had little experience in politics or activism, and they worked to maintain an organizational style that would remain flexible and provide leadership opportunities for all members.[40]

Participatory democracy remained a watchword throughout the sixties, but perhaps even more central to the identity of the New Left was direct action. One of the most significant differences between the New Left and the leftist politics that had preceded it, direct action was seen as an effective method to compel change, while the willingness to put one's body on the line was often a measure of the truly committed. Direct action had never entirely disappeared at Wisconsin in the 1950s, but it was the civil rights movement that especially sparked its revival. In declaring a rationale at the time of its first civil rights actions, in the spring of 1960, the Wisconsin Student Association's Human Relations Committee expressed its unwillingness to wait for the slow workings of the system. "We do not intend to wait placidly for those rights which are legally and morally ours to be meted out to us one at a time," the group declared. "We have then only one recourse in the matter of civil rights and civil liberties: direct and concerted action, not only in the federal and state legislatures, but also, as citizens, in our classrooms and communities." The next year, with leadership of the campus civil rights movement having passed to the Student Council for Civil Rights, the group's president, Tom Jacobson, argued that nonviolent direct action offered potential for confronting a largely apathetic public with the problems of racial discrimination in the United States. Not only is the "dedication and perseverance" of demonstration participants "very contagious," he told a meeting of the Wisconsin conference of NAACP branches, but direct action could achieve results much faster than the alternatives.[41]

For many, putting one's body on the line became the ultimate symbol of commitment to change. Rallies, marches, vigils, and other types of protest became ubiquitous in the early sixties even as more confrontational tactics became more prevalent later in the decade. In Madison, the 1964 Sears "shop-in" offered an example of an increasingly confrontational New Left, as members of the Madison chapter of CORE, most of them university students, entered the store to protest Sears' lack of African American hiring, especially in visible sales positions. With additional picketers outside, a group of twenty-five or thirty protesters sat down in an aisle in the shoe department and sang civil rights songs, while one student, Stanley Grand of Washington, D.C., was arrested for disorderly conduct. Grand was perhaps the first Wisconsin student arrested during the sixties protest era, but he would certainly not be the last.[42]

Even as civil disobedience — the nonviolent and purposeful violation of laws believed to be unjust — would become increasingly commonplace, it would also remain controversial. In addition to the criticism that came from various corners of the university, including the *Daily Cardinal*, whose opinions of demonstrations swung back and forth wildly in the early sixties, activists themselves were often torn over just what kind of action was appropriate and most effective. Almost immediately, the movement faced the prospect that its initial protests seemed to have little impact. Years later, former Madison student Frank Emspak recalled that many antiwar activists initially believed that the government simply needed more information and input, that a forthright and public discussion of American foreign policy would lead to an end of the war. When it quickly became clear that American involvement in Vietnam was not based on a lack of information but was part of a broad Cold War framework and highly resistant to change, activists were forced to adapt to the new reality. Teach-ins and other early actions across the country had been a success, but they were not enough. Escalation of the war in Vietnam continued, and there was no indication that the Johnson administration was considering a policy shift.[43]

It was the administration's pseudo-rebuttal to the spring 1965 teach-in movement that prompted one of the first extended discussions within CEWV and across the campus regarding the direction of the antiwar movement. That spring, led by State Department Vietnam specialist Thomas Conlon, a team of administration officials visited a number of midwestern universities to build support for the government's position. They came and went with little controversy at several universities, but their presentation in Madison, officially sponsored by the Madison Committee to Support the People of South Vietnam, made national headlines for the resulting confrontation. Inside a packed hall, and despite the pleas of some students and faculty members, about two hundred members of CEWV stood in the aisles and refused to let the event proceed. When the officials attempted to deliver their presentation, including answering questions from the audience, they were met by constant challenges: Was the National Liberation Front really communist? Why did the United States condone the use of torture? Why had there been no election in South Vietnam? Even when the officials tried to respond to the protesters, they were often shouted down, with the event devolving into chaos.[44]

The protest against the State Department representatives was perhaps the first genuine confrontation by the antiwar movement in Madison, polarizing the campus not just along the lines of those who supported the war and those who did not, but also between those who condoned and those who condemned the tactics of the Committee to End the War in Vietnam. The *Cardinal*'s editors labeled the protest "rude" and a "three-ring circus," while others called CEWV "anti-intellectual" and accused it of hypocrisy in its attempts to deny the officials an opportunity to speak. Even those who counted themselves part of the anti-war movement were torn. In a debate that played out in letters published in the campus paper, one antiwar student suggested that the group should have engaged in "real debate," and another, a member of CEWV, rejected the group's tactics even as she recognized students' frustration over not being heard. The organization's official response, penned by James Hawley, emphasized the committee's desire for an open and honest dialogue, something that was not forthcoming from the administration's representatives. Hawley argued that the group had a "moral obligation" to make clear its opposition to Vietnam, an obligation that superseded other concerns.[45]

Other activists seconded Hawley's defense and laid out a rationale that would be used over and over again to explain the New Left's increasingly disruptive tactics. Graduate student and future historian Joan Wallach Scott suggested that it would have been more troubling if students had *not* acted: "if . . . we had lost our passion, our ability to become indignant when we were insulted, when our serious questions were mocked or evaded, if we could not get angry when representatives of the government laughed while we were serious about people dying in war, then indeed we would have lost our humanity and there would have been great cause for concern!" Likewise, CEWV member Ellen Lehman spoke for many protesters when she declared defiantly that despite the condemnation from many corners of the university, she would not apologize for her behavior: "The subject of life and death is not a rational one to me. And if, in order to stop what is going on . . . I must be rude, then I will be rude. And if I can be more effective in bringing these atrocities to a halt by other unmannerly actions, then unmannerly I'll be. I can't be calm, cool, and detached any longer. . . . And I'll shout if that will make me heard. It is not I who am sick. I think rather that being able to sit back calmly and watch murder is what is sick."[46]

❖

Ellen Lehman's statement echoed many Americans' moral outrage against the war, and while the State Department protest was the first of its kind for the antiwar movement in Madison, it was certainly not the last. Just a few months later, eleven Wisconsin students were arrested at Truax Air Force Base outside of Madison as they attempted to perform a citizen's arrest of the base commander. The next year, the draft sit-in was the culmination of a campus politics that had been building since the 1950s at the same time that it was a sign of things to come. With students occupying the Administration Building for more than seventy-two hours to protest the university's cooperation with the Selective Service System, they demonstrated the emergence of a mass protest movement on campus, with the participation of hundreds of students at the sit-in and thousands for the Bascom Hill meeting and rally. At the same time, they highlighted the impact of direct action politics and the compelling moral idealism that had emerged with the civil rights, peace, and antiwar movements since the beginning of the decade. The sit-in ended peacefully, with some suggesting that Madison was somehow different from Berkeley and other campuses where protests had turned to violence, but the restraint that both sides had shown would not last. Any chance of a coalition between students and faculty was particularly weakened, with many faculty complaining of students' "coercive" behavior and many students accusing the faculty of "betrayal" for taking no action other than the formation of an official committee to review university policy.[47]

Finally, the sit-in points to the intersection of student activism and the realities of Cold War–era higher education. The protest movement that had developed in the early sixties was focused on civil rights, free speech, President Johnson's handling of Vietnam, and other national issues, but it would ultimately turn its attention to the University of Wisconsin's Cold War moorings even as it continued to be fueled by the Cold War's impact on the structures of higher education. Berkeley's Free Speech Movement was the New Left's first major assault on higher education, but the Berkeley confrontation would be replayed again and again at universities across the nation. Wisconsin administrators, like their colleagues at other universities, rejected students' characterization of the university as an agent of the federal government, but despite their claims of neutrality and no matter that many of these officials privately opposed the war, students would not be moved. The late sixties would see a huge expansion of the New Left, with students funneling their energy in many different directions, but the issue of the Cold War, and especially the role of higher education in the development and execution of American foreign policy, would remain near the center of the era's activism.

5

"We must stop
what we oppose"

Dow

D ow," as it came to be known by Madison activists and others, was the
culmination of the paradoxes of Cold War–era higher education at the
University of Wisconsin. Blending together protests against the war in Vietnam,
the role of corporations in supplying the American military, and especially the
university for its part in the "war machine," the October 1967 demonstration
against Dow Chemical Company's campus interviews shattered the increasingly
fragile peace that had existed since the conclusion of the draft sit-in just over
a year earlier. The demonstration included campus and city police forcibly
removing hundreds of protesters who were blocking the Dow interviews and
then skirmishing for more than two hours with a crowd of perhaps three
thousand protesters and onlookers. It represented a full-throttled shift from
"protest to resistance" among many in Madison's New Left, and it introduced
a period of late sixties activism that was marked by increasingly confrontational
tactics as the war in Vietnam continued to rage into the early 1970s.[1]

The contradictions in Cold War–era higher education had been building
since the years immediately after World War II, but it was not until the middle
and late sixties that they came fully into the open. Cooperation between universities and the federal government that had been haphazard in the years
following World War II had become organized and routine, with major universities like Wisconsin steadily increasing their research budgets and deriving
more and more of those dollars from an expanding menu of federal agencies,
including many with national security interests. Meanwhile, even as universities

had taken an increasingly central role in the Cold War struggle, they had also become centers for dissent against American foreign and domestic policy. With the growth of the student movement and the development of a network of student organizations, including journals like *Studies on the Left* and *Radical America* (the latter founded in Madison in 1967), there emerged the foundation key to a powerful protest movement. Just as significant, the increasing importance of university education and the flow of federal funds into university coffers under- wrote much of the massive expansion of student enrollment in the 1950s and 1960s. By the time that students met to prepare for Dow interviewers to arrive on campus in the fall of 1967, there were thirty-three thousand students in Madison, more than double the enrollment of a decade earlier.

Dow's manufacture of napalm for the U.S. military was a critical element in the demonstration, but it was only the catalyst for a much broader confronta- tion over the development of the Cold War university that was at the heart of much of sixties protest. It was the university's role in the war—"complicity" or even worse, many students argued—that heightened the stakes for this demon- stration, raising fundamental issues about the role of the university and the relationship between higher education and the federal government. "The work of the government cannot be separated from the daily operations of American corporations or the university," announced a leaflet distributed in the days before the demonstration. "To end the war, it is necessary to understand the extent to which major institutions such as this university and Dow Corporation are committed to its continuation. . . . We pick this week to demonstrate against Dow, against the university as a corporation and against the war because they are all one." The demonstration enveloped much of the campus, with nearly 40 percent of students claiming afterward that they participated in the original protest or the many activities that took place in its immediate aftermath. For many of those students, the university, the war, and their own role in campus and national politics would never be the same.[2]

❖

Though the May 1966 draft sit-in ended peacefully, with many students quickly heading home for the summer, the fall semester saw the campus movement pick up where it had left off. With the war in Vietnam escalating rapidly—there would be nearly four hundred thousand U.S. troops in Southeast Asia by the end of 1966 and nearly five hundred thousand a year later—the Madison left gained strength and moved in a number of directions at once. The movement to end the war in Vietnam was at the center of campus radicalism, but students also organized around draft resistance, black rights, the development of a parallel "free university," the broader Cold War, student housing, and the problems of campus teaching assistants, just to name some of the most prominent. The counterculture also emerged as a recognizable element on campus. Finally, students struggled over the best methods for an effective social movement. As the war escalated and the problems they faced seemed increasingly intractable, students continued to organize pickets, rallies, and marches even as they tried out more confrontational tactics meant to garner attention and compel change.[3]

That struggle over strategy within the New Left was on particular display at the October 1966 campus appearance of Senator Ted Kennedy, as the tactics of students from the Committee to End the War in Vietnam (CEWV) again set off a campus firestorm. Invited to speak by the UW Young Democrats, Kennedy was in Madison that fall to campaign for Democratic gubernatorial candidate Pat Lucey, but it was his status as the brother of former president John Kennedy and a major figure himself in the Democratic Party that made him a ripe target for antiwar activists. Shouted down by members of CEWV in the audience, he was unable to complete even his opening remarks, but he still managed to gain the upper hand. Relying on his keen political instincts, and with much of the crowd hostile to the antiwar protesters, he invited Robin David, the chairman of CEWV, onto the stage. With David announcing that the only solution to the crisis in Vietnam was immediate withdrawal, Kennedy proceeded to pick apart his position, laying out what he saw as the dangerous repercussions of a unilateral withdrawal and relying on arguments that were still persuasive to the large majority of Americans who supported President Johnson's policies in Southeast Asia.[4]

Even as Kennedy seemed to many to win the day, the event sparked a campus-wide controversy. Many of the arguments that had surrounded the confrontation with the State Department's "truth team" in April 1965 were replayed, but this time the stakes were even higher, as the war and the antiwar movement had both escalated, and the disruption of Kennedy's speech seemed to many on the campus like an especially egregious display of arrogance on the part of the university's antiwar movement. The *Daily Cardinal* claimed to speak for the vast majority of the student body when it called CEWV's action a "disgrace," and the paper hit the group for its hypocrisy, criticizing the campus left for supporting free speech only when it suited its own purposes. Meanwhile, a campus petition circulated in the days after the Kennedy incident and condemning the actions of CEWV collected a remarkable eight thousand signatures.[5]

The Committee to End the War in Vietnam, for its part, apologized for nothing other than its failure to raise the issue of the war more effectively. In a statement published in the campus paper, the group acknowledged the concerns raised throughout the university but declared that "freedom and democracy have meaning only in a moral context"; it was the federal government, with Kennedy as its representative, that was avoiding a public discussion of the war in Vietnam. Drawing on the New Left principle of participatory democracy, the group claimed that "the essence of democracy lies in the right of the people to discuss and decide upon the issues which determine their destiny. When the nation's decision-makers attempt to placate the people with jokes and platitudes instead of answering them about their policy, the people's right to decide is severely limited." In other words, the group declared, it was their "moral" duty to disrupt Kennedy's speech. Though some might consider it a violation of free speech, it was necessary in order to hold the federal government accountable and uphold the integrity of genuine democracy.[6]

Finally, the university's administration weighed in as well, issuing Kennedy an official apology while the faculty adopted a new resolution intended to preserve open discussion on campus. The resolution affirmed the right of students to freedom of speech, peaceable assembly, petition, and association, but it also made explicit that these rights could be exercised only insofar as they did not infringe on the rights of others. Students, the resolution declared, "may support causes by lawful means which do not disrupt the operations of the university, or organizations accorded the use of university facilities." A relatively generic statement of university policy, it was a starting point for efforts to rein in student protest, efforts that would escalate dramatically in the following year.[7]

As the university wrangled over the reasonable limits to student political activity, protests continued throughout the winter, spring, and summer. The Committee for Direct Action, a small group that engaged in civil disobedience, demonstrated against U.S. Marine recruiters in the campus union building, while a group of Madison students traveled to Milwaukee to protest outside of a military induction center, and another group protested off-campus interviews by recruiters from the CIA (the CIA often conducted its interviews off campus to avoid the kinds of problems that Dow would later encounter). Protesters remained a distinct minority on campus, but even as many students shied away from public participation in the antiwar movement, student opinion itself was beginning to shift. A fall 1965 poll by Harry Sharp, sociology professor and director of the Wisconsin Survey Research Laboratory, found that 72 percent of students favored "U.S. participation in the war in Vietnam" and only 16 percent opposed it. Two years later, however, what had been a decidedly minority opposition to the war had become much more mainstream. In a spring 1967 campus referendum, 30 percent of students favored immediate unilateral withdrawal of U.S. forces from Vietnam, while only 26 percent agreed that the U.S. should apply "whatever force is necessary for total military victory."[8]

The protest movement became large and powerful enough that it reached into many areas of campus life, a point highlighted by a "wrong-way" bus lane protest that took place in May 1967. The issue had received some attention throughout the spring, as a main campus thoroughfare had been turned into a one-way street while the city had left a single lane for buses heading in the opposite direction. Students argued that the traffic changes posed a danger to the large number of pedestrians that crossed the street daily, but despite a tragic accident in which a UW student lost her leg after being hit by a bus in the new lane, the university and city were initially unmoved. When a group of students organized a protest, a crowd of two to three thousand showed up, pointing to the growing willingness of students to engage in demonstrations and the increasing strength of campus activists.[9]

The fact that twenty-five students were arrested at the bus lane protest might have been shocking just two or three years earlier, but it was quickly becoming routine. In addition to the bus lane arrests, eleven members of the Wisconsin Draft Resistance Union were arrested at the Milwaukee induction center protest the same month, while eight students were arrested in July at a "paint-in," as students called their painting of a newly built and unpopular campus pedestrian bridge. After the Milwaukee demonstration, some members of the draft resistance group suggested that the arrests had helped to make the protest a "very good confrontation," while the police, for their part, were in no mood to allow the protest movement to escalate. In the aftermath of the bus lane conflict, Madison Police Chief Wilbur Emery, a veteran of the Marine Corps during World War II, declared that "We won't let the students run the city. . . . We'll crack their heads together if we have to, to protect our citizens." As happened across the country, it appeared that neither side was willing to give ground; both sides were prepared to escalate their tactics.[10]

Finally, the arrests at the summer "paint-in" highlight another important development on the campus left: the counterculture. Prominent throughout the country in the late sixties, the counterculture was a rejection of mainstream American social and cultural values, an exploration of alternatives to traditional institutions, norms, and authority. Young people in particular emphasized the importance of personal freedom and expression, and the counterculture affected every part of American life, from clothing, music, and drugs to politics and sex.

In Madison, members of the newly formed Open Arts Society organized the first in a series of "be-ins" in April 1967, following by a few months the first San Francisco be-in and featuring a plentiful dose of flowers, music, balloons, and, as the campus newspaper put it, "love."[11]

Of course, Madison had its own tradition of bohemian student culture long before the importation of the "be-in" from San Francisco and the late-sixties emergence of Mifffland—Madison's Mifflin Street neighborhood that resembled a smaller version of San Francisco's Haight-Ashbury. The Green Lantern, an eating co-operative, was an important hangout for political and cultural radicals in the fifties, and the Rathskeller, located in the university's Memorial Union and modeled after a traditional German tavern, was a crucial space as well. According to one student, the "Rat," as it was known, was the "bohemian center," home to existentialists, hard-core leftists, and not-so-hard-core leftists in the late 1950s and early 1960s. It was even at the center of controversy at times, as when Union administrators attempted to transform the space in 1959. The *Cardinal*'s editors described this effort as "the tangling tentacles of the Organization Men . . . spreading into one of the few remaining refuges of the individual," and letters poured into the newspaper over the next few weeks. Some of the letters praised the uniqueness of the Rat, while others called for an end to the predominance of "oddballs" and "radicals."[12]

Some political groups also had an early countercultural bent. While the communist Labor Youth League was usually focused on traditional political activity during its tenure in the early and middle 1950s, some campus leftists recall that later groups were more "fun." The Socialist Club and the Student Peace Center, active in the late 1950s and early 1960s, were independent of any national, adult organizations, and this helped give students the freedom to design their own program and mix politics with their youthful energy and creativity. Members of the Student Peace Center, for their part, organized perhaps the major countercultural event of the era, the annual antimilitary balls that began in 1957 and continued for several years. The balls were meant to counter the long tradition of annual military parties on campus, and they attracted hundreds of students and featured music and short plays, including at least two skits written by Madison student and future Woody Allen collaborator Marshall Brickman. According to Ron Radosh, one of his roommates at the time, Brickman was part of the campus left, but not very political; like some, he was more interested in working on the banjo than attending meetings.[13]

What started out as an effort to inject some creativity and even fun into political activity had, by the mid-1960s, developed into a crucial element of sixties culture. What might have been the first avowedly countercultural organization at the UW, the Ad Hoc Committee for Thinking, started in 1965, the brainchild of Stuart Ewen, Robert Gabriner, Russell Jacoby, and Paul Breines (interestingly, three of the four were veterans of the southern civil rights movement). Bound by a "sacred oath of antiauthoritarianism," they considered themselves akin to cultural pamphleteers, including one that they placed on campus desks: "Your Professor Does Not Really Exist." A year later, growing interest in the group led to the establishment of *Connections*, the campus's first countercultural newspaper and an attempt to blend politics and culture and to experiment with new forms of journalism. *Connections* would last only two years, but it would be followed by a number of other underground papers in Madison, including *Madison Kaleidoscope* and *Take Over*.[14]

Most students experienced the counterculture and the New Left as one seamless movement, but at least a few New Left activists questioned its value. In a piece in *Connections* around the time of the first be-in, student Ronnie Littenberg suggested that be-ins represented a "non-aggression pact with society." "The be-in is a reaction," he argued, "not an action; a state of being, not of doing." While Robert Cohen, a leader of the campus SDS, praised what he saw as the "activist" wing of the hippie movement, sociology graduate student and fiery New Left activist Evan Stark took the opposite tack, declaring later that year that "we can't build a resistance movement with degenerated hippies . . . people who believe freedom is all in the mind." Finally, another student proclaimed in *Connections* that a philosophy of love, such as the one championed by the campus's open arts group, was severely limited. Such a philosophy could be beneficial, but it could not stand alone; it needed "political" action to transform it from being an escape valve to an agent of change.[15]

Drug use was another part of the counterculture for many. Though drug use was not new in the sixties, there was a marked increase in the number of students who used drugs and the types of drugs with which they experimented. Drugs gained an early public hearing in December 1963, when the *Cardinal* ran a series of articles on the number of students who had tried marijuana (perhaps hundreds), how much it cost (about $5 for a "nickel bag"), its medical effects (not addictive), as well as police and university efforts to combat it. By the middle and late sixties drugs became a common topic in campus newspapers, while the administration, for its part, became increasingly anxious about the rise in drug use, including what official reports recognized as the worrying spread of LSD and heroin among students.[16]

Most students were much more accepting of drug use, but at least a few were concerned about its effect on the New Left. James Hawley, who had been active in New Left campus politics for several years, remarked in early 1966 that marijuana and LSD had become commonplace, and he suggested that pot was used by students to relax, a form of escapism and the result of apathy. The Committee to End the War in Vietnam publicly distanced itself from the campus Open Arts Society in 1967 because of the society's promotion of pot, while Ronnie Littenberg, the critic of be-ins, argued that drugs reduced users to impotence. At a time when youth needed to be politically active, Littenberg claimed, drugs destroyed critical thought and action. On the other side, however, some students argued that drugs were central to a complete rejection of contemporary American society and culture. In 1967, UW student Arnie Cohn criticized the limited, middle-class mind that was too narrow to understand the benefits of acid. "For the first time," he suggested of LSD use, "you transcend your little corpsy cell and invade the world of the sensual which has been denied to you since you learned good from bad." The New Left, or "politicos," as he called them, wanted to build a better world, but it was really just a new trip, this one with the New Left holding the keys.[17]

Despite the minor controversy that it sometimes engendered among students, the counterculture flourished in Madison just as it did in many parts of the nation. Not all students used drugs, grew their hair long, or engaged in casual sex, but the counterculture embodied a rejection of established authority that paralleled the New Left in many ways. Despite the distinction that is sometimes drawn between the counterculture and New Left, between hippies and politicos, the two often blended, and many in the sixties considered them both as part of one broad "movement." In practice, the counterculture's rejection of mainstream norms and authority often took on political tones, while political events increasingly incorporated countercultural elements like art, song, and drama. Indeed, at the beginning of the Dow protests in October 1967, it was the San Francisco Mime Troupe, a radical theater group that had been established several years earlier, that led students up Bascom Hill and toward a confrontation with university officials and police.

Despite the many changes to campus politics and the growth of the New Left from its beginnings in the 1950s and early 1960s, however, few had any idea of what was to come in Madison that fall. The Kennedy incident, the emergence of the counterculture, and the escalating pace of protests were unsettling developments to some, exciting turns to others, but the peaceful resolution of the draft sit-in had convinced many in the university administration that Madison was somehow different. After the sit-in, Chancellor Robben Fleming declared that Wisconsin faculty, students, and administration "have been almost alone among the great universities in our mutual willingness to tolerate strong differences of opinion among us without resorting to the kind of coercion which destroys a free society." Many believed that the events that had already shaken the University of California, Berkeley, could not happen in Madison, and just a few months before the Dow protests would begin, Wisconsin president Fred Harvey Harrington told the Board of Regents at their June meeting that the UW had been so successful in handling student demonstrations "that many institutions that are having new trouble are coming to us" for advice. Like others around the country, administrators in Madison were unprepared for the escalation of student protest; they had often welcomed the changes that had come to higher education in the previous two decades—the emergence of the Cold War university—and had little idea of what was to come.[18]

❖

Like the draft sit-in the year before, it was an ad hoc committee that organized the Dow protests, planning during the several weeks between the beginning of the fall semester and the dates that interviewers from Dow Chemical Company would be on campus: Tuesday, October 17, and Wednesday, October 18, 1967. Ad hoc committees limited the exposure of individual organizations to disciplinary action from the university, but they were also a reflection of the diversity within the Madison New Left, highlighting the rapid growth of campus activism in the middle and late sixties and recognizing that no single group commanded the attention of the entire campus left. Students for a Democratic Society had recently emerged as perhaps the most militant group on campus, replacing the Committee to End the War in Vietnam as the primary antiwar organization, but it was still only one campus group among many.[19]

In addition to SDS and CEWV, several other organizations were involved in planning and carrying out the Dow confrontation. Engineers and Scientists for Social Responsibility, the Teaching Assistants Association, and Concerned Law Students were three groups that played no direct role in the demonstration but that debated the issue in September and October and offered various forms of support. And though they were few in number, the involvement of Concerned Black People (which would become the Black People's Alliance a year or two later) was particularly important for the overwhelmingly white New Left. The group had been established the previous fall and reflected the growth of the Black Power movement in the middle and late sixties, especially the movement's increasing militancy and its emphasis on blacks controlling their own organizations and institutions. "Future leadership must essentially come from within," the Madison group announced in its first public statement in late 1966. "The negro has the ability, the rights, and, given the ideals of American

society, the duty to assume the forefront in the determination of its future."
The group was involved in a variety of activities related to black rights, including
fighting suspected discrimination from the Madison police and organizing a
demonstration against Chase Manhattan Bank over the bank's ties to South
Africa. Its involvement in the planning for Dow carried weight because of the
iconic status of the civil rights and Black Power movements among many white
activists.[20]

A final group that emerged in the wake of the draft sit-in to play an important
role in Dow was a new campus political party, University Community Action
(UCA, first named University Campus Action). The group had some success in
campus elections but is most significant in highlighting the controversy over the
New Left's participation in existing political institutions. Many in the New Left,
for example, derided the importance of congressional and presidential elections,
with some even suggesting that leftists sit out the 1966 reelection of Madison
congressman Robert Kastenmeier. According to this view, it didn't matter that
Kastenmeier was one of the most liberal members of Congress; he was too
deeply enmeshed in the political system to participate in a genuine reform
movement. UCA, however, represented the view that students must engage
existing political institutions if they hoped to make change. "The problem,"
declared history graduate student Fred Ciporen at an early UCA meeting, "is
a problem of power." Students could not simply demand change, Ciporen
argued, but must formulate a program and work within the existing political
structure.[21]

Despite skepticism in some parts of the New Left, many students were
already working in Democratic Party politics or third-party campaigns outside
the campus. Many would be involved, for example, in the Wisconsin Alliance,
a socialist political group that was founded in 1968 and organized in Madison
and many other parts of the state. Some students even ran for electoral office,
most notably Paul Soglin, a member of the campus New Left who would be
involved in Dow and who would be elected as a Madison alderman in 1968 and
the city's mayor in 1973. Soglin's candidacy would also benefit from the recent
passage of the twenty-sixth amendment, which lowered the voting age to
eighteen and was a response to the fact that many men were being drafted for
Vietnam even though they did not have the right to vote. Proposed by Congress
in March 1971 and ratified by thirty-eight states in less than four months, the
amendment would give young Americans a new means to participate in the
political system.[22]

More broadly, UCA was part of the development of a "student power"
movement. While civil rights, the Vietnam War, and a host of other national

and international issues occupied much of the New Left's attention, many students also targeted their own universities as important American institutions in need of radical change. In addition to such issues as a student-run cooperative bookstore, campus consumer and employee unions, and an end to in loco parentis rules that still governed much of student life, UCA pushed to establish a direct role for students in the educational process. This included areas like curriculum and campus planning, but it also meant a much broader rethinking of the role of the university in society. Specifically, UCA wanted to eliminate classified government research on campus, block campus interviews by companies that made products for the war in Vietnam, and prevent the university from issuing class rank information used by draft boards (an issue still unresolved after the draft sit-in).[23]

At its root, UCA represented the New Left's critique that American universities had drifted from their moorings as sites of independent inquiry, co-opted by their increasingly deep relations with large corporations and the federal government's national security apparatus. This point was first articulated during the May 1966 draft sit-in, as students questioned the university's role in the Selective Service System, and it rapidly became conventional wisdom among many on the left. In a handbook distributed by SDS as students arrived on campus in the fall of 1967, just two months before Dow, the group proclaimed that students had no meaningful say "either in broad educational policies or in the formulation of rules that determine where and how they may live at the university." The university's "overriding purpose," the handbook declared, "is not to stimulate independent thought, but to turn out graduates who will have the technical skills and the adaptive personalities needed by large business corporations and the government. It is so committed to the status quo in this country, and so dependent on the approval of those who will employ its graduates, that the needs of these institutions are the basic criteria for decision-making within the university." Put another way, wrote Russell Jacoby a few months earlier in *Connections*, "the proper functioning of the university is coercive: it cuts minds to fit the pattern of a society dedicated to suppressing the hopes and desires of free men."[24]

This was the contradiction in Cold War–era higher education laid bare. Universities had grown dramatically in the years since World War II, growth that had mirrored their importance to the Cold War struggle and the steadily increasing flow of federal dollars, but they had also become centers of dissent against those same Cold War policies. Indeed, the rapid growth of universities contributed to the development of a powerful protest movement in the sixties; Wisconsin had thirty-three thousand students at the time of Dow, compared to less than nineteen thousand at the beginning of the 1960s, while enrollment at universities and colleges throughout the United States now stood at more than six million, three times the 1951 number. In Madison, the growth was especially evident in the proliferation of political groups on campus as well as the fact that protests often attracted hundreds, and sometimes even thousands, of students.

Moreover, the growth of the campus contributed to the disillusionment with university education in Madison as well as the broader alienation of youth in the sixties. Concerns over the university's size had surfaced occasionally in earlier years, but they became a regular issue in the middle 1960s. In late 1964, the Student Peace Center drew on the protests then taking place at Berkeley in their criticism of Wisconsin as an increasingly impersonal "multiversity," while a special university committee chaired by law professor Frank Remington concluded the next year that the growth of the university had led to "a deep sense of frustration and dissatisfaction on the part of some students." Leon Epstein, dean of the College of Letters and Sciences in the late 1960s, recalls that rapid expansion during these years led to a certain amount of institutional instability, as rapid growth meant a shortage of experienced professors and put a particular strain on undergraduate education. An effort by several key professors to limit campus growth in the mid-1960s again brought the issue into the open, but they were unsuccessful in blunting the university's continued expansion.[25]

Connections between the university's expansion and the growing protest movement were evident for many. While the Remington committee suggested ominously that student frustration and dissatisfaction might result in "unacceptable behaviors," the *Daily Cardinal* in 1965 drew a direct line from the university's size to the rise in activism. The editors recognized the role of the Vietnam War but argued that the most important reason for the growth in activism was students' reaction against the "bigness" of the university and the transformation of higher education into a process of "mass production." Activism, the editors argued, "is a striving for a purpose other than sitting in the third seat of the fifteenth row of a lecture hall." Two years later, in the months preceding Dow, they concluded that higher education in Madison had shifted from its foundations. "The University of Wisconsin," they wrote, "is becoming a vast service station of the society, replete with high-octane, final-filtered education designed to trap and eliminate the last traces of lead that could clog up the Great Social Machine."[26]

In Madison and around the country, students were dissatisfied with the world they were inheriting and prepared to test the boundaries of their power. Writing in the *Call*, the Madison SDS newsletter, Carol Walton suggested in

1966 that universities' critical role in the corporate state and students' position as future workers gave them power, while a campus SDS statement the next year argued that because of the university's links to other institutions, student activism could "serve as a step toward the democratization of the entire society." Students also drew on the work of writers like C. Wright Mills, a sociologist and Wisconsin PhD whose 1960 "Letter to the New Left" was circulated widely in activist circles, including a 1961 reprinting in the Madison-based *Studies on the Left*. While traditional leftist theory had suggested that radicalism would emerge from within the working class, Mills argued that it was intellectuals who would lead the way to radical transformation in America.[27]

❖

As students arrived on campus for the fall 1967 semester, the decision to protest the Dow interviews, scheduled for October, was obvious. The interviews coincided with protests in Washington, D.C., that were being organized by the National Mobilization Committee to End the War in Vietnam and that would include the effort, led by Abbie Hoffman, to "levitate" the Pentagon. Also, though Dow was not especially well-known for its defense-related products— the company was best recognized at the time as the maker of household products like Saran Wrap—its production of napalm for the U.S. government had already brought it to the attention of antiwar activists across the country. A flammable gel that burned at high temperatures and removed oxygen from the atmosphere, napalm was first produced by Dow for the federal government in 1965, and by 1967 it had received wide press in the United States, symbolizing for many the horrors of the war. For students, its production also represented the broad cooperation between the federal government, American corporations, and higher education. Antiwar protests were often littered with pictures of Vietnamese civilians, especially children, horribly burned by napalm, and Dow had been targeted at university protests around the country beginning in 1966, including a protest at the UW–Milwaukee campus just a week before the events in Madison.[28]

Despite agreement over the need for a protest, consensus among student activists did not extend much further. There had always been disagreements within the left over what type of action was best, and many of the arguments were replayed in September and early October, complicated by the successes and failures of past protests as well as the question of just what this demonstration should be about. Some students, especially those in the Committee to End the War in Vietnam, wanted to focus specifically on the war, but many others saw the issue more broadly, connecting the war with corporations and universities that were, at the very minimum, complicit with what they considered America's destructive foreign policy. Other issues also emerged: some students argued that an effective movement needed a stronger organizational and ideological base than the Madison left possessed at the time and that more work was needed to create a strong foundation for the protest, others suggested that Dow was not the best choice if the goal was to maximize the public impact of the demonstration, and still others questioned the usefulness of the various types of protest under discussion. Meeting in the weeks before the middle of October, activists debated, voted, and debated some more.[29]

As the discussion evolved, some type of action was certain, but a serious divide emerged between those who wanted a more traditional protest—such as pickets, a rally, and a few speakers to draw attention to the issue—and others who wanted to use civil disobedience and physically obstruct the interviews. According to John Coatsworth, a longtime veteran of the campus left and a member of SDS and UCA, it was Robert Cohen and Evan Stark who pushed hardest to obstruct the interviews. Cohen, a philosophy graduate student, had already been arrested several times, most recently at the May bus lane protest, and had long advocated more confrontational tactics, including an unsuccessful effort to transform the draft sit-in into a complete takeover of the university's Administration Building the year before. Stark, too, had a long history in Madison, going back to the 1964 Sears sit-in and including leadership in the Committee to End the War in Vietnam, the Committee on the University and the Draft, and SDS. One member of the campus left suggested that Stark, a sociology graduate student well known for his incendiary speeches, had something of a "Jekyll-Hyde complex": he would sound quite logical at first, but then he would snap and would seemingly go mad.[30]

For those who advocated obstruction of Dow, it was time to escalate the antiwar movement. Inspired by the courage of civil rights protesters who had risked their lives for freedom and by the now-famous words of Berkeley activist Mario Savio—"you've got to put your bodies upon the gears and upon the wheels, upon the levers, upon all the apparatus, and you've got to make it stop!"—these students believed that more strident action was needed to bring an end to the war. "Publicity will not stop the war," a pamphlet distributed in the days before the protest declared. "Both the administration and the faculty know the true nature of Dow and yet they invite it to return. Two years ago, thousands of students demonstrated against class rank. The faculty laughed. . . . Even on this campus, protest has become a much publicized spectacle without an effect." Ultimately, the ad hoc committee organizing the protest worked out a compromise of sorts: the protest would be divided into two days, with the first day including a peaceful demonstration against Dow and the second day featuring physical obstruction of the interviewers in Commerce Hall, where the Business School was housed and where the interviews were scheduled to take place.[31]

The stage was set. Groups across the spectrum of the campus left had been organizing for weeks, with many of their plans making front-page news in the campus paper, and hundreds of students were ready for Dow's arrival in Madison. The university, for its part, said it was ready, too, rejecting efforts to cancel the interviews or move them off campus and promising a crackdown on protests that blocked campus activities. As the protesters described it, and as activists throughout the country reflected on the changes in the New Left in 1967 and 1968, the Dow confrontation represented a shift from "protest to resistance." It would test the resolve of students committed to ending the war in Vietnam and the lengths to which university administrators and faculty would go to block student protest, and, most importantly, it would highlight the paradoxes of Cold War–era higher education that had been developing for more than two decades and had finally erupted into open confrontation.

The confrontation over Dow Chemical Company interviews in Madison garnered a wide variety of descriptions at the time and since. In its lead the day after, the *Cardinal* described the event as "a bloody, glass-breaking, club-wielding, tear-gassing battle." John Cumbler, an undergraduate from Eau Claire, Wisconsin, who had worked for the Mississippi Freedom Democratic Party in 1966 and was a member of the campus Committee for Direct Action, mocked the university's proud tradition of "sifting and winnowing" in the confrontation's aftermath. Having been one of the several hundred students inside Commerce Hall when the police entered the building, he proclaimed later in the day that the administration's decision to eject students had "destroyed the image of the liberal university. The only thing we sifted and winnowed today was blood." Finally, many of the police officers who had battled with students expressed a conviction that they had done the right thing. "We would like to believe," a Madison police captain told a *Wisconsin State Journal* reporter, "we acted, under the circumstances, with tolerance."[32]

The first day of the demonstration, Tuesday, October 17, began and ended peacefully. The events planned that day had been a compromise with students who did not want to physically obstruct Dow, and the first pickets arrived at Commerce Hall about 9:30 a.m. A few students entered the building with signs, but most, perhaps two hundred, remained outside, with more gathering for an anti-Dow rally that continued throughout the afternoon. Robert Cohen and

Evan Stark were among the speakers, as was Seymour Kramer, a leader in the Committee to End the War in Vietnam. The steering committee that had organized the demonstration, including representatives from several campus groups, issued a statement claiming that the university should be a target of "revolutionary action" for its role in the "corporate system," but the day's events remained peaceful. "It's just too beautiful of a day for any trouble," declared Ralph Hanson, the head of the university police force and a likeable figure even among many in Madison's New Left. "I hope it stays that way."[33]

Whatever Hanson's hopes, and despite UW administrators' repeated warnings that students interfering with placement interviews would be subject to university discipline, the second day of the protest included a plan to physically obstruct the interviews. A "too orderly, too sweet, too nice" demonstration would be meaningless, Evan Stark had declared in the days before the obstruction, expressing a feeling that had been building over the past two years. "Four hours of marching around a flower bed at the Madison Capitol Building will satisfy the soul of a Wisconsin 'Radical,'" John Cumbler had written the year before, "but not save the life of a Vietnamese peasant." Similarly, another activist, James Rowen, remembers of Dow that "people were getting angrier and angrier and angrier about the war and the draft and the news that they were seeing, the images on television, the level of violence, the body counts, the bombings. It was all mounting."[34]

In the days leading up to Dow, groups planning the confrontation distributed at least two leaflets on campus, laying out the rationale for the upcoming demonstration and for the obstructionist tactics. "The alliance between the university and the corporation is clear," one pamphlet read. "Dow Chemical Corporation manufactures the napalm that burns and maims the people of Vietnam. The university is furnishing the technicians who create the tools of destruction as well as the facilities for hiring these technicians." Some students disagreed over the specific target of the demonstration—the university, Dow, or the war—but their ultimate rationale linked all three: "we sit in today to prevent the compliance of the university, the corporation, and the student in furthering the crimes of the war in Vietnam." "We must move from protest to resistance," read a short note that was distributed on the day that the obstruction was scheduled. "Before, we talked. Now we must act. We must stop what we oppose."[35]

On the morning of Wednesday, October 18, the San Francisco Mime Troupe, an experimental theater group that had performed on campus the previous evening, led several hundred students up Bascom Hill and toward Commerce Hall for the protest's second day. At 10:30, more than one hundred students filed into the building in order to obstruct the scheduled interviews, with more remaining outside to support the action. Over the course of the morning and into the early afternoon, more students gathered, until there were between three and four hundred inside the building, packed into the north-south and east-west corridors that intersected at Commerce Hall's main entrance. "We were packed in so tightly," remembers James Rowen, who had just finished his BA and started a master's program in English, "you literally couldn't move." Outside, a crowd of two to three thousand had gathered, some of them supporting the protest inside and some of them merely stopping to watch and witness the drama.[36]

With the demonstrators effectively preventing Dow representatives from meeting with interested students, and with the protest attracting more students throughout the morning, university officials were quickly faced with a decision on how to respond. Administrators had repeatedly affirmed their policy of holding placement interviews in university facilities and had delivered several warnings to activists in the days leading up to the protest; with these having failed to deter the confrontation, however, they were faced with a decisive moment. Ralph Hanson and his team of university police had been monitoring the situation, and Hanson had requested around noon that protesters leave the building, reminding them once again of the threat of disciplinary action. Stationed in a nearby parking lot were about thirty-five police officers from the city of Madison, outfitted in riot gear but waiting to hear whether their assistance would be requested by university officials and campus police.

The decision on whether and how to use the police that day fell to William Sewell, who had replaced Robben Fleming as the chancellor of the Madison campus that fall and who was responsible for the day-to-day operations of the university, with President Fred Harvey Harrington in charge of the several campuses that made up the University of Wisconsin and out of town on October 18. Before he became chancellor, Sewell had spent twenty years as a well-respected professor of sociology in Madison, but he was stepping into the chancellor's job at a particularly difficult time. It was even more complicated because Sewell himself, like Fleming before him and like many others in the administration, was opposed to the war in Vietnam. Sewell had experienced the horrors of war firsthand as part of the U.S. Strategic Bombing Survey that studied the effects of American air attacks on the Japanese during World War II, and he had signed his name to a December 1964 faculty petition that called on President Johnson to avoid escalation in Vietnam and to negotiate a withdrawal of American forces. He had also been involved in the Student-Faculty Committee to End the War in Vietnam, the short-lived group that had organized a series of antiwar events in the spring of 1965, including Madison's first teach-in; at the thousand-person rally that had culminated the week's events, Sewell was among a group of speakers that included radical historian William Appleman Williams, graduate student and antiwar activist Don Bluestone, and former National Security Council staff member turned Vietnam War critic Marcus Raskin.[37]

Sewell's dilemma was also complicated by the events of the last year, events that had taken place under his predecessor but that deeply influenced his own options. Looming particularly large was an earlier protest against Dow Chemical Company, a confrontation in February 1967 that had been carried out by the campus chapter of Students for a Democratic Society and had ended with eighteen student arrests as well as an increasingly resolute faculty. The arrests had taken place over two days, as students wrangled with campus police near the sites of Dow interviews, the initial group of about one hundred students swelling to a few hundred on the second day for a blockade of Chancellor Fleming's office in Bascom Hall. Student representatives met with Fleming and Dean of Students Joe Kauffman for over four hours in Fleming's office, but despite threats to prevent the administrators from leaving until they agreed to student demands—cancel placement interviews, drop charges against any students arrested during the demonstration, and open for inspection university records on contracts with the federal government—no agreement was struck, and Fleming made it clear that he would leave his office when he wanted to, which he did.[38]

Like many other protests during this era, the February confrontation over Dow interviews created a firestorm of controversy and recrimination over the following days and weeks. A short-lived student group calling itself "We Want No Berkeley Here" brought out eight hundred antiprotesters in the days after the demonstration, while the campus newspaper was full of the usual back and forth over tactics and principles. Declaring that "I do not like to conduct business with students on the basis of arrests," Chancellor Fleming received wide campus approval for his decision to pay more than a thousand dollars out of his own pocket to bail out jailed students; meanwhile, SDS conducted its own internal discussion on the successes and failures of the confrontation even as the group's role in the demonstration jeopardized its status as a university-recognized organization.[39]

Both student and university positions hardened in the aftermath of this first skirmish over Dow. President Harrington appeared before the state legislature in the following days, explaining that "We run a law and order institution. We don't intend to let things get out of hand," while the faculty also demonstrated that they were unwilling to tolerate disruptive student protests. Especially important was the faculty's vote to toughen the so-called "Kennedy incident resolution," the language that had been passed following the Kennedy protest the previous fall and that sought to guarantee free speech on campus. Despite Fleming's caution that enforcement might require the use of campus and city police as well as possible additional forces (a caution that turned out to be especially prescient), the faculty voted in the aftermath of the February protests to empower the administration to use whatever measures necessary to protect the continued operation of the university. Interestingly, Sewell was among the small minority of faculty who voted against the toughened stance, suggesting later that universities did not need to act as placement agencies for large corporations. Still, he was overruled, with the decision reverberating during Dow and for the rest of the sixties.[40]

By the time of the second day of Dow protests in October, Sewell was much more hemmed in than Fleming had ever been, caught in, among other things, the contradictions of the Cold War university. On one side, he had an increasingly restive student population, fueled by a deep tradition of dissent over American foreign policy and buoyed by rapidly growing enrollment. On the other, he had the university's obligations to the corporate world and to state and national governments. These obligations were not new in the decades of the Cold War, but they had grown rapidly with the increasing prominence of higher education in the struggle with the Soviet Union and the deepening financial relationship between the university and the federal government. The university's regents, for their part, had reacted negatively to Fleming's decision to post bail for students in February—Sewell recalls that they believed Fleming was "coddling" the students—and they had become much more conservative over the course of the sixties, with several of them appointed after Republican Warren Knowles replaced Democrat John Reynolds as governor in early 1965.[41]

Ultimately, Wisconsin administrators believed in the university's neutrality, and whatever the personal opinions of Sewell and Fleming, they, like other members of the administration, believed these distinct from their responsibilities as university officials. Some faculty voices had argued in March that the university should ban representatives of companies that made war materials, but they were badly overwhelmed by those who believed it was the university's responsibility to allow any legitimate interviewers on campus. "You can't block other students from doing what they want to do," Fleming had said to New Left activists during the February confrontation. "You can't make a moral decision and force it on others." Former dean Leon Epstein recalls that faculty and administrators discussed the issue often, and most agreed that it would have been entirely inconsistent if the university had decided to ban some interviewers from campus; the university had always provided a space for unpopular views, including communists and other radicals during the McCarthy years in the 1950s, and it was compelled to do the same for students who wanted to interview with Dow.[42]

With all of this providing the context for the administration's decision making that day, the force of about thirty-five Madison police officers not far from Commerce Hall received the call to engage the protesters at about 1:50 p.m. After hours of waiting, including attempted negotiation with student leaders, Chancellor Sewell had come to the conclusion that he no longer had any choice: the building must be cleared. Outfitted in riot gear, and supported by the campus police force, officers planned to start at the main entrance and clear the east-west corridor first, then the north-south corridor, emptying the building and then surrounding it in order to keep students from reentering. This was not the first time that campus and city police had scuffled with protesters, but with perhaps four hundred students inside the building, the outcome was far from clear.[43]

As officers gave one last warning and then entered the building, they found students in various states. Some went limp as police reached them, others linked arms, and still others fought back in an attempt to keep the police at bay. One of the officers, Keith Hackett, who had grown up in a farming community about forty miles from Madison and had been an army and navy reservist, recalls the process of wading into the halls filled with students: "You either grab somebody, you hit somebody, you knock them down, and you step over them. The line behind you picks that guy up, throws him back to the line behind, who takes him and throws him out the doors." Some students tried to cover their heads to avoid the worst of the blows from police nightsticks, and James Rowen remembers that he heard a new sound emerging from the commotion, "like somebody breaking watermelons with a baseball bat." It took the police about ten minutes to clear the east-west corridor before moving on to the north-south hallway; many students were dragged out, some were carried, and a few stumbled out on their own.[44]

Even after students were cleared out of the building, however, the atmosphere of confrontation continued outside, with the area taking on the appearance of a battle scene instead of a university campus. Police moved to form a line around the building to keep students out, while a large crowd, perhaps three thousand, including onlookers, remained. Both sides continued to jostle, police using nightsticks and tear gas to try and push back the crowd, students hurling taunts as well as items like rocks, bricks, and even shoes. Six students who had been among the first hauled out of Commerce Hall were released from a paddy wagon after students surrounded it and let the air out of its tires. Dozens of students made their way to the nearby University Hospital, which also treated thirteen police officers.[45]

As the violent scene unfolded, at least some students and professors appealed to Chancellor Sewell to call off the police. Sewell's son and daughter-in-law, both UW graduate students, warned him about the coming violence as they witnessed the police first enter Commerce Hall, while at least one group of professors also came to his office. Philosophy professor Haskell Fain remembers that he and other faculty pressed Sewell to pull back and stop the violence, but that Sewell, even as he was practically in tears, responded that there was nothing he could do, that the situation was now being managed by the police. Sewell himself recalled later that he had felt "powerless," acknowledging that he and other university officials had little idea of what to do in the days before the demonstration and as the confrontation unfolded.[46]

Calm finally did descend on the campus, about two hours after police and protesters had begun skirmishing in the area around Commerce Hall and with tear gas still heavy in the air, but even as the initial struggle was over, Dow's reverberations had only just begun; they would last for days, months, and even years. Later that night, perhaps five thousand students, faculty, and onlookers met at Library Mall, about a ten-minute walk from Commerce Hall, and though the meeting remained peaceful, police brutality quickly moved to the top of the list of student charges against the university. Three hundred faculty members created a physical ring of protection around the students, many of them voting unofficially to condemn the use of police earlier in the day, while protest leaders called for a student strike in order to shut down the university and force the faculty and administration to deal with student demands. A rally the next morning, with about a thousand students gathered in front of Abraham Lincoln's statue near the top of Bascom Hill, was followed by pickets throughout the day, appealing to students to support the strike.[47]

Even as students urged a strike, however, the majority of the faculty, even some of those who opposed the police presence that had invaded campus, were in no mood to change university policies, blaming students as much or more than the police for the violence. At a special faculty meeting on Thursday, the day after Dow, professors took an incredible six hours to debate what had happened and how to proceed. "This faculty has already put me in a precarious position in its past actions and here tonight," Sewell reported near the end of the meeting, referring to the faculty's earlier passage of the Kennedy incident resolution and with his emotions clearly visible: "You haven't had guts enough to admit that my reaction [to the sit-in] was an exact interpretation of what you intended." "This is not a time for weakness," added Eugene Cameron, geology professor and chair of the powerful University Committee, "but to hold fast to the rules we have adopted for the welfare of all in this community." Cameron introduced a resolution in support of Sewell, which passed 681 to 375; on their way out, professors had to walk past a silent watch of perhaps two thousand students who had come to monitor the meeting and make their presence felt.[48]

In addition to events on campus, there was also a surge of outrage from outside the university. With Madison police chief Emery defending the violence, claiming that "this was an organized resistance against law and order and we were overpowered, we were backed up to the walls," the state legislature and the university's regents had little sympathy for the protesters. "Long haired, greasy pigs" is how state assemblyman Edward Mertz, Democrat from Milwaukee, referred to student protesters, while state senator Leland McParland, Democrat from Cudahy, just south of Milwaukee, suggested that "we should shoot them if necessary. I would. I would because it's insurrection." The university's regents, for their part, had been unhappy with Fleming's "soft" treatment of protesters, and they now directed their frustration at Sewell. Sewell had called in the police, but the regents reacted negatively to his decision to cancel the Dow interviews after the outbreak of violence and to establish a committee to investigate the issue of campus placement interviews. Sewell would continue as chancellor through the end of the academic year, but it was clear after Dow that he had lost the regents' confidence.[49]

The Dow confrontation inflamed opinions on all sides and quickly cemented its place as a central event in the era's already tumultuous history. Though the student strike failed to disrupt the university in any meaningful way, with limited effect outside of the College of Letters and Sciences, activist students were undeterred. Nearly 40 percent of the Wisconsin student body reported in the aftermath that they had been involved with some aspect of Dow, and at least some of them were radicalized by their involvement, many by their outrage at the violence they had witnessed or even the physical blows they had personally received. Writing in the SDS campus newsletter, Paul Buhle, a history graduate student and the founder of *Radical America*, a journal established in Madison in 1967, declared in Dow's aftermath that "the student movement as a whole must move from protest to a struggle over control of the university." The events in the days after Dow, including demonstrations against the police, the faculty, the administration, and the state legislature, were "defensive actions," protests that failed "because our enemies were not outraged, or shamed, or scared enough to change." Meanwhile, in a letter published in *Connections*, one activist argued that "our administration is the henchmen behind the scenes. . . . What we are really doing is saying no to a world we did not create in the hope that we can find a better and more human place to live."[50]

More broadly, the Dow confrontation exposed even further the paradoxes of Cold War–era higher education that provided the foundation for so much of sixties protest. For members of SDS, the faculty's decision to create a committee to review the facts of Dow was just one more example of its lack of independence. "The faculty as a community of scholars," history graduate student and SDS member James O'Brien wrote mockingly in the weeks after Dow, "has demonstrated its decisive autonomy from extra university corporate power, by doing what those powers want without being told to do so." Paul Buhle agreed, suggesting that students were the only progressive force in the university and were at their strongest when they relied on themselves and didn't look to allies like the faculty. For James Rowen, who had been inside Commerce Hall on October 18, it was even simpler. "It just shocked me that the university, as I saw it, had chosen, had taken sides," Rowen later recalled. "They were with Dow; they were with the war profiteers; they were with weapons makers. You know, they were really part of the war."[51]

The *Daily Cardinal*, which had often expressed sympathy for the goals of student radicals even as it had criticized their tactics, now offered a full-throated denunciation of the university. While the students had indeed steered a collision course with the administration, the "university has been defined so that the profit motive is our guiding ethic, so that outside interests determine what topics will be researched and studied. The problem is that the administration of this university exerts little or no pressure on professors to teach, but is busy defending the colossal liberal hoax of selling or giving away university facilities to those who support the university financially." Though the administration believed it was preserving the university's integrity, the editors argued, it had it backward, as it was the student protesters who were most concerned with the future of the university: "There can be no peace on this campus until the present order is hauled down, taken apart, and built anew."[52]

This was the energy behind so much of sixties protest. The clash over the university, a clash that pitted oftentimes liberal faculty and administrators against radicalized students, that grew out of a long tradition of dissent in Madison and in other places, and that was sustained by a rapidly growing student body, was never resolved, but it provided an essential starting ground for much of what we know as "the sixties." The 1966 draft sit-in and especially the 1967 Dow demonstration exposed the contradictions of Cold War–era higher education, contradictions heightened by the Vietnam War, and these events served as touchstones for the rest of the era in Madison. "Dow" was not the last major confrontation between students and the university, but it was perhaps the most significant, the moment when students offered their most strident challenge to the functioning of the Cold War university. That challenge, whatever its merits, would transform the movement, a pivotal moment in an era that changed America.

6

Endings and Beginnings

The New Left in the Late Sixties

October 1967 was a climax of the tensions in Cold War–era higher education that had been building for more than two decades, but it was
hardly the end of the New Left in Madison. Protests continued to shake the
Wisconsin campus for the next several years, spurred by the continuing war in
Vietnam and the persistent critique of the university's ties to the Cold War; at
the same time, the movement, even more than before, simultaneously branched
out in a number of different directions. Many in the New Left continued to
work to radically transform America, attempting especially to overturn the
nation's racial hierarchies, its class system, and its imperialist foreign policy,
while new movements developed as well, including those for women's rights,
gay rights, and environmental conservation. Conservative students, too, asserted
themselves more forcefully in the late 1960s and early 1970s. They were often
overshadowed by happenings on the left, but their emergence helped fuel a
national conservative politics that continues to be felt today. Finally, the
counterculture blended with all of these movements, emphasizing a rejection of
traditional authority and, in the late sixties, the building of institutions that
embodied the values of the new society that many young people were trying to
create.

It was a moment of great promise as well as great conflict. While administrators in Madison worried that "the troubles" would never end, many leftist
students envisioned the coming of an entirely new society. "We imagined ourselves on the lip of changes in life and thought more sweeping than anyone had
proposed since the surrealists argued that true communism would abolish the
distinction between sleeping and waking states," writes Paul Buhle, a former

history graduate student, of the heady feeling of the late sixties. Young peoples' hopes and dreams "were swept along in an insurgent atmosphere so intoxicating that we hardly understood what had happened until the mood faded." Reality would soon dawn in Madison and elsewhere across the country as the New Left broke apart in the late sixties, but its influence would extend well beyond the era's end.[1]

❖

In the wake of the Dow demonstration, student activists and university officials continued the fierce contest that had started at the draft sit-in and had reached a peak in October 1967. In the months after Dow, the university worked to fend off state legislators' attempts to force a harsh crackdown on student activists, but most students were unimpressed by the university's commitment to student freedoms. The *Cardinal* and the campus underground newspaper, *Connections*, regularly attacked the university for its actions at Dow, and they followed closely the legal wrangling that developed in the confrontation's aftermath, including the expulsion of three students. Meanwhile, growing numbers of students registered their opposition to the war in the spring after Dow, while a sociology class under the direction of Harry Sharp, director of the Wisconsin Survey Research Center, found that nearly half of the student body believed that the administration had handled the Dow confrontation "poorly" and slightly more than half said the same of the police. Radical students in the New Left remained a minority on campus, even in the late sixties, but their position found increasing sympathy within the wider student body.[2]

Nor did the university's official attempt to deal with the issues raised at Dow satisfy student activists. The university created a student-faculty committee under the direction of Law professor Samuel Mermin and tasked it with evaluating the university's policies on placement interviews, but the committee had little success in defusing the issue. While its fourteen members, evenly split between faculty and student representatives, spent months collecting information and opinions, the group's majority report was rejected at a spring faculty meeting; supported by three professors and five students on the committee, the report had called for an end to placement interviews on campus, with future control of the issue placed in the hands of the Wisconsin Student Association. Instead, the faculty gave its overwhelming support to the committee's minority report, which viewed the interviews as an integral and necessary part of the university's educational functions and concluded that they should continue despite student opposition.[3]

Even as Dow continued to play out, however, the campus protest movement was already moving in other directions. Activists protested the arrival of U.S. Navy and Marine recruiters in November 1967, and nearly two hundred students rallied against Boeing interviewers in March 1968, with another group demonstrating in May to protest the Board of Regents' decision not to sell Chase Manhattan stock despite the bank's ties to South Africa's apartheid government. On April 5, a crowd in the thousands, including many community members, gathered on Bascom Hill and marched to the capitol to mark the assassination of Martin Luther King Jr. None of these events replayed the violent confrontation at Dow—indeed, representatives from Dow returned in the spring and drew little attention from protesters—but scattered examples of vandalism and property destruction were becoming more common. In March 1968, investigators suspected arson as the cause of an early morning fire that damaged a door outside of Bascom Hall, which housed the offices of many university officials. Two months later, a firebomb destroyed parts of the offices of the College of Letters and Sciences in the campus's historic South Hall; no group claimed responsibility, and no one was ever charged in the case.[4]

These events took place against the backdrop of a quickly growing and changing national movement. Students for a Democratic Society (SDS) had emerged as the most important New Left organization by the late sixties, with many activists drawn by the group's confrontational bent and its broad framework for understanding America's ills. Still, even as the group attracted ever more members, with overall membership reaching perhaps as high as one hundred thousand, the organization was never able to establish a coherent or lasting framework for influencing American policy. Events at the local level continued to push the movement forward, events such as the Dow demonstrations in Madison and the takeover of university buildings at Columbia University in April 1968, a protest that was aimed at the university's involvement with the Vietnam War as well as its disregard for the neighboring black community. Events at Columbia ended in a violent clash with police, as did the protests at the August 1968 Democratic National Convention in Chicago (which many from Madison attended). SDS was one of many groups that attempted to disrupt the convention, an attempt that ran into the well-prepared and uncompromising Chicago Police Department.[5]

The SDS national organization would flounder in 1969, splitting into two main factions at its summer convention and then dissolving completely the next year, but Madison's chapter worked to distinguish itself from the central office's rupture. Nationally, the split in SDS emerged between a faction that called itself Progressive Labor, a communist group that emphasized the need to organize in traditional working-class communities, and Revolutionary Youth Movement, which saw students, blacks, and others as part of a broader working class that could bring about revolutionary change. The latter would become the Weathermen within a few years, an organization that used bombings and other types of violence in an attempt to overthrow the U.S. government in the 1970s. In Madison, however, the factions competing at the national level held less sway. Though there were certainly leftists of all varieties in Madison, including some who reflected the national tensions, Paul Buhle recalls that sectarian activity on the Madison Left remained minor, even in the late sixties: "Trotskyists, Maoists, and Communist Party regulars attracted by 1967–1968 more personal sympathy than political sympathizers." After SDS's 1969 national convention ended in near-complete chaos, Madison's chapter passed a resolution severing its relationship with the national organization and continued operating independently into the early 1970s; the resolution criticized both of the main factions that emerged at the convention as undemocratic or, in the parlance of the times, "Stalinist."[6]

Local activists rejected some of the extreme infighting taking place on the national level, but the escalation of protest that marked Dow and continued into the late sixties was still accompanied by significant discord within Madison's New Left. Some of the arguments during these years replayed earlier disputes while others highlighted fresh disagreements, often revolving around the question of how the New Left could best build a new society. Sometimes the issues were even more fundamental: if a new society could be built, what would it look like?

One of the biggest divides in Madison's New Left continued around the relationship of activism and intellectual work. Madison had long possessed a strong leftist intellectual community, dating back at least to the Socialist Club in the 1950s and the beginnings of *Studies on the Left* in 1959, but many in Madison and around the country struggled to reconcile the need for building a strong theoretical foundation for a new politics with the urgency of stopping the Vietnam War. The demise of *Studies on the Left* in 1967 is at least partly due to the divide between those who wanted the journal to be closely involved with the activist movement of the middle and late sixties and those who wanted to focus on theoretical work for a new socialist politics. Similar tensions spilled over into much of the New Left.[7]

In Madison, history graduate student James O'Brien was a leader among those who believed that more theoretical work had to be done in order for the left to move past a fragmented and reformist activism. He was involved with an SDS program called the Radical Education Project, which operated nationally beginning in 1967 and included an active group in Madison. In a tentative program published in August 1967, just two months before Dow, the local group asked such questions as "What new constituencies should be organized [for the movement]? What are the basic causes of disaffection from the dominant patterns of life in our society? How do disaffected people become radicals? How do we understand and attack those institutions which are the seats of power and social control in America?" O'Brien was also one of several Madison students who worked on *Radical America*, a journal started by history graduate student Paul Buhle soon after he arrived in Madison in the fall of 1967. Like *Studies on the Left*, *Radical America*, which was affiliated with SDS in its early years, provided an important outlet for discussion and debate on the movement; it exemplified the continuing efforts of those in Madison and elsewhere in the New Left to ground their activism in an effective and sustainable politics.[8]

Many in Madison, however, believed that direct action was much more central to the New Left than the kind of theoretical work that went on in the pages of *Studies* or *Radical America*. Even among those involved with the Radical Education Project, there was concern that they not be labeled "intellectuals"; meanwhile, whatever attempts were made by some to step back and develop a solid ideological foundation for the movement were often swept away by the rapid current of late sixties events. As early as 1961, Tom Jacobson, chair of the Student Council for Civil Rights, had proclaimed the benefits of nonviolent direct action; those benefits seemed even more pronounced in the wake of the Vietnam War's escalation and students' belief in the university's collaboration with the federal government's national security apparatus. "Action," declared a leaflet distributed by SDS as students prepared for the arrival of Central Intelligence Agency recruiters in the months after Dow, "is a break with pro-grammed alienation and apathy; it is a creative act of self-realization." Another publication from SDS suggested that confrontation was the only form of protest left for students: "We have exhausted all means of obedient protest. Government policy abroad has become so repressive, brutal, and dangerous that we must simply do what we can to stop it directly." "Resistance" was necessary, wrote another member of Madison's New Left in 1968, because of the fundamental injustice of the "corporate liberal system"; it had the dual goals of hampering the functioning of that system and building a radical constituency.[9]

Two 1968 editorials in the *Cardinal*, which was increasingly influenced by radicals in the late sixties, also highlighted the growing acceptance of violent protest within at least some parts of the New Left. Writing in the weeks after students had taken over a building at Columbia University in April 1968 and engaged in a violent clash with police, the editors opined that "passionate expression" was the inevitable result of peaceful protest. "It takes a few arrests, some blood spilled, and a few days of classes called off," they wrote, "to get people thinking and reacting to issues which must be dissected and analyzed if we are to have meaningful communication and understanding." A month later, the editors declared that violence on university campuses was the result of the country's unsolved issues rather than a lack of morality on the part of the protesters. With the government using violence in Vietnam and the police initiating it on university campuses, violence would continue until there was a genuine effort to deal with America's underlying problems.[10]

Direct action and confrontational protests were sometimes stumbling blocks, however, when it came to the efforts of some in the New Left to reach out beyond the activist community. Though the promise of mainstream politics appeared to be an illusion for many in the New Left, a point seemingly confirmed by the treatment of protesters outside of the 1968 Democratic National Convention and the choice between establishment candidates Richard Nixon and Hubert Humphrey that fall, others believed that the only way for the New Left to make lasting change was to engage the existing political structure. Paul Soglin was one of several activists to run in local elections, and many Madison students attempted to reach out to the broader community in the city, believing that the left was doomed if it could not communicate to Madison residents and others the need to transform society, including withdrawal from Vietnam. Some students worked with faculty and community members on a city-wide antiwar referendum in the spring of 1968, while some were involved in the establishment of the Wisconsin Alliance that same year, a socialist political organization that attempted to build a coalition among students, small farmers, and workers throughout the state. The alliance found reasonable success in Madison, electing several representatives to the Madison City Council and the Dane County (Madison) Board of Supervisors.[11]

Some students also hoped to build a strong alliance with faculty members. A significant number of professors had been early opponents of the Vietnam War, with some of these helping to organize and lead teach-ins, circulating antiwar petitions among their colleagues, and speaking at antiwar meetings and rallies on campus and in the community. Professors would continue to organize in later years as well, including the UW Faculty for Peace, a group that was founded in the summer of 1967 and would claim more than one hundred members. The group would meet for several years in the late 1960s and early 1970s and drew faculty from across the campus, including biochemist Henry Lardy, sociologists Joseph Elder and Maurice Zeitlin, and historians Merle Curti, George Mosse, and Robert Starobin. Some of their early activities included work on the city's antiwar referendum, a variety of public speaking events, and assembling a collection of ten short essays published in 1968 to rebut some of the common arguments for the war. And while several professors had played an important role in the early development of the New Left, an even more radical contingent emerged in the middle and late sixties as champions of the movement. Many of them were junior faculty, like sociology professor Maurice Zeitlin, historian Robert Starobin, and English professors David Siff and Francis Bataglia, and at least some of them had conflicts with their colleagues because of their close ties to the student movement. Siff and Bataglia in particular were known for working closely with students in the New Left; in 1970, the English Department chose not to renew their contracts.[12]

Perhaps most important among the faculty on campus in the late sixties, at least within the antiwar movement and other parts of the New Left, was historian Harvey Goldberg. A Wisconsin PhD (1951—he and Williams graduated just a year apart and were friends for many years), he returned to the university in 1963 and taught there until his death in 1987. Other professors were more involved in the day-to-day workings of the movement, but it was Goldberg who provided inspiration to many on the left; his lectures on the history of political revolution were particularly relevant for students who sometimes had to dodge riot police on their way to class or who entered his lecture hall still recovering from the effects of tear gas. His dramatic style attracted hundreds of students, many of them not even enrolled in his courses, and his personal life—he was openly gay and regularly socialized with students, while he spent every third year in Paris—enhanced his appeal even further.[13]

Yet while Goldberg remained unapologetic in his support for the New Left in the late sixties, many of his senior colleagues, including some who had worked closely with students in previous years, became disillusioned with the movement's turn in the late sixties. Philosophy professor Haskell Fain sided with the majority of students as a member of the Mermin Committee after Dow, but despite his opposition to the war and his support for the New Left's position on campus placement interviews, he disagreed with students' confrontational direction, a point he made at a rally in Dow's immediate aftermath. Historian George Mosse, meanwhile, had been influential in the development of the New Left in the late 1950s and early 1960s and was a member of UW Faculty for Peace in later years, but he had little use for what he considered the "mindlessly violent activism" that he saw emerging around the time of Dow. Finally, radical historian William Appleman Williams, whose fierce criticism of American imperialism had been especially important to the early New Left, distanced himself from the movement as the era wore on. He remained important because of his scholarship, but he lost the personal connection that had defined his earlier relationship with the campus left. After the 1967–68 school year, he left Madison for Oregon State University, a move driven by personal considerations as well as his desire to escape Madison's political turmoil.[14]

Students, too, were often disappointed by even the liberal and left faculty on campus. The faculty as a whole had frustrated activists on a number of occasions, including the days following the draft sit-in and Dow, and many students saw professors as inextricably tied to the university and its policies. Departmental organizing became common across campus, with groups of students attempting to gain control over curriculum decisions, funding, and hiring, and this brought them into conflict with faculty who were reluctant to give up their traditional authority. In early 1968, one student argued in the Madison SDS newsletter that relying on faculty would hinder the radical movement; history graduate student James O'Brien commented a couple of years later that activists' relationship with faculty had become primarily "antagonistic." Many professors and students continued to work together, sometimes finding a commonality of interests, but despite the potential for a formidable alliance, the two sides often remained far apart.[15]

❖

Yet even as the campus New Left struggled to define itself in the late sixties and often remained cut off from the broader community, it continued to gain energy and momentum from outside events as well as its continuing efforts to transform the university. At the same time, the pace of events seemed to quicken. "Normal" campus happenings did not entirely disappear, but the continuing escalation of the war and the intransigence of American policymakers led to an increasing urgency in the antiwar movement. Headlines in 1968, 1969, and 1970 assailed the campus, including news of the Tet Offensive, the continuing failure of peace talks, the My Lai massacre, and President Nixon's order to bomb and, later, invade Cambodia. In Madison, these events and others prompted continued activism, with large demonstrations interspersed with much more regular and small-scale actions. Many of these were more confrontational, too, and property damage and other types of violence became regular features for some in the movement.

Just as the draft sit-in and Dow had attacked the relationship between the university and the federal government, this issue continued to fuel the movement. One attempt to investigate and publicize the university's ties with the

Cold War was the pamphlet "Business as Usual: The Social Uses of the University," published in 1969 by the campus's Anti-Imperialist Research and Action Project, a group established a year earlier by Madison's chapter of SDS. The pamphlet criticized the close relations between the UW and the federal government, noting that these ties had developed in the 1950s and had grown rapidly since; it drew the direct connection between the sources of higher education funding and the functioning of the university. Another target was the UW Land Tenure Center, a unit of the College of Agriculture that studied land ownership policies in developing countries. For students, the center was suspect since some of its funding came from the U.S. Agency for International Development, an agency created by President Kennedy in 1961 that many students saw as an arm of America's imperialist foreign policy.[16]

ROTC also continued to be a focus of the campus left. Although ROTC requirements had already eased considerably over the previous decade, with compulsory coursework for all male students ending in 1960 and a five-hour required orientation dropped in 1969, some students saw the mere presence of the ROTC program on the Madison campus as evidence of the university's collaboration with the war. One of these was James Rowen, an English graduate student, son of a *Washington Post* writer, and future chief of staff to Madison mayor Paul Soglin. In October 1969, Rowen published "The Case against ROTC," an investigative piece that was another attempt to make concrete the ties between the university and the Cold War. It included information on the program in Madison, which consisted of U.S. Army, Navy, and Air Force units and enrolled almost six hundred students, as well as the program's broader history in the United States. It emphasized especially ROTC's importance to the American armed forces, finding that ROTC was the primary source of officers for the military and arguing that it was crucial to America's ability to carry out its foreign policy.[17]

Yet even though the pamphlet contributed to the controversy over the issue, the ROTC program in Madison changed very little in the late sixties. ROTC was a center of controversy at campuses across the nation during these years, and some universities, most notably in the Ivy League, banned the program outright at the height of the war, determining at the time that it was incompatible with their universities' educational mission. Administrators in Madison, however, remained committed to ROTC despite the regular controversy it engendered. Drawing on arguments that had been raised since ROTC's beginnings, UW officials believed that the relationship between universities and the military was a benefit for both. Universities could play an important role in training future officers and in maintaining a much-needed bridge between the civilian and military worlds.[18]

One of the most dramatic confrontations of the late sixties in Madison was the so-called Black Strike, a series of actions that centered on demands made by black students and that captivated campus attention for much of February and March 1969. Black students had always been a small minority at the university, just as blacks made up a small percentage of the population in the Madison community, but the Black Power movement of the middle and late sixties led to the creation of Concerned Negro People in the fall of 1966, a student group that would later rename itself the Black People's Alliance. The group had made some efforts on behalf of increasing diversity at the university and had played a minor role at the Dow protests, but its symbolic importance was much more significant, a result of the almost iconic status of civil rights and, later, Black Power leaders among many white youth. The university, for its part, had already started to respond to the call for more diversity in the student body and the curriculum in the middle 1960s. It made efforts to recruit black students and faculty, expanded student services to assist minorities, and created courses in black literature, black history, and minority law. The university also established a committee led by education professor William Thiede in 1968 to investigate the status of race relations on campus and to make recommendations on future action, especially whether the university should create a black studies program or department.[19]

University committees were rarely known for their rapid progress, however, and black students and their allies in the New Left decided to take action, prompted especially by news that dozens of black students at Wisconsin State University–Oshkosh, a campus about eighty miles northeast of Madison, had been expelled after a confrontation with riot police. On February 7, representatives of the Black People's Alliance delivered to the administration a series of thirteen demands, a list focused on the creation of a black studies department with control in the hands of black students, including the ability to hire and fire professors and other staff. The list also included a demand that any of the Oshkosh students who wanted to be admitted to Madison be enrolled immediately. That same day, 250 students, including many members of the New Left, picketed and disrupted classes, with the protest growing in the following days. On February 9, the UW student government voted to support the strike and to provide bail money if needed; the next day, 1,500 students conducted a peaceful picket of classroom buildings.[20]

What had been a largely peaceful protest turned more confrontational in the following week. On February 11, students began to block access to a number of classroom buildings, and at least 180 police officers, some of them called in from surrounding areas, helped to clear the campus. The next day, as many as two thousand students returned, using hit-and-run tactics to elude the police and continue their strike. In response, Chancellor Edwin Young, a former professor of economics who had replaced William Sewell in the fall of 1968, called on Governor Warren Knowles to activate the National Guard. The campus took on the look of a military base as hundreds of Guard soldiers quickly arrived, buttressed by hundreds more in the following days; in an attempt to keep the university running, troops formed a perimeter around many classroom buildings. Still, over the next several days and weeks, protests continued, involving hundreds and sometimes thousands of students, and arrests were common. At the end of February, the Thiede Committee formally supported the creation of a Black Studies Department, with the faculty as a whole voting several days later to approve the plan. Black students and their allies were not entirely satisfied, but even as scattered protests continued, calm (or at least what passed for calm in the late sixties) generally returned to campus.[21]

The Black Strike set off an era of heightened confrontation in Madison. Protest continued on a number of fronts, but at least some in the movement believed in the need to raise the stakes, to shut down the university in order to transform it. The Madison Police Department and other law enforcement agencies contributed as well, as they took increasing steps to confuse and upset the movement. Even as the FBI used the COINTELPRO program to infiltrate and disrupt the New Left and other radical groups in the late sixties, Madison's local police created a similar program. They collected bulky files on activist leaders and began to use affinity squads, groups of plainclothes police officers who would sometimes spur controversy or even incite violence in order to disrupt campus protests. Secrecy and paranoia became increasingly common among many on the left, and some of the more radical members of SDS created a splinter group, the Mother Jones Revolutionary League, named after the famous early twentieth-century labor organizer; the group was meant to weed out the various informers and provocateurs that had become common in the larger SDS organization.[22]

Mass demonstrations became more and more routine. One of the largest was an October 1969 demonstration that brought out fifteen thousand students and community members, part of an international war moratorium that drew millions worldwide. In February 1970, a protest against General Electric recruiters pointed to the continuing contradictions of the Cold War university and replayed many of the themes that had emerged during the Dow protest; marching from the Library Mall on the university's east end to the Engineering Building on the relatively placid west end, the approximately 2,500 protesters clashed with police repeatedly. A successful strike by the Teaching Assistants Association, a group that had emerged around the time of the draft sit-in and was the nation's first graduate student employee union, upended the campus for several weeks in March and April, 1970, while in May students came out in large numbers again on news that the United States had invaded Cambodia as part of the widening war in Southeast Asia. Much of the Madison campus was engulfed in protests, and the stakes became even higher as word arrived about the students who had been killed during demonstrations at Ohio's Kent State University on May 4 and Mississippi's Jackson State University on May 14–15. Once again, the governor called out the National Guard in an attempt to keep the campus calm and open.[23]

Along with the demonstrations, which sometimes included confrontations with the police, other examples of violence also emerged, often targeting specific points of intersection between the university and the war. A small group of students that called itself the New Year's Gang carried out a number of generally unsuccessful firebombings in the winter of 1969–1970, using gasoline to try and destroy campus ROTC facilities and the local headquarters of the Selective Service. Some of the violence was more random. In February 1970, a group of students broke windows in campus buildings and nearby businesses when news reached Madison that five members of the Chicago Seven had been convicted; the group included several well-known New Left figures, including Tom Hayden and Abbie Hoffman, who had been prosecuted for their involvement in the 1968 demonstrations at the Democratic National Convention. Over the following months and years, window breaking and other types of "trashing" would become more common. One university group, the Campus Crusade for Christ, put out an informational flyer on how to treat a variety of medical issues that might result from rioting. For tear gas came the advice "do not rub eyes," while other topics included treatment for mace, nausea gas, shock, fractures, and bleeding. At the bottom of the flyer was a simple message: "Jesus loves you."[24]

Notably, it was always a very small minority of students who ever engaged in or even supported this kind of violence. While some members of the New Left argued from within the movement that confrontations with the police were ineffective, a line of reasoning that had emerged a few years earlier as the New Left was first taking a more confrontational turn, a survey of students taken at the end of 1970 provides interesting insight into the campus movement. Conducted by the Wisconsin Survey Research Laboratory, which had taken several surveys since the New Left had emerged as a significant force on campus, the poll asked about various forms of protest. Approval for some types of protest was high: 61 percent supported the right of students to stage sit-ins, while 66 percent approved of class boycotts, 80 percent approved of marches, and 93 percent approved of informational picketing. On the other end of the spectrum,

21 percent supported interrupting classes, 14 percent supported taking over university buildings, and between 3 percent and 4 percent supported trashing local businesses or destroying university property. The number of students who had actually engaged in some of these practices was even lower. A significant 53 percent of students said they had participated in a march and 28 percent had engaged in informational picketing, but only 4 percent had been involved with the takeover of a campus building. Even fewer, only 2 percent, had participated in trashing businesses or destroying campus property. With a university enrollment of approximately 35,000 at the end of the sixties, even 2 or 3 percent of students could have a significant impact, but the survey results represent a more complex view of the movement than the one that often appeared on the front pages of local and national newspapers.[25]

Within this complicated campus environment, another development in the late sixties was the emergence of a resurgent conservative movement, one that mirrored and helped fuel the growth of conservatism nationally. Of course, campus conservatives had never disappeared, and the Conservative Club and the campus chapter of Young Americans for Freedom (YAF), as well as the Young Republicans, had been active throughout the decade. Some of the largest campus disruptions, like the Dow protests, provoked disapproval among many students, often indicated in petition drives that collected thousands of signatures, while counterdemonstrations also became more common. YAF, which had been founded in 1960, the same year as Students for a Democratic Society, was especially known for its willingness to challenge the New Left. Confrontations between leftists and young conservatives became increasingly common in the late sixties at campuses across the country, sometimes leading to violence. At the time of the Black Strike, just hours before the National Guard arrived on campus in February 1969, a fight broke out between demonstrators on one side and members of YAF and the UW football team on the other; six arrests were made, and several minor injuries were reported. University vice-president Robert Taylor noted later that year that the campus right had grown significantly: "We often have as many objectors to the demonstrators as we have demonstrators," he said.[26]

A sign of the right's resurgence was the establishment of the *Badger Herald* in the fall of 1969. It joined several conservative student newspapers that began operations on campuses like Berkeley and Stanford in the late sixties, and it reflected the left's takeover of long-standing campus papers like the *Daily Cardinal* as well as the increased willingness of the campus right to fight for attention in places that had been dominated by liberals and leftists for years. In Madison, the *Herald* used an advertising slogan, "Dare to Join," to suggest that the campus right was unconventional and "cool," and it was not afraid to hit hard. In addition to occasional criticism of the *Cardinal*, the paper regularly supported ROTC and included sympathetic pieces on the Land Tenure Center and the Army Mathematics Research Center, two targets of the campus left. It also openly supported American involvement in Vietnam, including the publication of pictures of atrocities carried out by Vietnam's communist forces. Even as antiwar demonstrations were breaking out in Madison and across the country in May 1970 over the revelation of America's invasion of Cambodia, *Herald* editor and YAF member Patrick Korten penned an editorial supporting the widening of the war in Southeast Asia.[27]

At the same time, however, there were some interesting overlaps between the campus left and right in the late sixties. Even as young conservatives sometimes adopted the more confrontational stance of the left, a stance they had often disparaged just a few years earlier, many young conservatives also embraced the left's personal style, especially the counterculture. Long hair and bell bottoms, for example, became ubiquitous on the right as well as the left. Politically, too, there were a number of issues on which leftists and conservatives, especially the significant libertarian contingent among young conservatives, could agree. In Madison, the draft was one of those issues, as it was attacked by both the left and right in the late sixties, including an opinion piece in the second issue of the *Herald* that laid out the libertarian position against the draft as well as an editorial a couple of months later that attacked the Selective Service System as "selective slavery." The *Herald* also showed a good deal of sympathy for the early environmental movement in Madison, supported an end to campus in loco parentis policies, and reported generously on the early women's movement. Some of these positions would change over the following years, as libertarians in the campus and national right lost influence to more traditional conservatives, but they show how the sixties made a mark that extended beyond campus radicals and included an entire generation of Americans.[28]

Still, despite the resurgence of conservatism, it was the left that continued to make the most noise on campus, spurring an increasingly tough response from the nearby state legislature, the Board of Regents, and the campus administration. The state legislature was particularly hostile to the happenings on campus, and while the draft sit-in and the confrontation over Dow had provoked various expressions of outrage from state senators and representatives, the Black Strike led to a number of concrete efforts to stop the movement, including bills to increase the penalties for criminal behavior by students and limit out-of-state enrollment. Campus administrators as well as officials from the University of Wisconsin's central office, which had recently expanded to include the administration of several four- and two-year campuses throughout the state, were regularly called to appear before legislative committees; there they were questioned about the student movement as well as their efforts to keep the protests from getting out of control. The Board of Regents was also becoming more conservative during these years, with several members appointed since Republican Warren Knowles had been elected governor in 1964 (though it should be noted that some Democrats were among the fiercest critics of the student movement and that Knowles often worked to soften the legislature's attacks on the university). One member of the Board of Regents, Walter Renk, later recalled of the tough measures taken against students that it was a simple issue of maintaining order. "You can't let students take over the university," he said; the presence of National Guard troops on campus was "unfortunate" but necessary.[29]

For administrators in Madison, who dealt with the movement on a day-to-day basis, their responses were more complicated. On a practical level, they learned to live with what they sometimes called "the troubles," including such steps as scheduling meetings in the mornings and learning not to hold them at the end of hallways that were susceptible to student obstruction. They also attempted to navigate a course between the student activists on one side and the Board of Regents and the state legislature on the other. William Sewell recalls that in the months after Dow it was the forces on the right that were the hardest for him to deal with; he resigned in the spring of 1968, losing the confidence of the Board of Regents less than a year after he had become chancellor.[30]

Sewell was among many administrators in Madison who valued at least aspects of the student movement and who were torn personally and sometimes professionally over the issue of the Vietnam War. Likewise, President Harrington, the historian who had mentored William Appleman Williams and who had fit in easily with the iconoclastic members of the UW history department in the 1950s, publicly defended student protesters at numerous points during his presidency. As late as 1967 and 1968, with demonstrations engulfing campuses around the country, including Madison, he maintained that tolerance of dissent was part of the UW's proud tradition. Yet even as he parried some of the attempts by the regents and the legislature to crack down on student protesters, students gave him little or no credit for his efforts. The regents, for their part, were increasingly dissatisfied with his reluctance to take harsher measures to deal with the rising activism; by 1970 they finally forced him to resign.[31]

Of all of the campus events of the late sixties, perhaps the most remembered is the bombing of Sterling Hall. At the center of the controversy was the Army Mathematics Research Center (AMRC), a cooperative institute of the university and the U.S. Army that had been established in 1956 and that was housed in the building named after the university's first faculty member, mathematics professor John Sterling. The AMRC had occasioned little or no protest in its early days; indeed, it was celebrated by President E. B. Fred at the time as an opportunity for Wisconsin to contribute to "our national strength both military and scientific." By the late sixties, however, the center had come to symbolize for many activists the deep relationship between the university and the military, including the university's role in the war in Vietnam. The first student criticism of the AMRC to appear in the *Daily Cardinal* was published in December 1966, just a few months after the draft sit-in, and it continued in 1967 with a few pieces that explored the possibility that the center was producing classified research for the army.[32]

Controversy over the type of research done at the center and its relationship to the military continued over the next several years. Although the university maintained its denial that any classified research was taking place at the AMRC or anywhere else on campus, students remained unconvinced. Campus journalist James Rowen led the investigation into the center, with the *Cardinal* publishing numerous articles in 1969 on its activities and with Rowen and a few fellow students and professors issuing a pamphlet, "The Case against the Army Math Research Center," that same year. A few years later, after the bombing and with the center still the focus of significant controversy, Rowen published *The AMRC Papers*, more than one hundred pages of collected research that asserted a heavy involvement of the center in military affairs.[33]

The bombing took place in the early morning of August 24, as four members of the self-proclaimed New Year's Gang—Karl and Dwight Armstrong, brothers who had grown up in a Madison working-class family; Leo Burt, from a Catholic family near Philadelphia; and David Fine, a Jewish student from Delaware—parked a stolen Ford van packed with explosives behind Sterling Hall. They had already teamed up to target several other local symbols of the Vietnam War, including an unsuccessful attempt to drop homemade bombs from a stolen plane on the Badger Ordnance Plant, about forty miles from Madison. On the morning of the bombing, they placed a warning call to campus police, with the bomb exploding shortly after, at 3:54 a.m. The explosion destroyed much of Sterling Hall, though the offices of the AMRC were largely unaffected; in a twist of irony, the physics department was hardest hit even though many members of the department were vocal opponents of the war, and some had even tried to get the Army Math Center moved out of the building. More than two dozen nearby buildings were also damaged, while the most tragic outcome of the bombing was the death of physics postdoctoral researcher and father of three Robert Fassnacht, who was working on his research in the early morning hours when the bomb exploded.[34]

Just as the explosion could be felt by Madison residents throughout much of the city that morning, it reverberated through the Madison antiwar movement as well. For many, Fassnacht's death and the immense damage caused by the bomb—it is still one of the worst cases of domestic terrorism in U.S. history—forced a reevaluation of the movement, its methods, and its goals. Others, however, were undaunted, defending the bombing for its role in trying to end the war in Vietnam; occurring just a few months after several students were killed during protests at Kent State and Jackson State Universities, violence seemed routine to some in the New Left. And while it may have affected the mood in Madison, it did not end the movement, as large demonstrations continued into the early 1970s and often included the same kinds of confrontations with police that had marked earlier protests. The members of the New Year's Gang narrowly escaped capture in the bombing's immediate aftermath, and the FBI conducted a massive manhunt, ultimately capturing, trying, and jailing three members of the group over the next several years. The fourth, Leo Burt, was never found. More than four decades later, he is still wanted by the FBI, a small part of Madison's sixties history that is yet to be written.[35]

❖

The New Left was coming apart in the late sixties, a product of dissension in the movement, government repression, and increasing extremism in the face of the continuing war in Vietnam. Saul Landau, a member of the Labor Youth League and the Socialist Club and a founding editor of *Studies on the Left*, recalls that in addition to the mistake of turning to violence, the New Left lacked a sustainable vision that could outlast the era's convulsions. Likewise, Malcolm Sylvers, a member of the Madison left in the late sixties and a future historian, has written that the New Left's emphasis on "moral witness" was part of its failure, leading to "the sectarian push where what is most essential is to have the correct line and much less important is, who, if anyone, is following you." Both Landau and Sylvers, and many others, echo the claim of some sixties historians, namely that the activism of the late sixties failed to produce a lasting political movement. In this view, the New Left's descent into sectarianism and even violence, not to mention the drop-out mentality of the counterculture, left behind the principled vision constructed by members of the New Left in its early years.[36]

Yet even as the history of the sixties in Madison gives shape to some of these criticisms, it also suggests a more complicated legacy for the New Left. Campus activists were never able to sever the relationship between the university and the federal government, with Cold War tensions receding with the end of American involvement in Vietnam and not as the result of fundamental changes in higher education, but the upheaval of the sixties left a lasting mark on a generation of Americans. The New Left's efforts to radically restructure American society failed, but aspects of its critiques of capitalism, racism, and imperialism, all of these part of the movement's broader rejection of traditional authority and each of them formed in the cauldron of Cold War universities, proved more lasting. The energy unleashed by these efforts helped spur the diverse and powerful social movements that developed in the late 1960s and early 1970s. Conservatism may have reemerged to dominate national politics in the years since, a point that some have made to diminish the significance of the New Left, yet the movements of this era fundamentally altered America's social and cultural landscape.

By 1970, the proliferation of campus activism outside the confines of the New Left was plain. Gay students in Madison, for example, had mostly stayed behind the scenes until the late 1960s, gathering in a couple of friendly clubs in town, but New York City's 1969 Stonewall Inn riots, themselves a product of the era's youthful activism, ignited a gay rights movement in Madison and across the nation. Madison's gay community remained small, but it became more vocal, with groups like the Gay Liberation Front and the Gay Madison Sisters providing a place for gays and lesbians on campus and in the community to meet and push for more attention to gay issues. The campus also developed a significant constituency for environmental protection, which had been developing during the 1960s and gained visibility with the national celebration of the first Earth Day in 1970; among the founders of this inaugural event was Wisconsin senator Gaylord Nelson. Environmental issues such as pollution, the condition of local lakes, nuclear energy, and the impact of population growth were covered in the pages of the *Daily Cardinal*, which was firmly controlled by student radicals by the late sixties, but they also found a sometimes sympathetic hearing in the upstart *Badger Herald*.[37]

Another notable extension of New Left activism in the late sixties was the emergence of a variety of counter-institutions, organizations that reshaped the community even as they altered the definition of political activism. The counterculture has been celebrated by some and disparaged by others, but it was a central experience in the late sixties; while it is well known for affecting dress, musical tastes, and sexual practices, its rejection of conventional norms and authority also meant the creation of alternative institutions that would serve a new community. Grocery stores, theaters, newspapers, bookstores, apartment buildings—these were not meant to be political in the traditional sense, but in their shared rejection of mainstream cultural values and their embrace of experimentation they did more than envision a new society; they began the work of creating one. This was certainly the view of one writer in *Connections*, Madison's first underground newspaper, who described the growing co-op movement in Madison and argued that "rather than building electoral bases from above, we must participate in the creation of communities from within." Defying the stereotypes of hippies, the continued existence of some of these institutions today is a testament to the dedication and hard work of those who built them as well as the lasting power of their values.[38]

Perhaps the most important of the early counter-institutions that began in Madison was the Mifflin Street Community Cooperative, a grocery co-op that opened its doors on January 13, 1969. It offered just a few items and was run entirely by volunteer labor when it opened, and its bylaws point to an interesting mix of sixties values. The co-op, they read, "exists to embody a belief in community self-determination in opposition to the dominant trends in all communities in which control is increasingly concentrated outside the community and operated for profits which are not used for the betterment of the community." In a nod to the confrontational mood of the late sixties, the by-laws continued: "Our assets, as people and money, are committed to this struggle *by any means necessary*." For some of its founders, the co-op was an opportunity to work in their own neighborhoods, to do something that would bring people together and that would offer an alternative to the protests that were then so prevalent. It served as a meeting and community space, especially during its early years, while it also supported other co-ops and community organizations during its most successful years in the 1980s and 1990s.[39]

At least part of that success was its location in Madison's Mifflin Street neighborhood, the street named after a signer of the U.S. Constitution (Pennsylvania Quaker Thomas Mifflin) like most of the streets in downtown Madison. Situated just a few blocks southwest of the state capitol and home to a significant number of graduate students, "Miffland," as it came to be called, was already well known as a center of bohemian culture, and it would become famous for its annual block party. The first street party, organized in the spring of 1969 as a community gathering and a protest against the Vietnam War, attracted hundreds of students and community members and included three days of confrontation with the police. More than one hundred were arrested, including local alderman and future mayor Paul Soglin (who was actually arrested twice over the course of the three days), and more than seventy were injured. The block party cemented the neighborhood's status as a center of alternative culture in the city, and it became a Madison tradition in the years since, though the political overtones diminished over time even as the likelihood of violent clashes with the police did not.[40]

The Mifflin Street Co-op closed in 2006, but it was only one of many efforts to build an alternative community in Madison. While other grocery co-ops also emerged, including the still-thriving Willy Street Co-op, which was founded in another near-downtown neighborhood in 1974, the same spirit led to the experimental Broom Street Theater, established in 1969 and also still operating today. Madison's "Free University" started offering courses in 1966 and continued for at least a few years, emphasizing voluntary attendance, small-group discussion, student control, and no grades. Some of the courses in 1968 included "Land Ethic in America," "Contemporary Black Prose," "Guerrilla Theater," and "Women." Finally, students and others in Madison established a number of alternative newspapers during these years. *Connections*, founded in 1966, was the first, but it was soon joined by *Madison Kaleidoscope*, which operated in the late 1960s, *Take Over*, from 1971 to 1979, and several others. All of them varied, but each was an attempt to report on events related to the diverse movements that emerged in the wake of the New Left. Many of them also experimented with new forms of journalism, and some played their own roles in the era's activism.[41]

Finally, perhaps the most significant of the directions that students and other young people took in the late sixties was women's liberation. What had started as a reaction to sexism in the civil rights movement and the New Left quickly became a movement of its own, a powerful extension of the anti-hierarchical ideology that suffused much of the era's politics.

In Madison, women had always played an important role in the campus left, including *Studies on the Left* editor Eleanor Hakim, Student Peace Center founder Ellamae Calvert, Labor Youth League president Alita Letwin, and 1960s activists and leaders Vicki Gabriner, Elizabeth Ewen, and Ann Krooth; they had also managed to find a few female role models among the university's faculty and staff, especially French professor Germaine Bree and Dean of Women Martha Peterson. Yet despite the work that many women contributed, the New Left was still a male-dominated movement, with men holding leadership positions in most activist organizations throughout the 1950s and 1960s and taking prominent roles in almost all of the era's major campus demonstrations. Even as women became a larger percentage of the campus population, making up nearly 40 percent of students in the middle and late 1960s, including almost 30 percent of graduate students, the New Left remained dominated by male students as it turned to increasingly confrontational tactics. Some of the women who did rise to prominence in Madison, moreover, had boyfriends or husbands in leadership positions, suggesting that women had difficulty breaking into the movement's leadership without the strong personal support of male members.[42]

One of the first outward signs of women's discontent within the UW New Left came at a workshop on draft resistance held in Madison in March 1967, part of a regional SDS antidraft conference. Opposition to the Selective Service had always been a difficult issue for women in the New Left, as it was men who were susceptible to the draft, and women at the conference organized a workshop to help define their relationship to the movement. Their discussion ranged from women's role in the broader New Left to the possibility of forming their own organizations, and even as they determined to continue working alongside men within existing groups, they made clear their criticism of "male chauvinism" within the New Left. Members of the workshop called for an analysis of the draft's effect on women and asserted the need to create a system that allowed women and nondraftable men to serve in leadership positions. At least some of these women also signed an informal pledge against accepting typing duties, rejecting research and fund-raising positions as well in favor of what they considered more active and substantial roles.[43]

Women's activism continued in the late 1960s and early 1970s, part of the diversity of movements that emerged even as the New Left was losing strength. Gender had always been an issue on campus, but while social regulations had dominated earlier discussions, other issues proliferated in the late sixties, especially abortion, women's health, and sexual discrimination; the campus hosted a 1969 conference on women's liberation, and feminist students established a journal, *The Scarlet Letter*, in 1971. The journal provides an insightful look into the early women's movement, with its statement of purpose emphasizing women's shared oppression, the difficulties they face in a male-dominated world, and the importance of working collectively. It also provided space for a variety of women's groups on the campus and in the community to share their perspectives, including the Billie Holiday Collective, which focused on working women's issues, the Married Women's Collective, Madison Gay Sisters, and Women's Action Movement; articles covered such topics as women's health, pay inequity, welfare rights, the nature of love, and women's legal status. Though the journal itself was short-lived, its broad range and its strident criticism of

contemporary culture and politics highlight the breadth of leftist social movements in the late sixties.[44]

❖

Looking backward at the New Left and the sixties is a difficult task, and one
that has remained complicated even as the years have passed and the intense
emotions of the era have receded. A new generation of historians, one that did
not experience directly the upheaval of the sixties, has taken up the question of
the New Left and its legacy in the following decades, but a clear picture is still
elusive, a result, perhaps, of the diversity within the New Left as well as the
ways in which memories of the sixties remain tied to contemporary culture and
politics. "If you look back on the sixties and think there was more good than
bad, you're probably a Democrat," said former president Bill Clinton in 2004,
thinking about the way in which the sixties continue to influence modern
politics. "If you think there was more harm than good, you're probably a Republican." For many, the emergence of a powerful conservative movement in the
1970s and in the decades since has raised particularly stark questions about the
New Left's long-term influence.[45]

The history of the sixties in Madison gives shape to this complicated past. It
is a history that reveals the specific outlines of the movement on one campus as
well as the contradictions of Cold War–era higher education that existed
throughout the nation. In Madison, those contradictions contributed to the
early stirrings of political protest, as enrollment grew rapidly in the mid-1950s;
they were exposed more fully in the era's great dramas, including the draft
sit-in, the Dow confrontation, and the Sterling Hall bombing. During these
years, Madison and many other college and university campuses provided the
foundation for a movement that unleashed intellectual energy, bold activism,
and a powerful challenge to traditional American institutions and authority.
On the other hand, the same movement was sometimes plagued by infighting,
extremism, and even violence.

The New Left did not survive the era, breaking apart amid the great
upheavals of the late sixties, but the history of the UW–Madison points to the
movement's broad and continuing influence. Institutional changes in Madison
included an increased role for students in university governance, an end to in
loco parentis rules that had governed students' lives for more than a century,
the relaxation of ROTC requirements, the establishment of the Teaching
Assistants Association, and the creation of a Black Studies Department. Even

more important, the New Left engendered a spirit—democratic, experimental, opposed to hierarchy—that marked a generation of Americans, including some on the political right. And it helped spur various other movements, including those for gay rights, environmental conservation, and women's rights. The combined effect has been a shift in America's social, cultural, and political footing over the past several decades. In few places was the spirit of the sixties more prominent than in Madison. In a time when many of the era's struggles are still relevant, it is a spirit that continues to endure.

Notes

Introduction

1. *Daily Cardinal*, May 17, 1966.

2. George Flynn, *The Draft, 1940–1973* (Lawrence: University Press of Kansas, 1993), 166–87; *New York Times*, May 17, 1966, 8. For a discussion of changes in the draft as they affected the UW, see "Special University of Wisconsin Faculty Meeting," May 23, 1966, minutes, UW Archives, Series 4/19/1, Box 38, "Students—Sit-in—May 1966" and "Report and Recommendations on the University and Selective Service," June 10, 1966, UW Archives, Series 4/19/1, Box 38, "Students—Sit-in—May 1966."

3. "Why We Protest," 1966, UW Archives, Series 4/19/1, Box 38, "Students—Sit-in—May 1966"; "Special University of Wisconsin Faculty Meeting," May 23, 1966, minutes, UW Archives, Series 4/19/1, Box 38, "Students—Sit-in—May 1966"; *Daily Cardinal*, May 14, 1966.

4. "Why We Protest," 1966, UW Archives; "Special University of Wisconsin Faculty Meeting," May 23, 1966, UW Archives. The headlines were from the *Wisconsin State Journal*, May 19, 1966.

5. *Daily Cardinal*, May 19, 1966, and May 20, 1966; statement by campus clergy, 1966, UW Archives, Series 4/19/1, Box 38, "Students—Sit-in—May 1966"; "Sit-In Continues; Blockade's Out," *Wisconsin State Journal*, May 18, 1966; "Report and Recommendations on the University and Selective Service," June 10, 1966, UW Archives, Series 4/19/1, Box 38, "Students—Sit-in—May 1966." The bill to raise tuition for out-of-state students did not pass.

6. "Sit-In Gains, Still Threatens," *Wisconsin State Journal*, May 19, 1966; "Wisconsin U. Seeks to End Student Antidraft Sit-In," *New York Times*, May 19, 1966; Robben Fleming, "Faculty Document 89," October 3, 1966, UW Archives, Series 40/1/8/1, Box 10; Robben Fleming, *Tempests into Rainbows: Managing Turbulence* (Ann Arbor: University of Michigan Press, 1996), 147–61. The *Wisconsin State Journal* indicates that there were five thousand students at the meeting on Bascom Hill, while the article in the *New York Times* indicates there were ten thousand.

7. "Special University of Wisconsin Faculty Meeting," May 23, 1966, minutes, UW Archives, Series 4/19/1, Box 38, "Students—Sit-in—May 1966."

8. *Daily Cardinal*, May 24, 1966; June 20, 1966; and December 13, 1966.

9. The term "Cold War university" has been used elsewhere. See Rebecca Lowen, *Creating the Cold War University: The Transformation of Stanford* (Berkeley: University of California Press, 1997). Jeremi Suri uses the term "cultural contradictions of the Cold War" in a similar manner to describe the history of West Berlin's Free University, a university that was founded with the assistance of the United States to symbolize freedom and excellence in the West but that became the site of significant sixties-era protest. See Jeremi Suri, "The Cultural Contradictions of the Cold War: The Case of West Berlin," *Cold War History* 4 (April 2004): 1–20.

10. Ellen Schrecker's work is the best on McCarthyism in higher education. For her discussion of policies on student groups and campus speakers at the University of Michigan and the loyalty oath controversy at the University of California, see Schrecker, *No Ivory Tower: McCarthyism and the Universities* (New York: Oxford University Press, 1986), 85–92, 116–25. Other sources on Michigan and Berkeley include Mark Engberg, "McCarthyism and the Academic Profession: Power, Politics, and Faculty Purges at the University of Michigan," *American Education History Journal* 29 (2002): 53–62, and Bob Blauner, *Resisting McCarthyism: To Sign or Not to Sign California's Loyalty Oath* (Stanford, CA: Stanford University Press, 2009).

11. On the numbers of Jewish students in American higher education, see Marcia Graham Synnot, "Anti-Semitism and American Universities: Did Quotas Follow the Jews?" in David Gerber, ed., *Anti-Semitism in American History* (Urbana: University of Illinois Press, 1987), and Stephen Steinberg, *The Academic Melting Pot: Catholics and Jews in American Higher Education* (New York: McGraw-Hill, 1974). Jews' participation in the New Left is discussed in W. J. Rorabaugh, *Berkeley at War: The 1960s* (New York: Oxford University Press, 1989), 23–25, 33–34, and Kenneth Heineman, *Campus Wars: The Peace Movement at American State Universities in the Vietnam Era* (New York: New York University Press, 1993). A particularly interesting discussion of the distinctive mix of students in Madison is Paul Buhle, "Madison: An Introduction," in Buhle, ed., *History and the New Left: Madison, Wisconsin, 1950–1970* (Philadelphia: Temple University Press, 1990), while a history of Jewish students in Madison before World War II is provided in Jonathan Pollack, "'Is This We Have among Us Here a Jew?': The *Hillel Review* and Jewish Identity at the University of Wisconsin, 1925–1931," in Charles Cohen and Paul Boyer, eds., *Religion and the Culture of Print in Modern America* (Madison: University of Wisconsin Press, 2008). On the connections between the Old Left and the New Left, see Maurice Isserman, *If I Had a Hammer: The Death of the Old Left and the Birth of the New Left* (New York: Basic Books, 1987).

12. Two useful sources on Progressivism in Wisconsin are John D. Buenker, *The History of Wisconsin*, vol. 4: *The Progressive Era, 1893–1914* (Madison: State Historical Society of Wisconsin, 1998), and David Mollenhoff, *Madison: A History of the Formative Years* (1982; repr., Madison: University of Wisconsin Press, 2003). Robert LaFollette Jr. served as Wisconsin senator after winning the seat vacated on his father's death in 1925, but he lost the 1946 Republican Party primary to relative newcomer Joseph McCarthy.

13. "Wisconsin U. Seeks to End Student Antidraft Sit-In," *New York Times*, May 19, 1966. On Fred's view of communist professors, see "Red Editor's Speech Stirs Teapot Tempest," *Wisconsin Alumnus*, February 1954. On his opposition to a loyalty oath, see E. David Cronon and John W. Jenkins, *The University of Wisconsin: A History*, vol. 4: *Renewal to Revolution, 1945–1971* (Madison: University of Wisconsin Press, 1999), 92, and Henry Lardy, oral history, 1983, UW Oral History Project. The best source on the university's history is the multivolume *The University of Wisconsin: A History*, published by the University of Wisconsin Press. The first two volumes were authored by Merle Curti and Vernon Carstensen, the subsequent two volumes by E. David Cronon and John W. Jenkins. All four volumes are also available online as part of the University of Wisconsin's Digital Collection.

14. For more on the "military-industrial-academic complex" and other studies of the impact of the Cold War on American higher education, see Stuart Leslie, *The Cold War and Science: The Military-Industrial-Academic Complex at MIT and Stanford* (New York: Columbia University Press, 1993); Lowen, *Creating the Cold War University*; Roger Geiger, *Research and Relevant Knowledge: American Research Universities since World War II* (New York: Oxford University Press, 1993); Ron Robin, *The Making of the Cold War Enemy: Culture and Politics in the Military-Intellectual Complex* (Princeton, NJ: Princeton University Press, 2001); Noam Chomsky et al., *The Cold War and the University: Toward an Intellectual History of the Postwar Years* (New York: New Press, 1997); Sigmund Diamond, *Compromised Campus: The Collaboration of Universities with the Intelligence Community, 1945–1955* (New York: Oxford University Press, 1992); and Christopher Simpson, ed., *Universities and Empire: Money and Politics in the Social Sciences during the Cold War* (New York: New Press, 1998).

15. Lowen, *Creating the Cold War University*, 2.

16. One ranking of universities by overall federal funds is James Ridgeway, *The Closed Corporation: American Universities in Crisis* (New York: Random House, 1968), 236–37. For federal funds flowing into Madison, see Board of Regents, "Report to the Administrative Committee by its Ad Hoc Committee on Federal and Industrial Grants and Contracts," January 30, 1962, UW Archives, Record of the Minutes of the Regents of the University of Wisconsin, and "Federal Research Expenditures by Agency," September 16, 1969, UW Archives, Series 5/96/3, Box 5, "University-Military Relationship." For information on the Association of American Universities, including the founding members, see Ann Leigh Speicher, "The Association of American Universities: A Century of Service to Higher Education, 1900–2000," n.d., http://www.aau.edu/about/history_centennial.aspx. The link to the PDF article on this webpage is titled "AAU Beginnings." Other public universities did receive significant federal funding as well, and there was an effort in Congress in the 1950s and 1960s to spread research funds beyond those universities that had already developed close ties with the federal government. Kenneth Heineman, for example, discusses four universities that benefited from this wider distribution: Pennsylvania State University, Kent State University, Michigan State University, and the State University of New York at Buffalo. See Heineman, *Campus Wars*.

17. Kenneth Heineman has done the most to document the link between Cold War–related research and campus protests against this research. See Heineman, *Campus Wars*. Roger Geiger gives the fullest discussion of the concerns over the effects of federal funding on universities. See Geiger, *Research and Relevant Knowledge*, 199.

18. National enrollment figures are available at U.S. Department of Education, National Center for Education Statistics, Digest of Education Statistics, "Table 173: Total fall enrollment in degree-granting institutions, by attendance status, sex of student, and control of institution: 1947 to 1998," 2000, http://nces.ed.gov/programs/digest/doo/dt173.asp. UW enrollment figures are compiled from annual enrollment reports, UW Archives, Series 19/12/3/00–1, Boxes 1 and 2.

19. Jeremi Suri, *Power and Protest: Global Revolutions and the Rise of Détente* (Cambridge, MA: Harvard University Press, 2003), 88–89. For histories of the New Left at the University of Texas at Austin, Southern Illinois University, and Penn State University, see Doug Rossinow, *The Politics of Authenticity: Liberalism, Christianity, and the New Left in America* (New York: Columbia University Press, 1998); Robbie Lieberman, *Prairie Power: Voices of 1960s Midwestern Student Protest* (Columbia: University of Missouri Press, 2004); and Heineman, *Campus Wars*.

20. A good discussion of the periodization of "the sixties" is Andrew Hunt, "'When Did the Sixties Happen?': Searching for New Directions," *Journal of Social History* 33, no. 1 (1999): 147–61. Among the many books that have been published about 1968, see David Caute, *The Year of the Barricades: A Journey through 1968* (London: Paladin Books, 1988); David Farber, *Chicago '68* (Chicago: University of Chicago Press, 1988); Mark Kurlansky, *1968: The Year That Rocked the World* (New York: Ballantine, 2004); and Carole Fink, Philipp Gassert, and Detlef Junker, eds., *1968: The World Transformed* (New York: Cambridge University Press, 1998). Many of these works emphasize the global connections of 1968, a topic that was taken up as well in several articles in the *American Historical Review*, collected in the February and April 2009 issues in a forum titled "The International 1968." The rise of conservative youth politics in the 1960s has received considerable attention since the late 1990s. For a sample of books on the topic, see Rebecca Klatch, *Generation Divided: The New Left, the New Right, and the 1960s* (Berkeley: University of California Press, 1999); Lisa McGirr, *Suburban Warriors: The Origins of the New American Right* (Princeton, NJ: Princeton University Press, 2001); Gregory Schneider, *Cadres for Conservatism: Young Americans for Freedom and the Rise of the Contemporary Right* (New York: New York University Press, 1999); and John A. Andrew, *The Other Side of the Sixties: Young Americans for Freedom and the Rise of Conservative Politics* (New Brunswick, NJ: Rutgers University Press, 1997).

Chapter 1. Cold War University

1. Omar Bradley, commencement address, June 19, 1948, UW Archives, Series 5/00/5–15, Box 1. For a brief overview of other commencement speeches that summer, see *Time*, June 14, 1948, 48.

2. Bradley, commencement address.

3. The best source on the history of Wisconsin is the multivolume *The History of Wisconsin* published by the State Historical Society of Wisconsin with William Fletcher Thompson as general editor. For a history of the city of Madison through 1920, see David Mollenhoff, *Madison: A History of the Formative Years* (1982; repr., Madison: University of Wisconsin Press, 2003).

4. "The Good Life in Madison, Wisconsin," *Life*, September 6, 1948. Madison is still often ranked as one of the best places to live in the United States, including a number one ranking by *Money* magazine in 1996.

5. These details on the university's history are available in many places but are most accessible in the first two volumes of the multivolume history of the university published by the University of Wisconsin Press: Merle Curti and Vernon Carstensen, *The University of Wisconsin: A History, 1848–1925*, vols. 1 and 2 (Madison: University of Wisconsin Press, 1949). The subsequent two volumes are written by E. David Cronon and John W. Jenkins.

6. Again, the details of the university's organization can be found in many places. One useful source is "History and Organization of the University of Wisconsin System," University of Wisconsin, n.d., http://www.wisconsin.edu/about/history.htm.

7. *Daily Cardinal*, November 22, 1955. The *Daily Cardinal* devoted a good deal of space to issues of academic freedom and racial discrimination throughout this era, but it is less clear how important these issues were to the majority of students, as *Cardinal* editors and staff writers were often among the more politically active members on campus. I have used the paper extensively in my research, but I have made an effort not to take the editors' concerns for those of the student body as a whole without further additional evidence that this was the case.

8. Michael Neiberg, *Making Citizen Soldiers: ROTC and the Ideology of American Military Service* (Cambridge, MA: Harvard University Press, 2000); Donald Downs and Ilia Murtazashvili, *Arms and the University: Military Presence and the Civic Education of Non-Military Students* (Cambridge: Cambridge University Press, 2012).

9. *Daily Cardinal*, April 11, 1949; May 13, 1950; May 14, 1957; May 23, 1957. For an example of a student defense of ROTC, see *Daily Cardinal*, March 10, 1949. For information on the 1927 referendum, see E. David Cronon and John W. Jenkins, *The University of Wisconsin: A History*, vol. 3: *Politics, Depression, and War, 1925–1945* (Madison: University of Wisconsin Press, 1994), 130.

10. "UW May Be Evacuee Center in A-Bomb Raid," *Wisconsin Alumnus*, May 1951; Committee on Civil Defense, "Report on Civil Defense," April 1, 1955, UW Archives, Committee on Civil Defense Papers; Committee on Civil Defense, "Attention House Presidents," February 17, 1951, UW Archives, Committee on Civil Defense Papers, emphasis in original.

11. George Flynn, *The Draft, 1940–1973* (Lawrence: University Press of Kansas, 1993), 88–165; "The State of the University," *Wisconsin Alumnus*, October 1948; "Enrollment Highlights," October 23, 1952, UW Archives, Series 4/16/1, Box 188, "Enrollment"; "Student Life," *Wisconsin Alumnus*, June 1951.

12. *Daily Cardinal*, March 20, 1948.

13. *Daily Cardinal,* March 6, 1948; March 18, 1948; October 15, 1948.

14. *Daily Cardinal,* January 10, 1951; July 28, 1950; "Accelerated Program Offered Future GIs," *Wisconsin Alumnus,* March 1951.

15. Todd Gitlin, *The Sixties: Years of Hope, Days of Rage* (1987; repr., New York: Bantam Books, 1993), 21–26; *Daily Cardinal,* November 30, 1950; December 1, 1954.

16. *Daily Cardinal,* February 25, 1948; February 28, 1950; March 2, 1951. For more on Farrington Daniels's interest in peaceful uses of nuclear energy, see *Daily Cardinal,* March 1, 1950.

17. "Cold War," *Wisconsin Alumnus,* August 1948; Wayne Morse, "Sunrise or Sunset for Peace," *Wisconsin Alumnus,* March 1950; Dan Reich, senior address at honors convocation, June 19, 1952, UW Archives, Series 5/00/5-15, Box 1.

18. E. B. Fred, "The Age of the Draft," June 15, 1951, UW Archives, Series, 5/00/5-15, Box 1, emphasis in original.

19. "Be a Dorm Donor," *Spectator* (newsletter), October 25, 1951, UW Archives, Series 20/2/17-1, Box 1; *Daily Cardinal,* March 3, 1949.

20. "Fun with Atoms," *Octopus,* October 1948; "A Greeting to New Students . . . From the Editor," *Octopus,* April 1955; *Octopus,* November 1953, 12–13. The full issue of the *Octopus* that satirized ROTC is the April 1955 issue. For more editorial cartoons with military themes, see *Daily Cardinal,* January 13, 1951, and November 1, 1950. For the angry reaction to the ROTC issue by some ROTC students, see Dave Trubek, interview with the author, June 8, 2005.

21. C. Wright Mills, *The Power Elite* (1956; repr., New York: Oxford University Press, 1967), 198.

22. Rebecca Lowen, *Creating the Cold War University: The Transformation of Stanford* (Berkeley: University of California Press, 1997), 44; R. C. Lewontin, "The Cold War and the Transformation of the Academy," in Noam Chomsky et al., *The Cold War and the University: Toward an Intellectual History of the Postwar Years* (New York: New Press, 1997), 13; Roger Geiger, *Research and Relevant Knowledge: American Research Universities since World War II* (New York: Oxford University Press, 1993), 7–9. Along with Geiger's work on research universities after World War II, an excellent source on the federal government's role in funding university science before World War II is Roger Geiger, *To Advance Knowledge: The Growth of American Research Universities, 1900–1940* (New York: Oxford University Press, 1986).

23. Clay Schoenfeld, "University of Wisconsin Digest of War Services," June 29, 1950, UW Archives, Series 19/2/3-5, Box 3, "Civil Defense, 1950–1952"; E. David Cronon and John W. Jenkins, *The University of Wisconsin: A History,* vol. 4: *Renewal to Revolution, 1945–1971* (Madison: University of Wisconsin Press, 1999), 7–8; Mark Ingraham, "The University of Wisconsin, 1925–1950," in Allan Bogue and Robert Taylor, eds., *The University of Wisconsin: One Hundred and Twenty-Five Years* (Madison: University of Wisconsin Press, 1975); Ira Baldwin, oral history, 1974, 1985, and 1987, UW Oral History Project, 202–3. For UW contributions during World War I, see Stuart Levitan, *Madison: The Illustrated Sesquicentennial History, 1856–1931* (Madison: University of Wisconsin Press, 2006), 203.

24. Vannevar Bush, *Science: The Endless Frontier: A Report to the President on a Program for Postwar Scientific Research* (1945; repr., Washington, DC: National Science Foundation, 1960), 12. On the support by many for continued cooperation with academic scientists, including Eisenhower, see Geiger, *Research and Relevant Knowledge*, 3–29. The reference to Eisenhower is on pages 22–23.

25. Kenneth Heineman, *Campus Wars: The Peace Movement at American State Universities in the Vietnam Era* (New York: New York University Press, 1993), 14–17. Some scholars have discussed the postwar changes in the academy as the result of mostly external forces that warped higher education, while another perspective is to see the relationship as considerably more mutual. For a discussion of this topic, see David Engerman, "Rethinking Cold War Universities: Some Recent Histories," *Journal of Cold War Studies* 5, no. 3 (2003): 80–95.

26. E. B. Fred, speech, June 18, 1951, UW Archives, Series 4/16/5, Box 9.

27. *Daily Cardinal,* July 18, 1950; UW Defense Bulletin, January 5, 1951, UW Archives, Committee on Civil Defense Papers. For the UW's correspondence with the federal government concerning its war-related resources, see LeRoy Luberg to Stuart Symington, July 5, 1950, UW Archives, Series 19/2/3-5, Box 3, "Civil Defense, 1950–1952."

28. Oscar Rennebohm, speech, June 19, 1948, UW Archives, Series 5/00/5-15, Box 1; "University of Wisconsin Policies Committee Report: Wisconsin Legislative Council," *Wisconsin Alumnus,* January 15, 1955. An even more fervent supporter of integrating the university's scientific resources into a national defense system was chemistry professor and director of the UW's Naval Research Lab Joseph Hirschfelder. During World War II Hirschfelder worked at Los Alamos, and in a 1954 essay he argued that the nation's scientists were crucial for an effective national defense. He suggested more government planning on how to utilize scientific resources in the case of a national emergency, preparing scientists for defense work, and some kind of training for both professors and graduate students. See Joseph Hirschfelder, "How Can We Best Utilize Our Scientific Manpower," *Wisconsin Engineer,* December 1954.

29. Peterson is quoted in Lowen, *Creating the Cold War University,* 34; Geiger, *Research and Relevant Knowledge*, 13–19, 58–61, 157–58; "Crisis in the Colleges: Can They Pay Their Way?" *Time,* June 19, 1950; Wisconsin Legislative Council, "University of Wisconsin Policies," December 1, 1954, UW Archives, Series 19/2/6-1, Box 15, "Labor Youth League—SLIC Correspondence."

30. Lewontin, "Cold War"; Geiger, *Research and Relevant Knowledge*, 52–57. Geiger introduces the concept of the "federal research economy" on pages 19–29.

31. Lewontin, "Cold War," 15; Lowen, *Creating the Cold War University,* 2; Heineman, *Campus Wars,* 13–14.

32. Figures for the University of Michigan are from Howard H. Peckham, *The Making of the University of Michigan* (Ann Arbor: University of Michigan Press, 1967), 254, and James Ridgeway, *The Closed Corporation: American Universities in Crisis* (New York: Random House, 1968), 236–37. On Michigan's president Hatcher, see James Miller, *Democracy Is in the Streets: From Port Huron to the Siege of Chicago* (1987; repr., Cambridge, MA: Harvard University Press, 1994), 25. For information on Berkeley's Radiation Lab,

see Geiger, *Research and Relevant Knowledge*, 73–82. Other leading destinations for research dollars included public universities such as the University of Illinois, the University of Minnesota, the University of Washington, and the University of Texas. Leading private universities included Stanford University, Harvard University, Columbia University, the Massachusetts Institute of Technology, and the University of Pennsylvania.

33. Board of Regents, "The Reasons for the Decision to Expand the University Campus," October 25, 1952, UW Archives, Records of the Minutes of the Regents of the University of Wisconsin; Board of Regents, "Report to the Administrative Committee by Its Ad Hoc Committee on Federal and Industrial Grants and Contracts," January 30, 1962. The report is included with the meeting minutes for February 9, 1962.

34. Robert Divine, *The Sputnik Challenge* (New York: Oxford University Press, 1993); Barbara Clowse, *Brainpower for the Cold War: The Sputnik Crisis and the National Defense Education Act of 1958* (Westport, CT: Greenwood Press, 1981); Geiger, *Research and Relevant Knowledge*, 173–74.

35. "Federal Research Expenditures by Agency," September 16, 1969, UW Archives, Series 5/96/3, Box 5, "University-Military Relationship"; Cronon and Jenkins, *University of Wisconsin*, 4:598–99. Roger Geiger makes the point that the University of Wisconsin was the only university among the seventeen leading recipients of federal research funds in the immediate postwar years to significantly increase its share of federal dollars in the middle and late 1960s as Congress sought to spread the dollars more evenly through higher education. See Geiger, *Research and Relevant Knowledge*, 209.

36. This history of the meteorology department is from Cronon and Jenkins, *University of Wisconsin*, 4:274–79.

37. Geiger, *Research and Relevant Knowledge*, 58–59.

38. Jagdish Chandra and Stephen Robinson, *An Uneasy Alliance: The Mathematics Research Center at the University of Wisconsin, 1956–1987* (Philadelphia: Society for Industrial and Applied Mathematics, 2005), 11; "Mathematics Research Center: United States Army," booklet, 1959, UW Archives, Series 4/16/1, Box 321; Rudolf Langer, "Semi-Annual Report on the Mathematics Research Center, United States Army," April 25, 1960, UW Archives, Series 4/17/1, Box 4, "Army Mathematics Research Center"; Rudolf Langer to Colonel Mills, April 25, 1960, UW Archives, Series 4/17/1, Box 4, "Army Mathematics Research Center"; J. Barkley Rosser to Stephen Kleene, August 10, 1969, UW Archives, Series 5/96/3, Box 5, "University-Military Relationship." For a discussion of the lack of classified research on campus, see Eric Rude, oral history, 1999, UW Oral History Project.

39. Cronon and Jenkins, *University of Wisconsin*, 4:269–72. For figures on university research budgets from 1950/51 through 1960/61, including some figures on the AMRC, see Board of Regents, "Report to the Administrative Committee by Its Ad Hoc Committee on Federal and Industrial Grants and Contracts."

40. Clark Kerr, *The Uses of the University* (Cambridge, MA: Harvard University Press, 1964); Fred Harvey Harrington, "The Function of University Administration," *Journal of Higher Education* 3, no 1 (March 1963): 131–36.

41. LeRoy Luberg, "Characteristics of Recent Federal Support at the University of Wisconsin," 1964, UW Archives, Series 4/18/1, Box 84, "Luberg, L. E."

42. Divine, *Sputnik Challenge*.

43. Luberg, "Characteristics of Recent Federal Support"; Board of Regents, "Report to the Administrative Committee by Its Ad Hoc Committee on Federal and Industrial Grants and Contracts."

44. Cronon and Jenkins, *University of Wisconsin*, 4:132–33, 281. For information on the role of area studies in Cold War intelligence gathering, see Bruce Cumings, "Boundary Displacement: Area Studies and International Studies during and after the Cold War," *Bulletin of Concerned Asian Scholars* 29, no. 1 (January–March 1997), and Sigmund Diamond, *Compromised Campus: The Collaboration of Universities with the Intelligence Community, 1945–1955* (New York: Oxford University Press, 1992).

45. Robert Collins, *More: The Politics of Growth in Postwar America* (New York: Oxford University Press, 2000), 45–46; Steven Gillon, *Politics and Vision: The ADA and American Liberalism, 1947–1985* (New York: Oxford University Press, 1987). The quotation from Walter Lippmann is originally from the November 5, 1960, issue of the *Saturday Evening Post*.

46. Board of Regents, "Report to the Administrative Committee by Its Ad Hoc Committee on Federal and Industrial Grants and Contracts." For more general information on the expansion of business education in the postwar years, see Herrymon Maurer, "Should a Businessman Be Educated?" *Fortune*, April 1953, and Herrymon Maurer, "The Worst Shortage in Business," *Fortune*, April 1956. One example of the pre–World War II distrust of private capital at the University of Wisconsin was the so-called Grady resolution in 1925. Following Robert LaFollette's death that year, Daniel Grady and other UW Regents passed a resolution that banned all grants from private foundations. The resolution was rescinded soon after, but the board remained particularly skeptical of grants from the Carnegie and Rockefeller Foundations for several years. See Cronon and Jenkins, *University of Wisconsin*, 4:67–68, 125–28.

47. "Blueprint for Educational Planning in Wisconsin," *Wisconsin Alumnus*, April 1958; Board of Regents, "Findings Concerning Research Needs," February 9, 1962.

48. Merle Curti, oral history, 1973, UW Oral History Project; Cronon and Jenkins, *University of Wisconsin*, 4:107–8.

49. U.S. Department of Education, National Center for Education Statistics, Digest of Education Statistics, "Table 173: Total fall enrollment in degree-granting institutions, by attendance status, sex of student, and control of institution: 1947 to 1998," 2000, http://nces.ed.gov/programs/digest/d00/dt173.asp.

50. Peckham, *Making of the University of Michigan*, 254; W. J. Rorabaugh, *Berkeley at War: The 1960s* (New York: Oxford University Press, 1989), 180; UW annual enrollment reports, UW Archives, Series 19/12/3/00–1, Boxes 1 and 2.

51. Maurer, "Should a Businessman Be Educated?" For birth rates during the baby boom, see Centers for Disease Control and Prevention, National Center for Health Statistics, "Table 1-1. Live Births, Birth Rates, and Fertility Rates, by Race: United

States, 1909–2000," http://www.cdc.gov/nchs/data/statab/t001x01.pdf. At least one scholar has also suggested that the Cold War helped fuel the baby boom as well, highlighting the relative security of the family in contrast with the instability and danger of the Cold War world. See Elaine Tyler May, *Homeward Bound: American Families in the Cold War Era* (New York: Basic Books, 1988).

52. For a discussion of the importance of federal funding to the expansion of the UW Graduate School, see Robert Alberty, oral history, 1985, UW Oral History Project. Alberty was a chemistry professor and dean of the Graduate School in the 1960s.

53. *Daily Cardinal*, March 5, 1948; E. B. Fred, "High Enrollments: Should They Be Considered a Liability or an Asset," *Wisconsin Alumnus*, February 15, 1955; "Education in Review," *New York Times*, May 24, 1953. For other views on the rapid increase in enrollment, see E. B. Fred, "A Look at the Future," 1946, UW Archives, Series 4/16/1, Box 32, "Enrollment"; John Berge, "How Big Should Wisconsin Be?" *Wisconsin Alumnus*, July/August 1947; "Does Quantity Beget Mediocrity?" *Wisconsin Alumnus*, February 1958; Leon Epstein, interview with the author, February 8, 2006; James Villemonte, oral history, 1982, UW Oral History Project.

Chapter 2. "Let the rascal speak"

1. Jeffry Kaplow, "Parentheses: 1952–1956," in Paul Buhle, ed., *History and the New Left: Madison, Wisconsin, 1950–1970* (Philadelphia: Temple University Press, 1990). See Jeffry Kaplow, *Daily Cardinal*, December 9, 1955, for his contemporaneous opinion of civil liberties on campus. For a different perspective on LYL members' efforts to work in other campus groups, see Ron Radosh, *Commies: A Journey through the Old Left, the New Left, and the Leftover Left* (San Francisco: Encounter Books, 2001), 53–54.

2. Kaplow, "Parentheses"; Saul Landau, "From the Labor Youth League to the Cuban Revolution," in Buhle, *History and the New Left*, 108–9. Interestingly, in my interviews with former LYL members and others who were not in the league but knew people who were, there is still considerable reticence to name members of the group other than the league's public members. For another view of the FBI's attention to members of the UW, see Radosh, *Commies*, 57.

3. Kaplow, "Parentheses."

4. The most extensive source on the relationship between the Old Left and the New Left is Maurice Isserman, *If I Had a Hammer: The Death of the Old Left and the Birth of the New Left* (New York: Basic Books, 1987). Isserman argues that American radicals remade themselves in the late 1950s and early 1960s, rethinking many of their basic assumptions in response to the repression of the McCarthy years as well as changes in the Cold War.

5. Robert W. Iversen, *The Communists and the Schools* (New York: Harcourt, Brace, 1959); E. David Cronon and John W. Jenkins, *The University of Wisconsin: A History*, vol. 3: *Politics, Depression, and War, 1925–1945* (Madison: University of Wisconsin Press, 1994), 388–90; Leon Epstein, oral history, 1977, UW Oral History Project.

6. Two of the best general surveys of McCarthyism are Ellen Schrecker, *Many Are the Crimes: McCarthyism in America* (Boston: Little, Brown, 1998), and Stephen Whitfield, *The Culture of the Cold War* (Baltimore: Johns Hopkins University Press, 1991).

7. "College Freedoms Being Stifled by Students' Fear of Red Label," *New York Times*, May 10, 1951; "The Class of '49," *Fortune*, June 1949.

8. William Whyte, *The Organization Man* (New York: Simon and Schuster, 1956); Paul Goodman, *Growing Up Absurd: Problems of Youth in the Organized Society* (New York: Vintage Books, 1960); David Riesman, Nathan Glazer, and Reuel Denney, *The Lonely Crowd: A Study of the Changing American Character* (New Haven, CT: Yale University Press, 1950); David Riesman, "The Found Generation," *American Scholar*, Autumn 1956. For a broad discussion of intellectuals' response to the cultural changes in the 1950s, see Richard Pells, *The Liberal Mind in a Conservative Age: American Intellectuals in the 1940s and 1950s* (New York: Harper and Row, 1985), 183–261.

9. Student Conduct and Appeals Committee, UW Archives, Series 5/87, Box 1; *Daily Cardinal*, May 13, 1950; May 18, 1950; May 19, 1950; May 24, 1950. Harassment of LYL members is indicated in a letter to campus police from registrar Kenneth Little. See Kenneth Little to A. F. Ahearn, July 11, 1950, UW Archives, Series 19/2/6–5, Box 2, "Labor Youth League." The same folder also contains a 1953 letter from LYL member Henry Wortis to Dean of Students Theodore Zillman regarding a 1953 incident of harassment against Wortis. Nina Serrano, while chair of the Student Peace Center, also reported harassment from other students. See Serrano, "A Madison Bohemian," in Buhle, *History and the New Left*, 73–74. For Dave Trubek's account of his interrogation by military intelligence officials, see Dave Trubek, interview with the author, June 8, 2005.

10. *Daily Cardinal*, November 20, 1948; October 2, 1956; "Generation of Jellyfish: An Indictment of the Wisconsin Student," *Wisconsin Athenaean*, Spring 1951.

11. *Daily Cardinal*, September 29, 1953; December 10, 1957; January 15, 1955; "Campus Chronicle," *Wisconsin Alumnus*, June 1958.

12. Paul Boyer, *By the Bomb's Early Light: American Thought and Culture at the Dawn of the Atomic Age* (New York: Pantheon, 1985). Boyer's work focuses on the era between 1945 and 1950 but deals briefly with the 1950s as well.

13. "A Plea to a Sacred Generation," *New Idea*, April 5, 1957.

14. "Conformity on the Campus," *Wisconsin Alumnus*, January 1958. This is a transcript of a conversation that took place on the radio.

15. For a study of some of the most important groups in the 1950s left, see Isserman, *If I Had a Hammer*.

16. "Membership List," 1945, UW Archives, Series 19/2/6–5, Box 1, "American Youth for Democracy"; "UW Student Organization Annual Registration Form," 1955, Wisconsin Historical Society, Student Peace Center Records; "Annual Student Organization Registration Form," November 6, 1957, UW Archives, Series 19/9/4–2, Box 7. Various estimates put LYL's membership in this range. See Kaplow, "Parentheses"; *Daily Cardinal*, November 21, 1953; January 12, 1954; Henry Wortis, interview with the author, March 6, 2005. One estimate that stands out from the rest is from Ron Radosh,

who suggests that LYL in the middle 1950s had about one hundred committed activist members. See Radosh, *Commies*, 53–54. Alternately, Radosh wrote in 1956 that LYL had twenty members. See *Daily Cardinal*, October 3, 1956.

17. Henry Elson, "Here Is Your AYD," newsletter, May 1, 1946, UW Archives, 19/2/6-5, Box 1, "American Youth for Democracy"; *Daily Cardinal*, May 1, 1947; February 10, 1948; February 26, 1948.

18. "Hands Off Korea!" UW Archives, Series 19/2/6-5, Box 2, "Labor Youth League." One of the more popular speakers who came to campus under the auspices of the league was historian Herbert Aptheker. See *Daily Cardinal*, November 16, 1955. For a list of speakers that the league brought to campus, see "Off Campus Speakers—Labor Youth League," January 16, 1953, UW Archives, Series 19/2/6-5, Box 2, "LYL."

19. *Daily Cardinal*, May 22, 1958; July 17, 1958; July 22, 1958; April 21, 1961; April 22, 1961; April 26, 1961; April 27, 1961; October 19, 1963.

20. *Daily Cardinal*, March 20, 1957; April 9, 1957; April 24, 1958; April 25, 1959; April 9, 1960; April 29, 1961. It certainly didn't hurt that some of the skits, including 1959's "All Out for Fallout," were written by Marshall Brickman, who later collaborated with Woody Allen on *Annie Hall*. For a description of the Peace Center's goals, see "Constitution of the Student Peace Center," 1955, Wisconsin Historical Society, Student Peace Center Records.

21. Michael Nieberg, *Making Citizen Soldiers: ROTC and the Ideology of American Military Service* (Cambridge, MA: Harvard University Press, 2000). For the deliberations at the University of Wisconsin in the late 1950s, see the variety of reports and materials from the Wisconsin Student Association, the university's administration, and the United States Army. These are collected in the UW Archives, Series 5/75, Box 1, "Compulsory vs. Voluntary ROTC." For the SPC's 1957 poster walk, see "Press Release," 1957, Wisconsin Historical Society, Student Peace Center Records.

22. For information on AYD members, see AYD Membership List, UW Archives, Series 19/2/6-5, Box 1, "American Youth for Democracy"; Anita Kaufman to Paul Trump, February 21, 1947, UW Archives, Series 19/2/6-5, Box 1, "American Youth for Democracy." A few states contributed only one or two members to those listed on the 1945 registration form, which makes up for the remainder of those whose home towns were listed. Three students did not have home towns listed. For LYL members, see "LYL," February 3, 1953, UW Archives, Series 19/2/6-5, Box 2, "LYL." The university compiled its list of LYL members in 1953 during its internal deliberations on the group's status. It included only those who were officers and publicly identified themselves as members on university registration forms. For the 1950 ROTC picketers, see "List of Students Who Participated in the Picketing at the ROTC Review May 11, 1950," 1950, UW Archives, Series 19/2/3-5, Box 14, "Military—Miscellaneous, 1949–1952." It's unclear precisely how many students were involved in the 1950 protest. One source says nineteen, another says twenty.

23. On Jewish students at the University of Wisconsin in the decades before World War II, see Jonathan Pollack, "Jewish Problems: Eastern and Western Jewish Identities

in Conflict at the University of Wisconsin, 1919–1941," *American Jewish History* 89, no. 2 (June 2001); Jonathan Pollack, "'Is This We Have among Us Here a Jew?': The *Hillel Review* and Jewish Identity at the University of Wisconsin, 1925–1931," in Charles Cohen and Paul Boyer, eds., *Religion and the Culture of Print in Modern America* (Madison: University of Wisconsin Press, 2008); Cronon and Jenkins, *University of Wisconsin*, 3:557–60, 675–76. On admission restrictions against Jews at universities before World War II, see Marcia Graham Synnot, "Anti-Semitism and American Universities: Did Quotas Follow the Jews?" in David Gerber, ed., *Anti-Semitism in American History* (Urbana: University of Illinois Press, 1987). For information on campus enrollment, see UW annual enrollment reports, UW Archives, Series 19/12/3/00–1, Boxes 1 and 2. The University of Wisconsin's Hillel chapter opened a new building in 2009, a mark of the large Jewish student population that still exists today.

24. Pollack, "Jewish Problems"; A. W. Peterson to Robert Lynch, February 19, 1948, UW Archives, Series 4/16/1, Box 81, "Enrollment"; Trubek, interview with the author; Paul Breines, interview with the author, December 8, 2000; Cronon and Jenkins, *University of Wisconsin*, 3:389; *Daily Cardinal*, May 23, 1950; March 2, 1961; "Report and Recommendations on the University and Selective Service," 1966, UW Archives, Series 4/19/1, Box 38, "Students—Sit-in—May 1966." For another perspective, Henry Wortis, a New York Jew and a prominent member of the Labor Youth League in the mid-1950s, recalls that he experienced little anti-Semitism, though there was plenty of opposition to his ideological views. See Wortis, interview with the author. For an extended discussion of student views of Jews on campus, see the series of articles that ran on the topic in the *Daily Cardinal* during March 1961.

25. "UW Student Organization Annual Registration Form," 1955, Wisconsin Historical Society, Student Peace Center Records; *Daily Cardinal*, December 8, 1955; March 29, 1956. The Peace Center's Christian origins make for an interesting connection to Douglas Rossinow's study of the University of Texas in the 1950s and 1960s. Rossinow ties Christianity to the development of the New Left, especially in terms of civil rights activism at UT. See Doug Rossinow, *The Politics of Authenticity: Liberalism, Christianity, and the New Left in America* (New York: Columbia University Press, 1998).

26. Meeting minutes, Committee on Conscientious Objectors, November 3, 1954, UW Archives, Series 5/115; *Daily Cardinal*, December 8, 1955; March 20, 1957; Ken Knudson to Committee on Conscientious Objectors, October 8, 1959, UW Archives, Series 5/115; Serrano, "Madison Bohemian"; Francis Hole to Dick Lerner, December 11, 1960, Wisconsin Historical Society, Student Peace Center Records. For a colorful description of Knudson as an "anarchist-pacifist-vegetarian," see John Coatsworth, interview with the author, November 22, 2000. Citing time concerns, Hole ultimately withdrew as the group's faculty adviser the next year. Another interesting piece of evidence of the cross-over between the Socialist Club and the Peace Center is the copy of the script for the 1958 Anti-Military Ball skit in the Student Peace Center Records at the Wisconsin Historical Society. The script was typed on the back of old Socialist Club flyers.

27. Wortis, interview with the author. Paul Breines tells a somewhat similar story, recalling his time as a pledge in a Jewish fraternity in Madison. Making an announcement about a fundraiser to support the sit-in movement in the South, he remembers that his pledge father accused him of being a "nigger lover." See Breines, interview with the author. This tension also recalls the differences between Midwest and East Coast Jews before World War II, when many Midwest Jews resented the way in which the stereotypical image of East Coast Jews reflected on them. See Pollack, "Jewish Problems." Jack Holzhueter, an editor for the *Daily Cardinal* in the late 1950s and later a historian with the Wisconsin Historical Society, remembers that some New York students were more familiar with the socialists in Milwaukee than the Wisconsin natives on campus. Jack Holzhueter, interview with the author, February 18, 2005. There is also some evidence that even as Jews were overrepresented in leftist politics, they were also overrepresented in conservative campus politics. I did not collect information about conservative students in Wisconsin, but for statistics on Jews' involvement in pro-war student groups during the middle and late 1960s at several other university campuses, see Kenneth Heineman, *Campus Wars: The Peace Movement at American State Universities in the Vietnam Era* (New York: New York University Press, 1993).

28. Judy Kaplan and Linn Shapiro, eds., *Red Diapers: Growing Up in the Communist Left* (Urbana: University of Illinois Press, 1998). See especially the essay by Rosalyn Fraad Baxandall and Harriet Fraad, "Red Sisters of the Bourgeoisie." Baxandall was a student in Madison during the late 1950s and early 1960s and active in radical politics. Among the many UW students with ties to the Old Left, one that stands out is Michael Meeropol, the son of Julius and Ethel Rosenberg.

29. Breines, interview with the author; Roz Baxandall, "Another Madison Bohemian," in Buhle, *History and the New Left*, 134–35.

30. Franklynn Peterson, interview with the author, December 19, 2005, and follow-up correspondence. For another perspective on the relationship between Jewishness and radical politics in Madison, see Paul Buhle, "Madison: An Introduction," in Buhle, *History and the New Left*, 8.

31. Joshua M. Zeitz, *White Ethnic New York: Jews, Catholics, and the Shaping of Postwar Politics* (Chapel Hill: University of North Carolina Press, 2007); Rebecca Klatch, *A Generation Divided: The New Left, the New Right, and the 1960s* (Berkeley: University of California Press, 1999). W. J. Rorabaugh, *Berkeley at War: The 1960s* (New York: Oxford University Press, 1989), 33–34. Zeitz suggests that the Jewish-American emphasis placed on dissent has often been read backward into Jewish history and that it isn't a timeless Jewish value. He argues that Jewish immigrants brought a highly democratic culture with them, the result of conditions in nineteenth-century Europe, and that the democratic religious framework created by Jews in the United States, the result of a lack of centralized religious authority, also promoted intellectual freedom. Two examples of Jewish students drawing on the history of the Holocaust to justify their strident late sixties opposition to the war in Vietnam are Mark Greenside, "Two Days in October," film transcript, 2005, PBS, http://www.pbs.org/wgbh/amex/twodays/filmmore/pt.html;

and Adam Schesch, open letter to the Jewish Community of Madison, 1970, Wisconsin Historical Society, Adam Schesch Papers, Box 1, Folder 2. For the numbers of Jewish students in antiwar and pro-war student organizations in the late sixties on several campuses across the country, see Heineman, *Campus Wars*.

32. Merle Curti and Vernon Carstensen, *The University of Wisconsin: A History, 1848–1925* (Madison: University of Wisconsin Press, 1949), 2:508–25.

33. Cronon and Jenkins, *University of Wisconsin*, 3:129, 388–90; "Background of the Policy Established in 1922," March 16, 1953, UW Archives, Series 19/2/6-5, Box 2, "Labor Youth League"; Bob Blauner, *Resisting McCarthyism: To Sign or Not to Sign California's Loyalty Oath* (Stanford, CA: Stanford University Press, 2009), 58–59.

34. *Daily Cardinal*, December 3, 1947; December 5, 1947; December 10, 1947. For a variety of documents surrounding this controversy, see UW Archives, Series 19/2/6-5, Box 1, "American Youth for Democracy."

35. Ellen Schrecker, *No Ivory Tower: McCarthyism and the Universities* (New York: Oxford University Press, 1986), 85–93; Howard H. Peckham, *The Making of the University of Michigan* (Ann Arbor: University of Michigan Press, 1967), 225–26; W. J. Rorabaugh, *Berkeley at War*, 14.

36. Paul Trump to Bernard Gettelman, June 6, 1947, UW Archives, Series 19/2/6-5, Box 1, "American Youth for Democracy."

37. *Daily Cardinal*, December 9, 1947; December 12, 1947.

38. *Daily Cardinal*, December 4, 1947; December 10, 1947; December 12, 1947.

39. *Daily Cardinal*, October 6, 1948; Bernard Herschel to Paul Trump, October 8, 1948, UW Archives, Series 19/2/6-5, Box 1, "American Youth for Democracy"; Ivan Nestingen to Paul Trump, November 4, 1948, UW Archives, Series 19/9/4-3, Box 1, "American Veterans Committee." For more on the controversy, see the numerous *Daily Cardinal* articles and editorials on the issue in October and early November 1948.

40. Paul Trump to Edward King, March 10, 1947, UW Archives, Series 19/2/6-5, Box 1, "American Youth for Democracy"; Student Life and Interests Committee, "Proposed Statement of the University of Wisconsin Committee on Student Life and Interests with respect to the local chapter of AYD," UW Archives, Series 19/5/3/4-3. Although I was unable to determine whether this statement was ever officially published, it represents the general direction of university policy with regard to AYD. Some of the very same language is used in a press release from Dean Paul Trump regarding the university's recognition of the John Cookson Marxist Discussion Club in 1947. See "Press Release," November 4, 1947, UW Archives, Series 19/2/6-5, Box 2, "John Cookson Marxist Discussion Club."

41. Cronon and Jenkins, *University of Wisconsin*, 4:91–92; "Chronological Resume," December 30, 1953, UW Archives, Series 19/2/6-1, Box 15, "Labor Youth League— SLIC Correspondence." The latter source includes a chronology of the entire controversy. For a list of other speakers brought to campus by LYL between 1950 and 1953, see "Off-Campus Speakers, Labor Youth League," January 16, 1953, UW Archives, Series 19/2/6-5, Box 2, "Labor Youth League." For information on the controversy over

Owen Lattimore's campus appearance in 1952, see UW Archives, Series 4/16/1, Box 169, "Lattimore, Owen."

42. *Daily Cardinal,* January 15, 1953; March 7, 1953; Group letter to E. B. Fred, December 5, 1953, UW Archives, Series 19/2/6–5, Box 2, "Labor Youth League."

43. "Campus Young Republicans," UW Archives, Series 19/9/4–2, Box 7, "Young Republicans"; *Daily Cardinal,* January 7, 1953; May 16, 1953.

44. *Daily Cardinal,* March 1, 1955; March 16, 1955; March 25, 1955; April 22, 1955. Kolko was the initial organizer of Wisconsin's Student League for Industrial Democracy in fall 1954 (an earlier chapter had existed at some time in the 1930s). The Madison group changed its name to the Wisconsin Liberal Club in 1955 to avoid association with communism and dissolved some time in 1957. The national group changed its name in 1960 to Students for a Democratic Society. On the noncommunist left's fear of association with communists, see Serrano, "Madison Bohemian," 70. The graduate student journal *Studies on the Left,* established in Madison in 1959, also attempted to avoid a public association with communists. See Eleanor Hakim to Eugene Genovese, April 30, 1961, Wisconsin Historical Society, *Studies on the Left* Records, Box 3, Folder 16.

45. *Daily Cardinal,* March 7, 1953; November 21, 1953; February 26, 1954; March 24, 1953; May 9, 1953.

46. *Daily Cardinal,* April 8, 1953; April 15, 1953; April 16, 1953; April 17, 1953; July 17, 1953. See Cronon and Jenkins, *University of Wisconsin,* 3:93, for an account of McCarthy's 1951 campus appearance. For the letter urging repeal of the McCarran Act, see *Daily Cardinal,* December 1, 1955. In his autobiography, Ron Radosh writes about this letter and claims that most of those who signed were either LYL members or fellow travelers, though it is difficult to verify the truth of this claim. See Radosh, *Commies,* 53–54.

47. Wisconsin Legislative Council, "University of Wisconsin Policies," December 1, 1954, UW Archives, Series 19/2/6–1, Box 15, "Labor Youth League—SLIC Correspondence." For a discussion of the Council's efforts, see "Where Is the University Going?" *Wisconsin Alumnus,* May 15, 1954. For another perspective of relations between the university and the legislature in the context of the McCarthy era, see Holzhueter, interview with the author. Holzhueter claims that when he was working at the *Daily Cardinal* in the middle fifties (after the legislature's review of the university), President Fred called Wisconsin Student Association president Helen Rehbein into his office and requested that she help mute criticism of the state legislature at the *Cardinal,* which she did. According to Holzhueter, Fred was concerned about the student newspaper angering conservatives in the legislature and threatening increases in the university budget.

48. William F. Thompson, *The History of Wisconsin,* vol. 6: *Continuity and Change, 1940–1965* (Madison: State Historical Society of Wisconsin, 1988), 581, 595–96.

49. For a useful chronology of the events surrounding this controversy, see "Chronological Resume." Also see President's Fred letter asking faculty to sit on his ad hoc committee on outside speakers, April 2, 1953, UW Archives, Series 4/16/1, Box 184, "Committees (Appointive)."

50. Theodore Zillman to E. B. Fred, December 28, 1953, UW Archives, Series 19/2/6-5, Box 2, "Labor Youth League"; "Review of Policy and Regulations Applying to the Registration of Student Organizations," March 16, 1953, UW Archives, Series 19/2/6-5, Box 2, "Labor Youth League."

51. Quoted in Cronon and Jenkins, *University of Wisconsin,* 3:406; Fred Harvey Harrington to Lloyd Hoene, October 30, 1962, UW Archives, Series 4/0/3, Box 21, "Communism, Miscellaneous"; Theodore Zillman to LeRoy Luberg, April 16, 1962, UW Archives, 19/2/3-5, Box 6, "Off Campus Speakers (Gus Hall, May 3, 1962)."

52. For a more general review of the ways in which the left was recreating itself in the late 1950s and early 1960s, see Isserman, *If I Had a Hammer.* Henry Wortis and Ron Radosh, both members of the Labor Youth League, present two different views of the relationship between the LYL and the Communist Party. Wortis recalls only infrequent visits to Madison by party members and describes LYL as a break from the Old Left because of the independence with which the group operated. Radosh, on the other hand, cites regular contacts between the Communist Party and the group in Madison, describing the league as taking very seriously the instructions that it received. See Wortis, interview with the author; Radosh, interview with the author, December 29, 2005.

53. *Daily Cardinal,* October 3, 1957; June 28, 1963. For more on the factions within the Socialist Club, see Franklynn Peterson, oral history, 1985, UW Oral History Project. For another perspective on the blending of Madison and New York radicalism, see Buhle, "Madison," 8.

54. Serrano, "Madison Bohemian," 74; Saul Landau, interview with the author, December 12, 2005. Serrano's involvement in the campus left in the 1950s raises the issue of women's participation during this period. For further discussion of this issue, see Baxandall, "Another Madison Bohemian," and Elizabeth Ewen, "A Way of Seeing," in Buhle, *History and the New Left.*

55. *Daily Cardinal,* May 14, 1957; May 23, 1957; March 11, 1961; November 14, 1961. On the peace movement's protests against civil defense programs, see Charles DeBenedetti, *An American Ordeal: The Antiwar Movement of the Vietnam Era* (Syracuse, NY: Syracuse University Press, 1990), 24. For another discussion of the 1950s peace movement, see Isserman, *If I Had a Hammer,* 125–69. Isserman especially emphasizes the importance of radical pacifism's direct action politics for the New Left.

Chapter 3. "A constant struggle with ideas"

1. John McMillian explores the charges that the New Left was anti-intellectual and offers his own argument on the influence of ideas in "Love Letters to the Future: REP, *Radical America,* and New Left History," *Radical History Review* 77 (Spring 2000).

2. Ellen Schrecker, *No Ivory Tower: McCarthyism and the Universities* (New York: Oxford University Press, 1986), 340. For the redefinition of academic freedom, see pages 105–12. Schrecker's description of McCarthyism in higher education draws on events at a large

number of universities, but focuses especially on a smaller group that includes Harvard, Cornell, the University of Michigan, the University of California, and the University of Washington. She discusses the University of Wisconsin at a number of points but does not suggest that it differed significantly from other universities during the era.

3. Ibid., 94–111.

4. Ibid.; Mark Engberg, "McCarthyism and the Academic Profession: Power, Politics, and Faculty Purges at the University of Michigan," *American Educational History Journal* 29 (2002): 57.

5. Schrecker, *No Ivory Tower*, 194–218; Bob Blauner, *Resisting McCarthyism: To Sign or Not to Sign California's Loyalty Oath* (Stanford, CA: Stanford University Press, 2009), xiii. For exceptions to the treatment of faculty during the McCarthy era, see Schrecker, *No Ivory Tower*, 149–60 and 213–15.

6. Fred Harvey Harrington, interview by Tom Bates, January 8, 1988, UW Oral History Project; "Red Editor's Speech Stirs Teapot Tempest," *Wisconsin Alumnus*, February 1954; Association of American Universities, "The Rights and Responsibilities of Universities and Their Faculties," March 24, 1953, UW Archives, Series 4/16/1, Box 182, "AAU (Academic Freedom)." For Fred's objections to the statement, see Schrecker, *No Ivory Tower*, 189, and Sigmund Diamond, *Compromised Campus: The Collaboration of Universities with the Intelligence Community, 1945–1955* (New York: Oxford University Press, 1992), 221–24.

7. E. David Cronon and John W. Jenkins, *The University of Wisconsin: A History*, vol. 4: *Renewal to Revolution, 1945–1971* (Madison: University of Wisconsin Press, 1999), 92, 401; Henry Lardy, oral history, 1983, UW Oral History Project; Blauner, *Resisting McCarthyism*. There were no high-profile cases where McCarthyism played a role in hiring or firing decisions at Wisconsin, but there are some references to the impact of McCarthyism that I have come across. Paul Buhle and Edward Rice-Maximin mention that several young professors were denied tenure for political reasons in the fifties, while Ron Radosh recalls that Dick Herschcopf, who had been a member of AYD, was denied a PhD by the History Department because of his political affiliations. See Paul Buhle and Edward Rice-Maximin, *William Appleman Williams: The Tragedy of Empire* (New York: Routledge, 1995), 45; and Ron Radosh, interview with the author, December 29, 2005. For a discussion of the impact of faculty radical politics on professional advancement in the late sixties in Madison, see James C. Scott, oral history, 1976, UW Oral History Project.

8. Daniel Bell, *The End of Ideology: On the Exhaustion of Political Ideas in the Fifties* (Glencoe, IL: Free Press, 1960). For more discussion of these trends, see Schrecker, *No Ivory Tower*; Ron Robin, *The Making of the Cold War Enemy: Culture and Politics in the Military-Intellectual Complex* (Princeton, NJ: Princeton University Press, 2001); and Noam Chomsky et al., *The Cold War and the University: Toward an Intellectual History of the Postwar Years* (New York: New Press, 1997).

9. The Higham quotation is from Jon Weiner, "Radical Historians and the Crisis in American History," *Journal of American History* 76 (1989): 402. For more on consensus

history, see Peter Novick, *That Noble Dream: The "Objectivity Question" and the American Historical Profession* (Cambridge: Cambridge University Press, 1988), 281–92, 320–60.

10. Conyers Read, "The Social Responsibilities of the Historian," December 29, 1949, American Historical Association, http://www.historians.org/info/AHA_History /cread.htm. For more on Read's speech and its context, see Novick, *That Noble Dream*, 318.

11. Francis Hole to E. B. Fred, April 15, 1953, UW Archives, Series 4/16/1, Box 182, "AAU (Academic Freedom)." For information on Link's activities, see Henry Lardy, oral history; Karl Paul Link, "Faculty Adviser's Report on the University of Wisconsin Chapter of the Labor Youth League, 1950–1956," January 14, 1957, UW Archives, Series 4/0/23, "Karl Paul Link Report."

12. *Daily Cardinal*, December 13, 1947; February 22, 1961. For Rice's involvement in campus civil liberties issues in the 1920s, see William Rice, oral history, 1974, UW Oral History Project.

13. Henry Lardy, oral history; James Crow, oral history, 1983, UW Oral History Project; Henry Wortis, interview with the author, March 6, 2005. See also Leon Epstein, interview with the author, February 8, 2006, for a discussion of the anti-McCarthy atmosphere in Madison as well as the caution that faculty exercised during the era.

14. For background on Gerth as well as his relationship with Mills, which included later collaboration on a number of projects, see Guy Oakes and Arthur Vidich, *Collaboration, Reputation, and Ethics in American Academic Life: Hans H. Gerth and C. Wright Mills* (Urbana: University of Illinois Press, 1999). For more on Gerth, see Buhle and Rice-Maximin, *William Appleman Williams*, 40–41; Eleanor Hakim, "The Tragedy of Hans Gerth," in Paul Buhle, ed., *History and the New Left: Madison, Wisconsin, 1950–1970* (Philadelphia: Temple University Press, 1990); Evan Stark, "In Exile," in Buhle, *History and the New Left*; Franklynn Peterson, interview with the author, December 19, 2005; Franklynn Peterson, oral history, 1985, UW Oral History Project.

15. George Mosse, *Confronting History: A Memoir* (Madison: University of Wisconsin Press, 2000); Paul Breines, interview with the author, December 8, 2000; Radosh, interview with the author; Paul Breines, "Remembering Madison, Mosse, and Mississippi," UW–Madison Department of History Newsletter, Fall 2007. Paul Breines has written in several places about Mosse and his influence in Madison during these years. See also Paul Breines, "The Mosse Milieu," in Buhle, *History and the New Left*.

16. "UW News," October 4, 1961, UW News Service, http://digital.library.wisc .edu/1711.dl/UW.HistoryDept, 242; Tom McCormick and Lloyd Gardner, "Walter LaFeber: The Making of a Wisconsin School Revisionist," *Diplomatic History* 28, no. 5 (November 2004).

17. McCormick and Gardner, "Walter LaFeber"; Tom McCormick, interview with the author, March 14, 2005; Buhle and Rice-Maximin, *William Appleman Williams*, 37. For neo-Beardian history in Madison, see Paul Buhle, "Madison: An Introduction," in *History and the New Left*. For Beale's campus activities, see *Daily Cardinal*, March 1, 1955; April 6, 1955; April 21, 1955; October 21, 1955; "Stick Your Neck Out," *Wisconsin Alumnus*, June 1952.

18. Merle Curti, "Intellectuals and Other People," December 29, 1954, American Historical Association, http://www.historians.org/info/AHA_History/mcurti.htm. On Curti and consensus history, see Novick, *That Noble Dream*, 318, 325; Buhle and Rice-Maximin, *William Appleman Williams*, 52; Buhle, "Madison: An Introduction," 21.

19. Rawick, "I Dissent," in Buhle, *History and the New Left*, 57; Saul Landau, "From the Labor Youth League to the Cuban Revolution," in Buhle, *History and the New Left*, 110; Paul Breines, "Mosse Milieu," 249. Although Rawick has little positive to say about most of the history faculty, he notes that Howard Beale protected him from another professor's attempt to red-bait him.

20. William Appleman Williams, *The Contours of American History* (1961; repr., Cleveland: World, 1966), 9. On Williams's brand of socialism, see McCormick, interview with the author; and Eleanor Hakim to Saul Landau, David Eakins, and Bob Blanchard, March 25, 1961, Wisconsin Historical Society, *Studies on the Left* Records. The best general source on Williams is Buhle and Rice-Maximin, *William Appleman Williams*.

21. William Appleman Williams, "Raymond Robbins and Russian-American Relations, 1917–1938," PhD diss., University of Wisconsin, 1950; William Appleman Williams, *American-Russian Relations, 1781–1947* (New York: Rinehart, 1952).

22. Williams, *American-Russian Relations*, 258–83.

23. William Appleman Williams, *The Tragedy of American Diplomacy* (Cleveland: World, 1959).

24. Ibid., 19, 209–10.

25. Buhle and Rice-Maximin, *William Appleman Williams*, 95–96, 114–16; Jon Weiner, "Radical Historians," 399, 404; William Appleman Williams FBI file.

26. Radosh, interview with the author; McCormick, interview with the author. For one example of Williams's influence outside of Madison, see James Miller, *Democracy Is in the Streets: From Port Huron to the Siege of Chicago* (1987; repr., Cambridge, MA: Harvard University Press, 1994), 170–72. Miller discusses the ways that Williams's work was understood by some of the early thinkers in Students for a Democratic Society.

27. Buhle and Rice-Maximin, *William Appleman Williams*, 104. The same event is recounted in Radosh, interview with the author; and the *Daily Cardinal*, February 22, 1961.

28. McCormick, interview with the author.

29. Bertell Ollman, "From Liberal, to Social Democrat, to Marxist: My Political Itinerary through Madison in the Late 1950s," in Buhle, *History and the New Left*, 106; Breines, interview with the author; Saul Landau, interview with author, December 12, 2005.

30. James Weinstein, "*Studies on the Left*," in Buhle, *History and the New Left*, 116–17. For the debate within *Studies* over intellectual work versus activism, see James Weinstein to Saul Landau, May 3, 1966, Wisconsin Historical Society, *Studies on the Left* Records, Box 5, Folder 18; and McCormick, interview with the author.

31. James Weinstein and David Eakins, eds., *For a New America: Essays in History and Politics from 'Studies on the Left': 1959–1967* (New York: Vintage Books, 1970), 6; "A Statement by the Editors," *Studies on the Left* 2, no. 3 (1962): 3. *Studies* mirrored the New Left in its

criticism of the infighting and sectarianism of the Old Left, but it could not entirely escape this past, as the editors decided in 1961 that it would be best to maintain distance from another journal, *Science and Society*, that was known at the time for its "Stalinist" (pro-Soviet Union) leanings. See Eleanor Hakim to Eugene Genovese, June 18, 1961, Wisconsin Historical Society, *Studies on the Left* Records, Box 3, Folder 16.

32. For Hakim's reference to dying young, see Lee Baxandall, "New York Meets Oshkosh," in Buhle, *History and the New Left*, 131; and Radosh, interview with the author. The list of initial *Studies on the Left* editors included Joan Bromberg, Lloyd Gardner, Saul Landau, Nancy O'Connor, William Rouff, Dena Samberg, Steve Scheinberg, Marty Sklar, and Carl Weiner. James Weinstein, who would soon move to Madison and become a pivotal player throughout the journal's life, was listed as New York correspondent in the first issue. On the importance of the distance from Old Left centers on the coasts, see Kevin Mattson, "Between Despair and Hope: Revisiting *Studies on the Left*," in Paul Buhle and John McMillian, eds., *The New Left Revisited* (Philadelphia: Temple University Press, 2003), 29–30.

33. "The Radicalism of Disclosure," *Studies on the Left* 1, no. 1 (1959).

34. Lloyd Gardner, "From New Deal to New Frontiers, 1937–1941," *Studies on the Left* 1, no. 1 (1959).

35. Van Gosse, *Where the Boys Are: Cuba, Cold War America, and the Making of a New Left* (New York: Verso, 1993), 1, 162–65; Landau, interview with the author.

36. "The Cuban Revolution: The New Crisis in Cold War Ideology," *Studies on the Left* 1, no. 3 (1960): 3.

37. Ibid.

38. John Kenneth Galbraith, *American Capitalism: The Concept of Countervailing Power* (Boston: Houghton Mifflin, 1952). A good source on the changes in liberalism from the 1930s to the postwar era is Alan Brinkley, *The End of Reform: New Deal Liberalism in Recession and War* (New York: Alfred A. Knopf, 1995). For a history of the ADA, see Steven Gillon, *Politics and Vision: The ADA and American Liberalism, 1947–1985* (New York: Oxford University Press, 1987).

39. Williams, *Contours of American History*, 439.

40. Marty Sklar, "Woodrow Wilson and the Political Economy of Modern United States Liberalism," in *Studies on the Left* 1, no. 3 (1960). For the evolution of Sklar's thinking about corporate liberalism, see Marty Sklar, *The Corporate Reconstruction of American Capitalism, 1890–1916: The Market, the Law, and Politics* (Cambridge: Cambridge University Press, 1988). For another example of the critique of liberalism from a *Studies* editor, see James Weinstein, *The Corporate Ideal in the Liberal State: 1900–1918* (Boston: Beacon Press, 1968).

41. "The Ultra-Right and Cold War Liberalism," *Studies on the Left* 3, no. 1 (1962): 3, 5.

42. The "Port Huron Statement" is available in a number of places. One that is easily accessible is at the end of Miller, *Democracy Is in the Streets*. For Carl Oglesby's speech, see "Let Us Shape the Future," November 27, 1965, http://www.antiauthoritarian.net/sds_wuo/sds_documents/oglesby_future.html.

43. Saul Landau to *Studies on the Left* office, November 10, 1961, Wisconsin Historical Society, *Studies on the Left* Records.

44. "Civil Rights and the Birth of Community," *Studies on the Left* 1, no. 2 (1960): 2; *Studies on the Left* office to C. Clark Kissinger, May 13, 1963, Wisconsin Historical Society, *Studies on the Left* Records, Box 5, Folder 8.

Chapter 4. "I can't be calm, cool, and detached any longer"

1. American Veterans Committee, "Just a Little Thing," leaflet, UW Archives, Series 19/2/6-5, Box 1, "American Veterans Committee." After his graduation from the UW Law School, Theodore Coggs and his wife Pauline moved to Milwaukee where they became active in civil rights and state politics. For the Committee Against Discrimination report, see Board of Regents, "Document 933," January 9, 1950, UW Archives, Records of the Minutes of the Regents of the University of Wisconsin. For an even longer history of efforts against housing discrimination at the university, including discrimination against Jews, see Jonathan Pollack, "Jewish Problems: Eastern and Western Jewish Identities in Conflict at the University of Wisconsin, 1919–1941," *American Jewish History* 89, no. 2 (June 2001).

2. Board of Regents, minutes, November 11, 1950; December 9, 1950. In 1952, the Regents approved Faculty Document 1041, which included the substance of 933. For more on the SLIC report and early university efforts on discrimination, see E. David Cronon and John W. Jenkins, *The University of Wisconsin: A History*, vol. 4: *Renewal to Revolution, 1945–1971* (Madison: University of Wisconsin Press, 1999), 386–98. For one critical view of the university's efforts in the mid-1950s, see *Daily Cardinal*, May 22, 1956. The attempt by the faculty to force university organizations to remove discriminatory clauses from their charters was put into place when the Board of Regents approved it in 1952. The result was the "1960 clause," which gave existing campus organizations until 1960 to comply with the policy while denying recognition to any new organization with a discriminatory clause in its charter.

3. *Daily Cardinal*, February 27, 1960; March 1, 1960. See also Saul Landau, interview with the author, December 12, 2005; Paul Breines, interview with the author, December 8, 2000; Franklynn Peterson, interview with the author, December 19, 2005.

4. James O'Brien, "The Development of a New Left in the United States," PhD diss., University of Wisconsin–Madison, 1971, 83–84, 89; *Daily Cardinal*, March 1, 1960; March 4, 1960; May 18, 1960.

5. *Daily Cardinal*, March 3, 1960; March 4, 1960; May 18, 1960; May 19, 1960; Gaylord Nelson, speech, March 3, 1960, UW Archives, Series 19/2/3-5, Box 4, "Discrimination—Rallies, Marches, Picketing, Spring of 1960."

6. *Daily Cardinal*, March 3, 1960; March 4, 1960; March 8, 1960. For a history of the WSA Human Relations Committee during this period, see "History Fact Sheet," July

1960, UW Archives, Series 19/9/4–3, Box 8, "Student Council for Civil Rights." Some students also raised broader critiques of the civil rights movement. See, for example, *Daily Cardinal*, March 2, 1960. The critique of "emotion" was not new in 1960. In the 1950s, the campus paper praised the use of "reason" in the place of "emotion" in dealing with the campus race problem and criticized the Wisconsin Liberal Club for its "emotionalism" during a public spat with the American Legion. See *Daily Cardinal*, October 15, 1954; February 17, 1956.

7. *Daily Cardinal*, March 4, 1960; "Students Picket Woolworth Store to Protest Southern Segregation," *Capital Times*, February 27, 1960. In the days leading up the campus demonstration, the administration expressed a degree of caution about the upcoming march. See *Daily Cardinal*, March 2, 1960.

8. *Daily Cardinal*, June 23, 1961; October 6, 1962; June 30, 1964; "Rights March Here Disrupted," *Wisconsin State Journal*, September 23, 1963. Civil rights leaders were sponsored by a variety of campus groups in their trips to Madison. Others who came to campus included James Farmer, the national director of CORE, minister and King associate Ralph Abernathy, and minister and Birmingham leader Fred Shuttlesworth. Martin Luther King Jr. and Malcolm X came to campus within two weeks of each other in 1962, King invited by the university for a campus symposium and Malcolm X invited by a student group.

9. *Daily Cardinal*, March 10, 1965; March 16, 1965; March 17, 1965; March 18, 1965; March 19, 1965; March 20, 1965; Robben Fleming, *Tempests into Rainbows: Managing Turbulence* (Ann Arbor: University of Michigan Press, 1996), 147–48.

10. *Daily Cardinal*, December 13, 1960. For information on the number of black students at the university, see Ruth Doyle, "Profile of the Negro Student," May 13, 1965, Wisconsin Historical Society, Ruth Doyle Papers. For information on the number of black faculty, see *Daily Cardinal*, May 7, 1964.

11. "NAACP Denies Part in Picketing of Sears," *Wisconsin State Journal*, March 23, 1964. For Colston's 1963 hints about possible demonstrations in Madison, see *Capital Times*, July 25, 1963; July 30, 1963. For information on Madison's black population, see William F. Thompson, *The History of Wisconsin*, vol. 6: *Continuity and Change, 1940–1965* (Madison: State Historical Society of Wisconsin, 1988); and Naomi Lede, *Madison's Negro Population: A Report Made for the Community Welfare Council of Madison, National Urban League* (Madison, 1966).

12. "NAACP 2nd Shift on Capitol Vigil," *Capital Times*, August 1, 1961; "Governor's Sister Joins Vigil of Capitol 'Liberty Lobbyists,'" *Capital Times*, August 2, 1961; "Lonely Weekend for Rights 'Lobby,'" *Capital Times*, August 5, 1961; James McWilliams to Lloyd Barbee, September 23, 1961, Wisconsin Historical Society, Lloyd Barbee Papers, Box 13, Folder 17; Odell Taliaferro to James McWilliams, September 26, 1961, Box 14, Folder 11.

13. Breines, interview with the author. For more on Dylan's stop in Madison, see Breines, interview with the author; and Ron Radosh, *Commies: A Journey through the Old*

Left, the New Left, and the Leftover Left (San Francisco: Encounter Books, 2001), 76–77. Danny Kalb went on to play guitar and vocals for The Blues Project in the 1960s and 1970s and continues to work as a musician.

14. Stuart Ewen, "The Intellectual New Left," in Paul Buhle, ed., *History and the New Left: Madison, Wisconsin, 1950–1970* (Philadelphia: Temple University Press, 1990), 180.

15. W. J. Rorabaugh, *Berkeley at War: The 1960s* (New York: Oxford University Press, 1989), 19–20. On Freedom Summer, see Doug McAdam, *Freedom Summer* (New York: Oxford University Press, 1988). For another perspective from Madison students on the dangers of working in the South, see Robert and Vicki Gabriner, open letter, June 19, 1964, Wisconsin Historical Society, Robert and Vicki Gabriner Papers, Box 1.

16. Ewen, "Intellectual New Left," 180.

17. *Daily Cardinal*, March 7, 1963. For SDS's founding, see C. Clark Kissinger to James Weinstein, November 26, 1963, Wisconsin Historical Society, *Studies on the Left* Records, Box 5, Folder 8.

18. Elizabeth Ewen, "A Way of Seeing," in Buhle, *History and the New Left*, 149–50 (emphasis in the original); Joseph Kauffman in Joan Page, "News Bureau: University of North Carolina-Chapel Hill," February 19, 1966, UW Archives, Series 4/19/1, Box 38, "Student Affairs—Miscellaneous—1965–66."

19. *Daily Cardinal*, February 5, 1960; symposium participant statements, Wisconsin Historical Society, John Patrick Hunter Papers, Box 1, "The Sixties: Challenge to our Generation Symposium." A number of historians have written about the connections between the Cold War and the civil rights movement. See Mary Dudziak, *Cold War Civil Rights: Race and the Image of American Democracy* (Princeton, NJ: Princeton University Press, 2000); Thomas Borstelmann, *The Cold War and the Color Line* (Cambridge, MA.: Harvard University Press, 2001); Penny Von Eschen, *Race against Empire: Black Americans and Anti-colonialism, 1937–1957* (Ithaca, NY: Cornell University Press, 1997); and Brenda Plummer, *Rising Wind: Black Americans and U.S. Foreign Affairs, 1935–1960* (Chapel Hill: University of North Carolina Press, 1996). In Madison, there was always significant overlap between student groups working on civil rights and those working on issues related to the Cold War. Interestingly, it was a Pete Seeger concert to raise money for the Montgomery Bus Boycott in 1956 that proved to be the immediate cause of the UW Labor Youth League's dissolution. A scheduling mistake by the LYL brought penalties against the group's two officers, and with no other members willing to take public leadership roles (a university requirement), the group soon folded.

20. For more information on SANE and other individuals and groups involved in the fight against U.S. Cold War policies in the 1950s and early 1960s, see Charles DeBenedetti, *An American Ordeal: The Antiwar Movement of the Vietnam Era* (Syracuse, NY: Syracuse University Press, 1990), 9–80.

21. O'Brien, "Development of a New Left," 167–202; *Daily Cardinal*, March 10, 1961; November 14, 1961; March 27, 1962.

22. James Hawley, interview with the author, November 22, 2000; John Coatsworth, interview with the author, November 22, 2000. Hawley is perhaps most

notorious for his minor role at SDS's Port Huron conference. Hawley attended the conference as a nonvoting delegate. The decision by SDS to allow him to observe despite his membership in a Communist Party–affiliated group had significant implications for the group's positioning relative to the Old Left. For an account of Hawley's involvement in the conference, see James Miller, *Democracy Is in the Streets: From Port Huron to the Siege of Chicago* (New York: Simon and Schuster, 1987), 116.

23. DeBenedetti, *American Ordeal*, 83.

24. Vietnam troop numbers are available in many places. For one source, see David Farber and Beth Bailey, *The Columbia Guide to the 1960s* (New York: Columbia University Press, 2001), 387.

25. *Daily Cardinal*, February 10, 1965; February 13, 1965. "Vietnam" has become the common usage in the United States, but in the 1960s it was often referred to as "Viet Nam," and the organization's acronym was sometimes written as CEWVN.

26. *Daily Cardinal*, March 30, 1965; DeBenedetti, *American Ordeal*, 114–15.

27. *Daily Cardinal*, May 6, 1965.

28. Petition, December 3, 1964, UW Archives, Series 4/18/1, Box 84, "Madison Chancellor"; *Daily Cardinal*, March 21, 1967.

29. *Daily Cardinal*, March 31, 1965; April 2, 1965.

30. *Daily Cardinal*, April 2, 1965. Williams's speech is reprinted as "Our Leaders Are Following the Wrong Rainbows," in Ron Radosh and Louis Menashe, eds., *Teach-Ins: U.S.A.: Reports, Opinions, Documents* (New York: Frederick A. Praeger, 1967). For another view from Williams, see his testimony to a panel convened by Madison-area Democratic congressman Robert Kastenmeier in 1965. The testimony is included in *Vietnam Hearings: Voices from the Grassroots* (Waterloo, WI: Artcraft Press, 1965).

31. Committee to End the War in Vietnam, "Organizing a Vietnam Protest Committee," [1965?], Wisconsin Historical Society Pamphlet Collection.

32. The *Newsweek* poll is cited in O'Brien, "The Development of a New Left," 403; "Background of the Committee to Support the People of South Vietnam," April 1965, Wisconsin Historical Society, Judith Faber Papers; *Daily Cardinal*, July 22, 1965. Interestingly, Gordon did not make mention of "New Yorkers," a common euphemism for out-of-state and/or Jewish students. Of the two Robert Gordons listed in the UW student directory that year, one was from New York City and the other from Highland Park, a Chicago suburb known for its large Jewish population.

33. *Daily Cardinal*, November 1, 1956; November 2, 1960; Howard H. Peckham, *The Making of the University of Michigan* (Ann Arbor: University of Michigan Press, 1967), 249. For information on *Insight and Outlook*, see "Insight and Outlook," *Wisconsin Alumnus*, December 1963; *Daily Cardinal*, Fall Registration Issue, 1965.

34. The best source on the origins of Young Americans for Freedom is John Andrew, *The Other Side of the Sixties: Young Americans for Freedom and the Rise of Conservative Politics* (New Brunswick, NJ: Rutgers University Press, 1997).

35. *Daily Cardinal*, July 8, 1965; May 5, 1965; August 3, 1965. For two views on the effectiveness of the campus right during this period, see *Daily Cardinal*, April 15, 1965,

208 ◆ *Notes to pages 129–132*

and April 28, 1965. Interestingly, conservative student groups sometimes took positions at odds with adult conservatives. In 1965, for example, the campus chapter of Young Americans for Freedom came out publicly in support of black voting rights in Alabama. See *Daily Cardinal*, March 12, 1965.

36. For Madison activities during the International Days of Protest, see *Daily Cardinal*, October 13, 1965. For national activities as well as background information on the National Coordinating Committee to End the War in Vietnam, see DeBenedetti, *American Ordeal*, 121–22, 125–26.

37. For a small sample of the many SDS-centric histories of the sixties, which were especially prevalent in early histories written about the era, see Kirkpatrick Sale, *SDS* (New York: Random House, 1973); James Miller, *Democracy Is in the Streets*; and Todd Gitlin, *The Sixties: Years of Hope, Days of Rage* (New York: Bantam, 1987). Membership numbers for student organizations are notoriously difficult to pin down. CEWV claimed 150 members in a pamphlet issued in 1965 or 1966, a number repeated in the *Daily Cardinal*. Another observer, a regional coordinator for the communist W. E. B. DuBois Club, put the number of members at 450 in fall 1965. See Committee to End the War in Vietnam, "Organizing a Vietnam Protest Committee"; *Daily Cardinal*, February 23, 1966; Michael Eisenscher, "Midwest Regional Coordinator Report," September 29, 1965, Wisconsin Historical Society, Michael Eisenscher Papers, Box 1, Folder 3. Finally, on the role of Madison's SDS chapter during these early years of the antiwar movement, one survey of the liberal and left groups on campus placed it near the middle of the pack, to the left of the liberal Americans for Democratic Action but to the right of groups like the Socialist Club, the Young People's Socialist League, and the W. E. B. DuBois Club. See *Daily Cardinal*, April 28, 1965.

38. Hawley, interview with the author; Coatsworth, interview with the author; *Daily Cardinal*, Fall New Student Edition, 1965.

39. Committee to End the War in Vietnam, "Organizing a Vietnam Protest Committee."

40. Eisenscher, "Midwest Regional Coordinator Report"; *Daily Cardinal*, February 23, 1966; Committee to End the War in Vietnam, "Organizing a Vietnam Protest Committee."

41. *Daily Cardinal*, April 14, 1960; Thomas Jacobson, address to the State Conference of NAACP Branches, October 21, 1961, Wisconsin Historical Society, Lloyd Barbee Papers.

42. *Daily Cardinal*, March 24, 1964.

43. Frank Emspak made these remarks at a panel discussion titled "The War at Home Continued" at the UW–Madison, September 23, 2003. Other panelists included former UW student and Madison mayor Paul Soglin and former UW sociology professor Maurice Zeitlin. For some of the varying opinions regarding direct action expressed by the editors of the *Cardinal*, see, for example, *Daily Cardinal*, May 12, 1961; June 22, 1961; October 3, 1962; March 9, 1963; November 9, 1963; June 19, 1964.

44. Donald Janson, *Nation*, May 24, 1965 (reprinted in Radosh and Menashe, *Teach-Ins*); *Daily Cardinal*, May 7, 1965.

45. *Daily Cardinal*, May 8, 1965; May 12, 1965; May 13, 1965.

46. *Daily Cardinal*, May 12, 1965; May 20, 1965.

47. *Daily Cardinal*, October 19, 1965; May 24, 1966; "Special University of Wisconsin Faculty Meeting," May 23, 1966, minutes, UW Archives, Series 4/19/1, Box 38, "Students—Sit-in—May 1966."

Chapter 5. "We must stop what we oppose"

1. Dow has been written about in several other places, most prominently David Maraniss's *They Marched into Sunlight: War and Peace, Vietnam and America, October 1967* (New York: Simon and Schuster, 2003).

2. Students for a Democratic Society, leaflet, October 1967, Wisconsin Historical Society, James P. O'Brien Papers, Box 1; *Daily Cardinal*, February 14, 1968.

3. One source with information on troop numbers in Vietnam is David Farber and Beth Bailey, *The Columbia Guide to the 1960s* (New York: Columbia University Press, 2001), 387.

4. *Daily Cardinal*, October 28, 1966.

5. Ibid.; Tyler Kennedy and David Null, "The History of 20th Century Protests and Social Action at UW–Madison," UW–Madison Libraries, http://archives.library .wisc.edu/uw-archives/exhibits/protests/1960s.html. For a sympathetic, but critical, perspective on the incident, see Michael Meeropol and Gerald Markowitz, "Neighborhood Politics," in Paul Buhle, ed., *History and the New Left: Madison, Wisconsin, 1950–1970* (Philadelphia: Temple University Press, 1990), 213–14.

6. Madison Committee to End the War in Vietnam, October 30, 1966, Wisconsin Historical Society, Madison Committee to End the War in Vietnam Records, Box 2, Folder 3. The statement was also published in the *Daily Cardinal*, November 2, 1966.

7. Robben Fleming, "The Enforcement of Chapter 11 of the Laws and Regulations Governing the University of Wisconsin," March 6, 1967, Wisconsin Historical Society, Adam Schesch Papers, Box 1, Folder 5; *Daily Cardinal*, December 13, 1966.

8. *Daily Cardinal*, December 7, 1966; April 12, 1967; "A Brief Chronology of the Development of the Student Protest Movement on the University of Wisconsin, Madison Campus, 1965 to Sterling Hall Bombing," 1972, UW Archives; "Class Level by Selected Attitudes of All Degree Seeking Students at the University of Wisconsin–Madison," January 7, 1966, UW Archives, Series 4/19/1, Box 38, "Student Affairs—Miscellaneous—1965–66"; *Daily Cardinal*, April 5, 1967. The chronology referenced here was compiled by the office of Robert Taylor, vice president for university relations. Although it often focuses on official university developments, it provides an invaluable reference on the late sixties in Madison. For another account of the protest at the Milwaukee induction

center, see Jody Chandler, "Wisconsin Draft Resistance Union," 1968, Wisconsin Historical Society Pamphlet Collection.

9. *Daily Cardinal*, March 3, 1967; May 18, 1967.

10. "A Brief Chronology"; Chandler, "Wisconsin Draft Resistance Union."

11. *Daily Cardinal*, April 15, 1967; May 9, 1967.

12. Ken Lundgren, "A Brief Description, History and Appreciation of the Green Lantern Eating Cooperative," 1963, Wisconsin Historical Society, Green Lantern Eating Cooperative Records, Box 1, Folder 1; Franklynn Peterson, interview with the author, December 19, 2005; *Daily Cardinal*, October 31, 1959. The Rat is a recurring topic in recollections of Madison during these years, including the interviews I conducted. For a more general history of the Rathskeller, see Robert Gard, *University-Madison-USA* (Madison: Straus, 1970), 127–31.

13. Henry Wortis, interview with the author, March 6, 2005; Saul Landau, interview with the author, December 12, 2005; *Daily Cardinal*, March 20, 1957; April 9, 1957. The Anti-Military Ball continued at least through 1965. See "Ninth Annual Military Ball," *Crisis* [Madison], April 2, 1965. Some of the skits performed at Anti-Military Balls in the late 1950s, including those written by Marshall Brickman, are collected in the Student Peace Center Records at the Wisconsin Historical Society. On Marshall Brickman, see Ron Radosh, interview with the author, December 29. 2005; Ron Radosh, *Commies: A Journey through the Old Left, the New Left, and the Leftover Left* (San Francisco: Encounter Books, 2001), 49–63.

14. Stuart Ewen, "The Intellectual New Left," in Buhle, *History and the New Left*, 181.

15. *Connections*, April 1, 1967; *Daily Cardinal*, April 7, 1967; October 18, 1967; *Connections*, October 2, 1967. The relationship between the counterculture and the New Left has been taken up in many places. One interesting perspective is from Doug Rossinow, "The New Left in the Counterculture: Hypotheses and Evidence," *Radical History Review* 67 (Winter 1997).

16. *Daily Cardinal*, December 18, 1963; December 19, 1963; December 20, 1963; Ralph Hanson, "The Madison Campus and the Dangerous Drug Problem: A Report and Recommendations," 1970, UW Archives, Series 1/4/3, Box 1.

17. "Advisory Committee on Student Problems," February 17, 1966, UW Archives, Series 19/2/3–7, Box 1, "Advisory Committee on Student Problems, 1965–66"; *Daily Cardinal*, May 10, 1967; *Connections*, April 1, 1967.

18. Fleming is quoted in E. David Cronon and John W. Jenkins, *The University of Wisconsin: A History*, vol. 4: *Renewal to Revolution, 1945–1971* (Madison: University of Wisconsin Press, 1999), 458; Leon Epstein, interview with the author, February 8, 2006; "A Brief Chronology of the Development of the Student Protest Movement."

19. On SDS's lack of a formal role in Dow, see James O'Brien, "An Informal History of Madison SDS," n.d., Wisconsin Historical Society, Students for a Democratic Society Records, Box 43.

20. *Daily Cardinal*, December 8, 1966; March 11, 1967; April 6, 1967; April 11, 1967; October 17, 1967.

21. *Daily Cardinal,* October 7, 1966; December 14, 1966; March 23, 1967. For a list of the some of the group's early leaders, see *Daily Cardinal,* September 27, 1967.

22. Paul Soglin was mayor of Madison from 1973 until 1979, from 1989 until 1997, and was elected again in 2011.

23. *Daily Cardinal,* December 9, 1966; September 28, 1967; Madison SDS, "A Student Handbook," September 1967, Wisconsin Historical Society, Social Action Vertical File, Box 49, "SDS—UW." While student groups made increasing noise about classified research taking place on campus, the university generally denied that any such projects existed at the UW, though it did acknowledge that some university faculty and staff might be engaged in classified work as consultants or in off-campus duties. See University Committee, "Dear Colleagues," November 12, 1969, UW Archives, Series 5/96/3, Box 5, "University-Military Relationship"; and Eric Rude, oral history, 1999, UW Oral History Project. There is evidence, however, that the university was aware of some classified research. See, for example, Board of Regents, May 9, 1953, Records of the Minutes of the Regents of the University of Wisconsin, UW Archives and University Committee, "University Policy on Publication or Research Results," January 28, 1967, UW Archives, Series 4/19/1, Box 45, "Committee—University—1966–1967."

24. Madison SDS, "A Student Handbook"; *Connections,* April 16, 1967. This critique of the university and society owed much to Herbert Marcuse, especially his argument, stated most explicitly in 1964's *One-Dimensional Man,* on the ways that contemporary capitalism integrated men and women into the status quo and limited oppositional thinking and behavior. For a brief discussion of Marcuse's influence, see Ewen, "Intellectual New Left," 181.

25. Student Peace Center, "Some Observations on University Life at Wisconsin," December 15, 1964, UW Archives, Series 4/19/1, Box 31, "Free Speech Movement (California)"; Committee on the Noncurricular Life of Students, "Report of the Noncurricular Life of Students Committee," August 12, 1965, UW Archives, Series 5/106, Box 1; Leon Epstein, interview with the author; James Villemonte, oral history, 1982, UW Oral History Project.

26. *Daily Cardinal,* February 28, 1967.

27. Carol Walton, "The University as an Independent Radical Base," *Call,* October 12, 1966; *Daily Cardinal,* May 12, 1967; C. Wright Mills, "Letter to the New Left," in *New Left Review* 5 (September–October 1960). The view that university-based protest could reverberate into radical social change was repeated after Dow as well. See Paul Buhle, "The Key: Student Spontaneity," *Call,* November 1967.

28. Maraniss, *They Marched into Sunlight,* 69–76; Dick Krooth, "Dow Chemical Company, Vietnam, Napalm, and You," n.d., Wisconsin Historical Society, James P. O'Brien Papers, Box 1.

29. *Daily Cardinal,* October 10, 1967; October 12, 1967; October 14, 1967; John Coatsworth, interview with the author, November 22, 2000; James O'Brien, "Some Muddled Thoughts on the Need for Clarity of Ideas," *Call,* October 6, 1967; Bob Kent, "When Dow Comes," *Call,* October 6, 1967; O'Brien, "Informal History of Madison

SDS." Protests earlier in 1967 prompted similar discussions about how best to confront the university and stop the war. See, for example, *Connections*, April 16, 1967, and Chandler, "Wisconsin Draft Resistance Union."

30. Coatsworth, interview with the author; "Sit-In by UW Students Protests Draft 'Tie-In,'" *Wisconsin State Journal*, May 17, 1966; James Gilbert to James Weinstein, n.d., Wisconsin Historical Society, *Studies on the Left* Records, Box 3, Folder 19. In recalling the debates leading up to Dow, Coatsworth points out that the New Left was not a democracy and that Cohen, Stark, and a group of other like-minded activists were prepared to obstruct Dow no matter what the majority decided. For William Sewell's perspective on Cohen and Stark, see Sewell, oral history, 1977, UW Oral History Project.

31. Madison SDS, leaflet, October 1967, Wisconsin Historical Society, James P. O'Brien Papers, Box 1.

32. *Daily Cardinal*, October 19, 1967; October 20, 1967; "After a Warning, the Clubs Swing," *Wisconsin State Journal*, October 19, 1967. I have leaned heavily on the accounts of the demonstration in the *Daily Cardinal* and the *Wisconsin State Journal*, though Madison's other daily newspaper, the *Capital Times*, also reported on the demonstration, and *Connections*, Madison's countercultural newspaper, published a long recap of the events in the weeks following.

33. *Daily Cardinal*, October 18, 1967; "UW Protesters Hit Dow's Line Again," *Wisconsin State Journal*, October 18, 1967.

34. *Daily Cardinal*, October 10, 1967; John Cumbler, "Effectiveness of the New Left," *Call* 1, no. 3 (1966); James Rowen, transcript, "Two Days in October," 2005, PBS, http://www.pbs.org/wgbh/amex/twodays/filmmore/pt.html.

35. Madison SDS, "Why We Sit In," 1967, Wisconsin Historical Society, Students for a Democratic Society Records, Box 43; Madison SDS, leaflet, October 1967, Wisconsin Historical Society, James P. O'Brien Papers, Box 1.

36. *Daily Cardinal*, October 19, 1967; "After a Warning, the Clubs Swing," *Wisconsin State Journal*, October 19, 1967; Rowen, "Two Days in October." For background on the San Francisco Mime Troupe, see Maraniss, *They Marched into Sunlight*, 166–70.

37. Petition, December 3, 1964, UW Archives, Series 4/18/1, Box 84, "Madison Chancellor"; *Daily Cardinal*, April 3, 1965; Robben Fleming, *Tempests into Rainbows: Managing Turbulence* (Ann Arbor: University of Michigan Press, 1996), 149; Sewell, oral history. For an extended discussion of the background and antiwar views of Sewell and Dean of Students Joe Kauffman, see Maraniss, *They Marched into Sunlight*, 119–38.

38. *Daily Cardinal*, February 23, 1967; February 24, 1967. For a detailed account of the February protest from a member of SDS, see Hank Haslach, "Dow Chemical Protest," 1967, Wisconsin Historical Society, Students for a Democratic Society Records, Box 43.

39. *Daily Cardinal*, February 28, 1967; February 24, 1967; Fleming, *Tempests into Rainbows*, 150–52; *Connections*, April 16, 1967; O'Brien, "Informal History of Madison SDS."

40. University of Wisconsin–Madison News Service, "Fact Sheet," January 26, 1973, UW Archives, http://digicoll.library.wisc.edu/cgi-bin/UW/UW-idx?id=UW .DemProDisGen; Fleming, "Enforcement of Chapter 11"; *Daily Cardinal*, February 24, 1967; Sewell, oral history.

41. Sewell, oral history. Fred Harvey Harrington also confirms the increasingly conservative turn of the Board of Regents in the middle and late 1960s. See Fred Harvey Harrington, interview by Tom Bates, January 8, 1988, UW Oral History Project.

42. "A Brief Chronology"; *Daily Cardinal*, February 23, 1967; Leon Epstein, interview with the author. For another faculty perspective on "neutrality," see R. H. Dott Jr. and C. J. Bowser, *Daily Cardinal*, April 5, 1967.

43. "76 Hurt in UW Rioting," *Wisconsin State Journal*, October 19, 1967; "After a Warning, the Clubs Swing," *Wisconsin State Journal*, October 19, 1967; *Daily Cardinal*, October 19, 1967.

44. Ibid.; Keith Hackett and James Rowen, "Two Days in October."

45. "76 Hurt in UW Rioting," *Wisconsin State Journal*, October 19, 1967; "After a Warning, the Clubs Swing," *Wisconsin State Journal*, October 19, 1967; *Daily Cardinal*, October 19, 1967.

46. Sewell, oral history; Haskell Fain, oral history, 1976, UW Oral History Project.

47. "Students, Faculty Vote Strike Today," *Wisconsin State Journal*, October 19, 1967; "13 Protesters Suspended," *Wisconsin State Journal*, October 20, 1967; *Daily Cardinal*, October 19, 1967; October 20, 1967.

48. "Faculty Backs Sewell's Handling of UW Riots," *Wisconsin State Journal*, October 20, 1967. Haskell Fain was one of the antiwar faculty who parted with students on the Dow protests. Even as he had pleaded with Sewell to call off the police, he spoke at one of the student rallies in the following days and gave an "angry" speech, "scolding" students for precipitating the violence on campus. See Fain, oral history.

49. "Chief Looks Back on 'Fight for Life,'" *Wisconsin State Journal*, October 20, 1967; *Daily Cardinal*, October 19, 1967; Sewell, oral history; Cronon and Jenkins, *University of Wisconsin*, 4:463.

50. *Daily Cardinal*, February 14, 1968; James Rowen, oral history, 1978, UW Oral History Project; Paul Buhle, "The Key: Student Spontaneity"; *Connections*, November 1, 1967.

51. Madison SDS, "Pre History," October 1967, Wisconsin Historical Society, James P. O'Brien Papers, Box 1; Buhle, "Key"; Rowen, "Two Days in October."

52. *Daily Cardinal*, October 28, 1967.

Chapter 6. Endings and Beginnings

1. Paul Buhle, "*Radical America* and Me," in Buhle, ed., *History and the New Left: Madison, Wisconsin, 1950–1970* (Philadelphia: Temple University Press, 1990), 229. For administrators' reference to "the troubles," see Leon Epstein, interview with the author,

February 8, 2006, and Fred Harvey Harrington, oral history, January 8, 1988, UW Oral History Project.

2. *Daily Cardinal*, February 14, 1968; May 11, 1968. In addition to the regular articles in the *Cardinal*, two manuscript sources on Dow's aftermath are "Injunction, Subpoena, Suspension, Violence—The Guns of a Great University," November 16, 1967, Wisconsin Historical Society, James O'Brien Papers, Box 1; and "A Brief Chronology of the Development of the Student Protest Movement on the University of Wisconsin, Madison Campus, 1965 to Sterling Hall Bombing," 1972, UW Archives.

3. *Daily Cardinal*, March 6, 1968; March 14, 1968. For accounts by two faculty members on the committee, see Haskell Fain, oral history, 1976, UW Oral History Project, and Samuel Mermin, "Student Protest and the American University: A Case Study," *Kobe University Law Review*, International Edition 8 (1972).

4. In addition to the regular *Daily Cardinal* coverage of campus protests during this era, two additional sources include "Brief Chronology"; and Tyler C. Kennedy and David Null, "The History of 20th Century Protests and Social Action at UW–Madison," UW–Madison Libraries, http://archives.library.wisc.edu/uw-archives/exhibits/protests/1970s.html.

5. A useful discussion of the changing demographics of the New Left is Robbie Lieberman, *Prairie Power: Voices of 1960s Midwestern Student Protest* (Columbia: University of Missouri Press, 2004).

6. Buhle, "*Radical America* and Me," 220; Madison SDS, "On the Relationship between Madison SDS and the SDS National Organization," July 1969, Wisconsin Historical Society, James O'Brien Papers, Box 1. Other sources on Madison's divergence from the national direction of SDS include *Badger Herald*, September 25, 1969, and James Rowen, oral history, 1978, UW Oral History Project. One of the best sources on the history of SDS, including the 1969 convention, is still Kirkpatrick Sale, *SDS* (New York: Random House, 1973).

7. For more information on the dissolution of *Studies on the Left*, see *Studies on the Left* Editorial Board to Dear Friend, August 9, 1967, Wisconsin Historical Society, *Studies on the Left* Records, Box 15, Folder 4; and the introductory essay in James Weinstein and David Eakins, eds., *For a New America: Essays in History and Politics from "Studies on the Left," 1959–1967* (New York: Random House, 1970).

8. James O'Brien, "Spring Offensive," 1968, Wisconsin Historical Society, James P. O'Brien Papers, Box 1; "Tentative Program Outline for the Radical Education Project," Wisconsin Historical Society, James P. O'Brien Papers, Box 2; Buhle, "*Radical America* and Me." For a history of the Radical Education Project and *Radical America*, see John McMillian, "Love Letters to the Future: REP, *Radical America*, and New Left History," *Radical History Review* 77 (2000).

9. Robert McBride, "SDS and Radical Education: One View," *Call*, October 6, 1967; Thomas Jacobson, address to the State Conference of NAACP Branches, October 21, 1961, Wisconsin Historical Society, Lloyd Barbee Papers; Madison SDS, "Obstruct the CIA," November 1967, Wisconsin Historical Society, James P. O'Brien Papers, Box

1; Madison SDS, "SDS and the Obstruction of the CIA," n.d., Wisconsin Historical Society, James P. O'Brien Papers, Box 1; *Daily Cardinal*, February 8, 1968.

10. *Daily Cardinal*, May 1, 1968; June 25, 1968.

11. "The Politics of Obstruction: An Analysis," n.d., Wisconsin Historical Society, Patrick Quinn Papers, Box 2, Folder 2; Michael Meeropol and Gerald Markowitz, "Neighborhood Politics," in Buhle, *History and the New Left*, 213; Michael Meeropol, "How Did an 'Old Left' Background Guide One Individual's 'Take' on the Explosion of New Left Activity after 1966?" *Vietnam Generation* 7, no. 1–2 (1996); *Daily Cardinal*, February 8, 1968; "Wisconsin Alliance Party: What We Believe and Why We Believe It," October 2, 1970, Wisconsin Historical Society Pamphlet Collection. For some of the many critiques of involvement in electoral politics, see *Connections*, March 12, 1968; James O'Brien to Stan Caine, August 15, 1968, Wisconsin Historical Society, James P. O'Brien Papers, Box 1; Madison SDS, "SDS," 1968, Wisconsin Historical Society, James P. O'Brien Papers, Box 1.

12. *Daily Cardinal*, June 22, 1967; UW Faculty for Peace, "Papers on Vietnam," 1968, Wisconsin Historical Society, UW Faculty for Peace Records; Rowen, oral history; E. David Cronon and John W. Jenkins, *The University of Wisconsin: A History*, vol. 4: *Renewal to Revolution, 1945–1971* (Madison: University of Wisconsin Press, 1999), 476. For the perspective of one young radical faculty member in Madison in the late 1960s and early 1970s, see James C. Scott, oral history, 1976, UW Oral History Project.

13. Ron McCrea and Dave Wagner, "Harvey Goldberg," in Buhle, *History and the New Left*.

14. Fain, oral history; George Mosse, "New Left Intellectuals / New Left Politics," in Buhle, *History and the New Left*, 234; Paul Buhle and Edward Rice-Maximin, *William Appleman Williams: The Tragedy of Empire* (New York: Routledge, 1995). For more on George Mosse's relationship with the New Left, see George Mosse, *Confronting History: A Memoir* (Madison: University of Wisconsin Press, 2000). One example of the split between student activists and antiwar faculty was a faculty antiwar group's decision to support the right of Secretary of Defense Melvin Laird to speak on campus in 1971. See UW Faculty for Peace, press release, January 1971, Wisconsin Historical Society, UW Faculty for Peace Records.

15. Abner Spence, "On the Correct Handling of Contradictions among the People," *Call*, April 5, 1968; James O'Brien, "General Ideas on the Radical History Issue," August 23, 2970, Wisconsin Historical Society, James P. O'Brien Papers, Box 1, "RA-Radical History Issue." For one source of information on departmental organizing, see "Inter-Departmental Coordinating Committee Meeting," minutes, September 24, 1968, Wisconsin Historical Society, James P. O'Brien Papers, Box 1. There is also a good discussion of these efforts, including the perspective of faculty members, in Cronon and Jenkins, *University of Wisconsin*, 4:470.

16. SDS/WDRU Anti-Imperialist Research and Action Project, "Business as Usual: Social Uses of the University," 1969, Wisconsin Historical Society, Robert Gabriner Papers, Box 2, Folder 6; Cronon and Jenkins, *University of Wisconsin*, 4:487.

17. James Rowen, "The Case against ROTC," October 1969, Wisconsin Historical Society Pamphlet Collection.

18. Carlisle Runge, oral history, 1982, UW Oral History Project. Two excellent sources on ROTC are Michael Nieberg, *Making Citizen Soldiers: ROTC and the Ideology of American Military Service* (Cambridge, MA: Harvard University Press, 2000), and Donald Downs and Ilia Murtazashvili, *Arms and the University: Military Presence and the Civic Education of Non-Military Students* (Cambridge: Cambridge University Press, 2012).

19. Edwin Young, "Statement by the Madison Chancellor," February 8, 1969, UW Archives, http://digital.library.wisc.edu/1711.dl/UW.CampusDisrupt, pp. 5–7; Cronon and Jenkins, *University of Wisconsin*, 4:466–67, 482–83.

20. Black People's Alliance, list of demands, February 1969, Wisconsin Historical Society, James P. O'Brien Papers, Box 1; "Chronology of Activity Regarding Black Students," UW Archives, Series 4/21/1, Box 20, "Black Students—Individual—1968–1969."

21. "Chronology of Activity."

22. Rowen, oral history; "Mother Jones Reborn," Wisconsin Historical Society, James P. O'Brien Papers, Box 1. Though there are restrictions on access, FBI and local police files on Madison activists and leftist organizations are archived at the Wisconsin Historical Society in the papers of Michael Fellner, who was a UW student and an editor of *Take Over*, an underground newspaper in Madison during the 1970s.

23. *Badger Herald*, October 24, 1969; Kennedy and Null, "History of 20th Century Protests"; William Sewell to Bryant Kearl, May 18, 1970, UW Archives, Series 7/33/8, Box 2, Folder 7. For an early history of the Teaching Assistants Association, before the 1970 strike, see Henry Haslach, "The University of Wisconsin Teaching Assistants Association," Wisconsin Historical Society, James P. O'Brien Papers, Box 1.

24. Kennedy and Null, "History of 20th Century Protests"; Campus Crusade for Christ, "Medical Info Bulletin," 1970, UW Archives, http://archives.library.wisc.edu/uw-archives/exhibits/protests/campus_crusade_first_aid.jpg.

25. UW News and Publications Services, "UW News," April 21, 1971, UW Archives, http://digital.library.wisc.edu/1711.dl/UW.DemProDisGen, p. 20.

26. "Chronology of Activity"; "Unrest Spurs Growth of Conservative Student Groups," *New York Times*, October 12, 1969. An excellent source on Young Americans for Freedom is Gregory Schneider, *Cadres for Conservatism: Young Americans for Freedom and the Rise of the Contemporary Right* (New York: New York University Press, 1999).

27. "Unrest Spurs Growth," *New York Times*; *Badger Herald*, September 18, 1969; September 25, 1969; November 14, 1969; December 5, 1969; May 1, 1970.

28. "Unrest Spurs Growth," *New York Times*; *Badger Herald*, September 18, 1969; November 7, 1969; December 5, 1969; February 13, 1970; March 13, 1970; April 10, 1970; April 17, 1970; April 24, 1970. Another source on the overlaps (and the differences) between the left and the right in the sixties is Rebecca Klatch, *Generation Divided: The New Left, the New Right, and the 1960s* (Berkeley: University of California Press, 1999).

29. "Brief Chronology"; Fred Harvey Harrington, interview by Tom Bates, January 8, 1988, UW Oral History Project; Walter Renk, oral history, 1977, UW Oral History Project.

30. Harrington, interview by Tom Bates; Paul Ginsberg, oral history, 1988, UW Oral History Project; William Sewell to Herbert Hyman, March 6, 1968, UW Archives, Series 7/33/8, Box 2, Folder 4.

31. William Sewell, oral history, 1977, UW Oral History Project; Cronon and Jenkins, *University of Wisconsin*, 4:214–15, 460; *Daily Cardinal*, October 16, 1968.

32. Jagdish Chandra and Stephen Robinson, *An Uneasy Alliance: The Mathematics Research Center at the University of Wisconsin, 1956–1987* (Philadelphia: Society for Industrial and Applied Mathematics, 2005), 11; *Daily Cardinal*, December 15, 1966; May 10, 1967; July 13, 1967; July 18, 1967.

33. University Committee, "Dear Colleagues," November 12, 1969, UW Archives, Series 5/96/3, Box 5, "University-Military Relationship"; "The Case against the Army Math Research Center," 1969, Wisconsin Historical Society Pamphlet Collection; Science for the People, *AMRC Papers* (Madison: 1973).

34. The most comprehensive source on the bombing and the events and personalities surrounding it is Tom Bates, *RADS: The 1970 Bombing of the Army Math Research Center at the University of Wisconsin and Its Aftermath* (New York: HarperCollins, 1992). A lesser-known work is Michael Morris, *Madison Bombings: The Story of One of the Two Largest Vehicle Bombings Ever* (London: Research House, 1988). For a significant number of official university documents related to the bombing, see the UW Archives collection at http://digital.library.wisc.edu/1711.dl/UW.MathResearch.

35. Kennedy and Null, "History of 20th Century Protests." For the aftermath of the bombing, especially the manhunt for members of the New Year's Gang and their trials, see Bates, *RADS*. An update on the case and the search for Leo Burt can be found in "A Statement for Peace, an Act of War," CBS News, http://www.cbsnews.com/stories/2011/08/28/sunday/main20098388.shtml?tag=contentBody;cbsCarousel.

36. Saul Landau, interview with the author, December 12, 2005; Malcolm Sylvers, "Memories from the Periphery," in Buhle, *History and the New Left*, 188. Two key sixties histories that have argued this "declension" thesis are Todd Gitlin, *The Sixties: Years of Hope, Days of Rage* (New York: Bantam Books, 1987); and James Miller, *Democracy Is in the Streets: From Port Huron to the Siege of Chicago* (New York: Simon & Schuster, 1987). Perhaps the first direct challenge to this view of the sixties came from former Wisconsin student Wini Breines, "Whose New Left?" *Journal of American History* 75 (1988).

37. Two sources on the emergence of gay activism on campus are Scott Seyforth, "Close to Home," *On Wisconsin*, Fall 2007; and Kenneth Burns, "A New Chapter," *Isthmus* [Madison], April 12, 2007. The UW Oral History Project has also collected a series of interviews in a collection titled "Madison's LGBT Community: 1960s to Present." An introduction to these interviews can be found at http://archives.library.wisc.edu/oral-history/by-subject/lgbt/index.html. For articles on environmental issues, see *Badger*

Herald, December 12, 1969; February 13, 1970; February 20, 1970; March 13, 1970; April 10, 1970; April 17, 1970; April 24, 1970.

38. *Connections,* March 12, 1968.

39. The most detailed history of the Mifflin Street Community Co-op that I've found was written by Michael Bodden and edited by Paul Soglin: "People's History: A History of the Mifflin Street Community Co-op," Waxing America, http://www.waxingamerica.com/2006/11/history_of_the_.html. There were also a number of newspaper articles on the co-op's history around the time that it shut down, in 2006. See, for example, "Mifflin Street Co-op," *Wisconsin State Journal,* December 6, 2006.

40. *Badger Herald,* April 28, 2010.

41. *Daily Cardinal,* October 26, 1966; October 5, 1967; "Free University Timetable," Summer 1968, Wisconsin Historical Society, James P. O'Brien Papers, Box 2.

42. For the history of the women's liberation movement's development within the civil rights movement and the New Left, see Sara Evans, *Personal Politics: The Roots of Women's Liberation in the Civil Rights Movement and the New Left* (New York: Vintage Books, 1979). For a discussion of male dominance in the campus left, see Nina Serrano, "A Madison Bohemian," in Buhle, *History and the New Left,* 72–73; and Rowen, oral history. Many of the other women with contributions in *History and the New Left* also discuss women's role in the left. UW enrollment figures are compiled from annual enrollment reports, UW Archives, Series 19/12/3/00–1, Boxes 1 and 2.

43. Ann Gordon, "On the Women's Workshop," March 1967, Wisconsin Historical Society, James P. O'Brien Papers, Box 1, "Madison SDS, 1966–67."

44. *Badger Herald,* December 5, 1969; December 12, 1969.

45. Rick Perlstein, "Who Owns the Sixties? The Opening of a Scholarly Generation Gap," *Lingua Franca* 6 (May/June 1996). Former president Clinton is quoted by Michael Heale, "The Sixties as History: A Review of the Political Historiography," in *Reviews in American History* 33 (March 2005): 134. The original quotation is from the *Independent* (London) on June 5, 2004.

Index

219

❖ STUDIES IN AMERICAN THOUGHT ❖
AND CULTURE
